T0113868

Warning to the
CHURCHES....

There is No Pre-Tribulation Rapture of the Church!

RAY C PEARSON SR

WESTBOW
PRESS®
A DIVISION OF THOMAS NELSON
& ZONDERVAN

Copyright © 2022 Ray C Pearson Sr.

All rights reserved. No part of this book may be used or reproduced by any means, graphic, electronic, or mechanical, including photocopying, recording, taping or by any information storage retrieval system without the written permission of the author except in the case of brief quotations embodied in critical articles and reviews.

WestBow Press books may be ordered through booksellers or by contacting:

WestBow Press
A Division of Thomas Nelson & Zondervan
1663 Liberty Drive
Bloomington, IN 47403
www.westbowpress.com
844-714-3454

Because of the dynamic nature of the Internet, any web addresses or links contained in this book may have changed since publication and may no longer be valid. The views expressed in this work are solely those of the author and do not necessarily reflect the views of the publisher, and the publisher hereby disclaims any responsibility for them.

Any people depicted in stock imagery provided by Getty Images are models, and such images are being used for illustrative purposes only. Certain stock imagery © Getty Images.

Unless otherwise indicated, all Scripture taken from the King James Version of the Bible.

Scripture quotations marked (NIV) are taken from the Holy Bible, New International Version®, NIV®. Copyright © 1973, 1978, 1984, 2011 by Biblica, Inc.® Used by permission of Zondervan. All rights reserved worldwide. www.zondervan.com The "NIV" and "New International Version" are trademarks registered in the United States Patent and Trademark Office by Biblica, Inc.®

ISBN: 978-1-6642-8012-0 (sc)
ISBN: 978-1-6642-8011-3 (e)

Print information available on the last page.

WestBow Press rev. date: 11/28/2022

Author's Disclaimer

Due to the "political correctness" of today's society; I'm not allowed to use, "questionable, unwholesome, or profane language" in this book. Nor am I allowed to quote "verbatim" the words that were spoken and the description of the events that took place in the presentation of this book. Therefore, I had to revise it, and present, for your reading a, "watered- down" version of the exact words spoken; and a diluted description of the events that took place.

Furthermore, I'm not allowed to use certain, exact quotations, from the King James Version of the Bible that might be "offensive" to some readers. An example can be found in Revelation Chapter 17:1-18 (read) where God describes the idolatrous nation of the United States of America as, "*the great* [expletive] that *sitteth upon many waters.*"

In such instances, I will note: (read) and you can open your Bible and read the Scripture(s) to get the Truth of what God, our Heavenly Father, the Creator of the universe has said. Also further, due to "*political correctness*" of today's culture; it's ironic to me that people don't want to 'offend' others with the truth, but they have no problem *offending God* with distorted and watered-down words of His Holy Book! Be as it may. It is written, "*Verily, there is a reward for the righteous; verily he is a God that judgeth in the earth*" (Psalm 58:11).

Contents

Introduction

You may believe or been taught, *"The Rapture of the Church could occur at any moment."* This is a false doctrine and false teachings to the core! The church must go all the way through the seven (7) years of the tribulation period. Please, for your own soul's salvation's sake, [and those whom you are misleading] I beg of you to put away your false doctrine, belief, and teachings, and let the Bible, which is the Word of God teach you- *The Truth* (John 8:32; 17:17).

Why I Wrote This Book

Because of the false teachings I've heard and had been taught in the past has led me to teach *Bible Truth,* mainly regarding the timing of the Rapture of the Church. I used to let people believe whatever they wanted to believe, and I did not go out of my way to correct their misunderstanding. However, after being called into the ministry and with my pastoral office and duty, I now have a different perspective on life; especially with the unlearned [Christians] and the unsaved.

I've come to realize that since *"God is not willing that any should perish, but that all should come to repentance"* (2 Peter 3:9). I question myself, "Who am I that I should not warn them?" Furthermore, Ezekiel said that it's the watchman's [pastors and teachers] duty to warn people of coming danger and judgment; otherwise, *"their blood will be on* [his] *the watchman's hands"* (Ezekiel 33:1-9).

This false doctrine has become a 'thorn in my flesh'; somehow, and for some reason I get irate when I hear one of those false teachers saying, "The Rapture of the Church could happen at any given moment." Whenever I hear it, I immediately write them letting them know that they're misleading God's people. In getting the truth out I can relate to the prophet Jeremiah, who said, [the truth of God's Word-is] *"as a burning fire shut up in my bones"* (Jeremiah 3:9).

This book exposes many of the false doctrines that's been taught and believed among the Christian community. I have written many popular and well-known TV evangelist, pastors, teachers, and radio talk show host informing them of this false doctrine that they are propagating for Satan. [incidentally] I 've stopped supporting those false teachers' ministries! I will not mention them by name, nor will I tell what church or radio program that they are from.

I've warned them that their false doctrine and teachings, is a *lie* which Satan has *planted* in the churches and among believers to deceive the unlearn. If you are one of them, ["Pre-trib" Rapture teaches] you've probably received a letter from me. The Apostle Paul said that this 'doctrine' is the *"strong delusion"* that God will send [allow] to perpetrate the church in the End Times (2 Thess. 2:9-11).

Foremost, Jesus warned the church of the End Times deception that will be prevalent before His return. He said, *"For there shall arise false Christs and false prophets, and shall show great signs and wonders: insomuch that, if it were possible, they shall deceive the very elect"* (Matt. 24:24). Question: How can the *very elect* [true believers] be deceived by those false teachers if the church is suddenly caught up in a Pre-Tribulation Rapture? Remember, the Bible says, *"Whom shall He [God] teach knowledge? And whom shall He make to understand doctrine?... For precept must be upon precept;... line upon line...*(Isiah 28:9,10).

This "Pre-Tribulation" Rapture doctrine does not line up with Scripture! There will be a succession of events to occur that will lead up to the rapture of the church which I will explain later in this book. But first, if you are one of those whom I've written in my many letters; I ask that you read this book and, *"Search the Scriptures"* to see if you're teaching *Bible Truth* or Religious Doctrine? Note: There are two kinds of teachers in the church; Bible teachers [those who teach the written Word of God, and religious teachers, which teaches religious doctrines, i.e., man's opinions and ideologies, etc.]

Question: Which are you? After reading this book and *"Rightly Dividing"* the Word of Truth, you will know for sure. And, if you reject the Truth of this book; remember, Jesus foresaw it, He said, *"But in vain they do worship Me, teaching for doctrines the commandments of men"* (Matt. 15:9). That is exactly what the "Pre-Tribulation Rapture of the Church" is- a man-made doctrine and not the 'Rightly Divided' Word of God! In your reading of this book, you will be surprised to learn; what the Bible really teaches on this subject.

After reading this book, some will still outright reject Bible Truth and will hold on to their religious beliefs. However, Jesus foresaw this as well. He said, *"For laying aside the commandment of God, ye hold the tradition of men,...Full well ye reject the commandment* [teaching] *of God that ye may keep your own tradition"* (Mark 7:8,9). I believe the Lord is addressing the "Pre" and "Mid" Tribulation Rapture doctrine. Furthermore, God said, *"My people* [church folks] *are destroyed for the lack of knowledge"* [i.e., the Truth of His Word] (Hosea 4:6).

Many books have been written and many movies have been made regarding the Rapture of the Church, some entitled "Left Behind" which teaches the Pre-Tribulation Rapture doctrine. Truth is that the ones to be 'left behind' are the ones to be saved! According to the Bible, the first ones to be *'taken'* will be taken by the Antichrist, [he's coming first to *deceive*] Jesus gave us this *Truth*. He said, "But *he that endure unto the end* [of the Great Tribulation period] *the same shall be saved."* (Matt. 10:22; 24:13).

If you can understand plain English Jesus Christ said those who will be "left behind" are the ones that will be saved. Satan is good at twisting Scriptures; he started in the Garden of Eden and has continued his diabolical plan to deceive God's people ever since. Remember, Jesus said, *"Satan is the father of lies"* (John 8:44).

If those false teachers would read and teach the Bible, without man's finite interpretation they will learn the *Truth* regarding the rapture, that, John the Revelator saw the church *"coming out"* of the Great Tribulation (Rev. 7:13,14). I question this teaching: How could the church "come out" of the Great Tribulation if it had already been 'caught up' [Raptured] in a Pre -Tribulation Rapture? Also consider Rev. 2:7,11,17; Rev. 3:5,12,21; Rev. 21:7. All these passages of Scriptures talks about the Saints that *"overcometh"* i.e., holds fast to their faith during the tribulation period.

So as one can plainly see, this "pre" tribulation rapture doctrine is false teaching to the core! If you're one of them, I'm not going to wish you "God's Speed" the Apostle Paul said that we should not do that. By doing so, one would become 'partakers' of their evil deeds (Eph. 5:6,7). In obedience to this passage of scripture, I've stopped supporting those ministries that teaches the *Big lie* of a Pre-Tribulation Rapture of the Church. However, I'm following the instructions of Isiah 58:1 where he recorded that God said, *"Cry aloud, spare not, lift up your voice like a trumpet, and show my people their transgression."*

Again, there are many events recorded in the Scriptures that are to occur before the rapture of the church. God is going to inflict the world with plagues and disasters to get man's attention because, *"He is not willing that any should perish, but that all men might be saved"* (2 Peter 3:9). If anyone does perish, they will perish because of their lack of understanding [of God's Word and their own corruption] (2 Peter 2:12; Hosea 4:6). God has provided mankind a Savior, His only begotten Son, Jesus Christ (John 3:16).

However, according to Scriptures many souls are still going to perish [in the lake of fire] because of deception, defiance, and unbelief. And if a Christian perish, it will be because they would "deny" the Savior during the tribulation period (Matt. 10: 32, 33). So then my friend, God has written a book, it's called the Holy Bible. It is written *"All scripture is given by inspiration of God, and is profitable for doctrine, for reproof, for correction, for instruction in righteousness: That the man of God may be perfect,* [in teaching His Word] *thoroughly furnished* [equipped] *unto all good works"* (2 Timothy 3:16, 17).

If you really want to know the Truth about the timing of the Rapture of the Church, and if you let the Bible speak for itself, then the Word of God will plainly explain it to you. Jesus Christ said, *"Immediately after the* [Great] *Tribulation He would send His angels to gather* [Rapture] *His saints"* (Matt. 24:29-31). The Apostle Paul said, *"Let no man deceive you...For that day* [the Rapture of the Church] *shall not come, except there come a falling away first, and that man of sin* [the Antichrist] *be revealed, the son of perdition..."* (2 Thess. 2: 3,4).

Paul also declared that the rapture would occur at the" last" [7ᵗʰ] *trumpet* (1 Corinthians 15: 51,52). Therefore, I say again, if you let the Bible speak for itself, then you will, *"know the truth, and the truth will make you free"* of religious doctrines and man's ideologies [emphasis mine]. It is recorded in Revelation 7:1-12 that John said the Saints, one hundred forty-four thousand Jews and a great multitude of Gentile believers [the universal church] will be sealed here on earth [for protection] during the Great Tribulation period (vs. 3). Take notice that it doesn't say that we will be "Raptured" from it! Notice also verses 13 & 14, *"they came out of the Great Tribulation."* Question: How could one *"come out"* of something that they didn't go through? The Bible tells us that Daniel *"came out"* of the lions' den and the three Hebrew boys *"came out"* of the fiery furnace, but first they had to go *through* it!

Ray C. Pearson Sr, PASTOR,
ETERNAL LIFE FULL GOSPEL CHURCH
(Non -denominational) Milwaukee, WI

1

Laying the Foundation:

I grew up in a church that taught this 'theory' of a Pre-Tribulation Rapture of the Church. I will not name the denomination, but you will recognize it by its teachings. As a matter of fact, you may even pastor or belong to one of them. Therefore, "you will know a tree by its fruit." [Emphasis Mine]. I joined this church because I used to work with the pastor, he seemed to be an upright, sincere and devoted man of God. In my eyesight, he carried himself as, "a true man of God."

I grew up without a father in the home; this pastor, in his lifestyle lived a life that I wish I could have had in my own father, of whom I could pattern my life after and that I could learn lessons in life from. So, I looked up to him as my, 'father figure.' I would go to him for advice about life and spiritual matters as well. He would tell me that, "God has the answers to whatever problems that we have in life, but God doesn't answer a sinner's prayer unless the person is willing to turn his life around." He would quote St. John 9:31. He always would advise me to, "give my life over to Jesus Christ and be saved from hell's fire."

He invited me to come to church and be saved, and that I could learn to live the Christian lifestyle through Sunday school and weekly Bible studies. I joined the church on my first visit; it was a church of the same denomination that I was used to. I was comfortable with the songs, order of service and the teaching. Everyone seemed so nice, they all welcomed me, and I felt loved and appreciated. In his sermon it seemed as though he was talking directly to me, [which he probably was] warning me that, *"There is Eternal Life or Eternal Damnation After My Physical Death, and that, if I Die Without Accepting Jesus Christ As My Lord And Personal Savior; That I Would Have Automatically Chosen Hell Over Heaven!"*

He read and explained Luke 16: 19-31 as proof that, if a person dies *unsaved*, they will wake up in Hell! And if that person's name was not found written in the Book of Life at the Great White Throne Judgment Seat of God: that that person would be cast into the "Lake of Fire" alone with the devil and his demons for all eternity! He delivered a powerful message. If I didn't know the Lord; the dynamic presentation of his message would have probably, "scared me to death!" I knew about heaven and hell because I was brought up in church. My mother died when I was five years old, my father left us [nine children] with his mother in Memphis, Tennessee and he moved to Chicago, Illinois where he remarried and started another family. My grandmother was very strict, and she was a devoted church goer, she served on the usher's board which required her to be at church regularly. She was a disciplinary, and she made sure that all the children would go to church as well.

Because of her discipline and strict house rules, all my siblings either got married early, or ran away from home. And years later only one of my sisters came back home. My grandmother passed away in 1968 five months before my sixteenth birthday. Several months before she died, she would have me to read Proverbs 22:6, *"Train up a child in the way he should go: and when he is old, he will not depart from it."* I had to read this passage of Scripture twice daily, at the breakfast table and at bedtime. I had read it so much that I memorized it; however, she wouldn't let me just recite it, I had to read it aloud. I once asked her, "why did I have to read the same Scripture every day?" She said, "I would understand it better by and by" which I didn't understand.

When she died, I was left with her house, all the furnishing, her life savings, and the proceeds from her life insurance policy.

She had also named me as her beneficiary, and she had added my name on her bank account with instructions that; I should have access and full control of the account on my sixteenth birthday. Her house was valued at $20,000 and my total cash assets was well above $45,000.00. In 1968 that was a lot of money for an unsupervised teenager to have. I felt like a millionaire, at the economy of those days I probably was.

I never question my grandmother as to how she had accumulated so much wealth. She was the type of person that believed, "a child should stay out of grown-ups business." But judging from what I had heard from conversations that she shared with her friends: I learned that she was from Marvell, Arkansas and my grandfather was from Helena, Arkansas. I heard her tell her friends that, "they both were sole heirs of their family's land. She had inherited sixty-five acres of land and my grandfather was left with one hundred and twenty-four acres."

"After they married, they decided to least out her land to a mercantile company that produced cotton and they lived on his plot.... And after thirty-four years of marriage, my grandfather was farming the land one day when their bull broke out of his pen-trying to get into a fenced pasture where their cows was grazing. And that he was gored by the bull while trying to lure him back into his pen: and his injuries was so severe that he couldn't farm anymore, so they sold their land and moved to Memphis, Tennessee." I never got to meet my grandfather, he died thirteen years before I was born.

I had no contact with most of my other siblings after they left home. As of this day, I still haven't heard from two of my older brothers, I don't know if they're still living or not. None of my siblings attended our grandmother's funeral, therefore, I couldn't share my good fortune with them. However, I kept $20,000.00 in a separate account on deposit in the bank to be divided among them if they ever showed up.

At sixteen years of age this was a great achievement. I was the richest kid in school and the neighborhood. It seemed that everyone really respected me and wanted to be my friend.

3

I never had an argument nor a fight with any of the boys in the neighborhood. I knew the kid's parents in the neighborhood didn't have much money, so on Saturdays and during summer months when school was out, and most of the kids was on the playground, I would buy a big bag of candy and take it to the playground, and I shared it with them. When the ice cream truck was in the area, I would buy popsicles and sodas for everyone. I would spend an average of ten to fifteen dollars daily on refreshments for myself and the other kids. It seemed that every kid in the neighborhood came out to the playground. As the crowd grew, it was getting too expensive to maintain and I had to draw a line. Therefore, I told everyone that I could buy refreshments every Saturday and only once a week. I chose Wednesdays from Noon to three o'clock and if it was raining on Wednesday, then "refreshment time" would be on Thursdays or the next clear day afterwards.

At school, my teachers seemed to have a great level of respect for me as well. I wasn't the smartest kid in my classes; most of my grades were C's & C +'s. I was able to maintain that grade average with the help of my girlfriend. She was very smart, a straight- A student and she had ambitions of following in her mother's footsteps and becoming a nurse after graduating from college. Most of my teachers offered to help me after school in my studies if I wanted or needed them.

Many of the neighbors would ask to borrow money until their next payday, most of them would repay as promised and I told them, "As long as they fulfilled their obligations that I would make loans to them." My grandmother had warned me that people would come to me wanting to borrow money and that I should be careful of whom I made loans to. She also advised me that I should set a limit as to how much money I loaned out. And she told me, "If they didn't pay me back, then don't let them come back to borrow more." Therefore, I set fifty dollars limit on personal loans to those that repaid, and I kept $500.00 in cash at home as an 'emergency benevolent fund' just in case someone with a need wanted to borrow.

After she died some of her friends and neighbors came to me to repay money that they owed her. I thanked them for their honesty, but I let them keep the money. I told them, "She didn't tell me her business, nor did she make a note of it, and I didn't know about it anyway, therefore, I wouldn't miss it." I totaled the amount to be three hundred and eighty-five dollars from those that offered to repay her. From this, many of the neighbors seemed to watch over me more than their own kids. After her death I often wondered if she was well liked and respected because she was always there for her friends and the neighbors in their time of financial need? I once (jokingly) told her that, "she should start an in-home loan company and charge interest on the loans."

She said, "that would be usury, and the Bible speaks against it." She had me to read Deuteronomy 23:19, 20 and she explained to me that it would be wrong to charge her friends interest on the loans, but it would be okay to charge strangers, but she didn't loan money to people that she didn't know."

As an unsupervised teenager with a pocket full of money and with no adult supervision in the home; I stopped going to church and started hanging out with my friends, some of whom I knew that my grandmother would not have approved of. I bought my first car on my seventeenth birthday, I paid $800.00 for a low milage 1964 Plymouth Belvedere that was owned by an elderly man, a widower and an acquaintance of my grandmothers from church. He used to take her grocery shopping and other places where she had to go, but his health was failing him. I heard him tell my grandmother that, "because of his condition, he wouldn't be able to drive much longer." I told him, "If he teaches me how to drive, that I would take the both of them on their errands and to their doctor's appointments."

With the approval of my grandmother, he started giving me driving lessons and I learned very quickly how to control a car. It was easy because I used to go- go karting with a friend and his dad at the community amusement park which was outside of my neighborhood. His dad was a youth counselor at church, he and his wife often took the kids on outings and field trips. His wife would take the girls on trips and sleepovers, and he would take the boys fishing and camping and together they would take us roller skating and when the Cotton Carnival and the State Fair was in town, they, and several volunteers from church would chaperone the kids to those events as well.

I obtained a booklet from the Tennessee Department of Transportation which I studied, and I learned all the road signs, laws and regulations for operating a vehicle. After I obtained my learner's permit, I drove them as promised to their grocery shopping and doctor's appointments. There were times when they didn't feel up to traveling, so I told them to fill out a grocery list and I would take the car and do their shopping for them, which was very convenient for them.

It was a pleasure for me because I was the only fifteen-year-old boy that I knew of or observed that had privilege and access to a car. It became a sense of pride and a show-off to me, because it drew lots of attention from many girls, especially those from church and school who knew me. They would give me their address or phone number for me to call them, but because of my faithfulness to my girlfriend, I never called nor pursued any of them. I gave most of them an application form to fill out asking about their personal interest, goals and what positive things that they could contribute to a relationship. I told all the girls that I was a "one lady's man, and that I would put them on my 'list' and I would call them if an opening for a long-term relationship comes up."

I kept a notebook and the last count that I remembered, I had collected eighty-seven names and addresses from girls that wanted to get to know me. My grandmother often checked my room to make sure that I didn't have any hidden adult materials in it. She came across my notebook and asked me about it, I told her that many girls at church, in the neighborhood and at school wanted to get to know me and it was my way of saying "no" to them.

She advised me, "not to play with people's emotions, that those girls were probably serious." I told her, "They were indeed, that most of them wanted more than just friendship, that they wanted to have an intimate sexual relationship with me." And I reminded her of her warnings to me that, "most girls would be after me, seeking a financially secured lifestyle." And it was my way of turning them down without embarrassing them or getting involved in an unwanted sexual relationship with any of them. She seemed pleased with my answer, and I was allowed to keep my notebook.

Her friend seemed to have taken a liking to me as well, he trusted me with the car, he said that I was a "responsible and well-behaved kid." He didn't have any children nor grandchildren of his own. I learned that his only son was killed in the Korean war and his grandson died in a house fire while trying to rescue his wife, they both were killed in the fire. He never told me so, but I think he saw something in me that he wished he could have had or experienced in his own son or grandson had they lived. He gave me a set of keys to the car, and he told me that I could come by and get it and drive to school during impudent weather conditions. He would let me keep the car on weekends if I wanted to, he said, "just in case I wanted to take my girlfriend out." He lived within walking distance from church, the only times that he drove the car was on the first of the month to take care of business when he received his pension, and social security disability checks; or when he and my grandmother went grocery shopping or had their doctor's appointments.

She told me not to abuse the privilege of using the car, so I only used it on the weekends when I had a date with my girlfriend or to pick her up or drop her off at her school during bad weather conditions. I would then drive to my school; we lived in different neighborhoods and attended different schools. He had promised to sell me the car, but he didn't sell it to me until after she had passed. I could have afforded to buy a brand-new car, but I was taught not to be wasteful in money matters. Therefore, I waited until he was ready to sell me the car. I didn't know at the time that he was keeping it for me as my seventeenth birthday present. When he passed, I received a cashier's check from his bank, he had left instructions in his estate to issue me ten thousand dollars upon his death.

I don't know what his total assets were, but it was divided among his other siblings. He had three brothers and two sisters, one of his sisters also attended church with us, she was left with his house and some cash. She was the choir director in the Elders Gospel Choir. I once overheard him telling my grandmother that, "he and his sister was the only saved ones in the family, therefore she will get his house and most of his money when he's gone."

I had my house parties, but only with a selected group of close friends, which was mostly guys, my girlfriend and their girlfriends. One of my friend's dad owned a pool hall, it was a multi-purpose building that operated the pool hall, a barber shop and a beauty salon.

And it contained a rooming house above the building which he rented rooms by the hours, days, weeks, and month. Oftentimes we would go to the pool hall and shoot pool most of the night, and when the pool hall closed for the night, we would come back to my house and spend the rest of the night partying with our girlfriends. I respected my elderly neighbors and my grandmother's friends, so I didn't cross the line.

She had asked them to keep watch over me and keep me away from, "bad company." And in fulfilling of their promise to her, they constantly showed up making sure that I lived up to her wishes and expectations of me. Not only that, but several of them could be seen sitting in their windows watching my house and weather permitted, they would sit on their porches most of the day watching to see who was coming and going from my house. They didn't hide it; it was their way of letting me know that they were fulfilling their promise that they made to her. It seemed that their lives were centered around me.

I got tired of people watching me all the time. I didn't have much privacy because it seemed that, all eyes were on me. They knew that I had stopped going to church; most of them would phone me and invite me to attend church with them and their families. I got tired of the invitations so I had the number changed so that they couldn't call me anymore. After that, many times they would come to my house and knock on the door but if I didn't want to be bothered, I wouldn't answer it.

I made a deal with my friend's father that owned the rooming house, that he would reserve a room for me for a couple of hours and sometimes overnight and on weekends when I wanted to escape my 'nosy neighbors' or to have private time with my girlfriend. I didn't want most of them to see her, she was a Christian, but they didn't know her. They most likely would have questioned her about her faith, because they knew that my grandmother didn't want me to have an unsaved girlfriend. She had the mindset that, "unsaved girls would be more sexually active than those who were church goers." I didn't want my guardian neighbors to annoy her as they did me. They often asked me questions about my dreams and goals for my future. I assumed it was to ensure that I lived up to my grandmother's wishes for me. She wanted me to be a preacher of the Gospel, and she had told her friends so.

I learned that her father was a preacher and my grandfather had ambitions of becoming one as well, but he had to put it off to farm his land and raise his family. She said that his life, dreams, and goals were cut short when he was injured by the bull. She wanted my father, who was her only son to be a preacher as well, but she had said that "he was more interested in women than anything else."

Therefore, she wanted to live her dreams and expectations through me since I was the only one of her grandsons that stayed home. She didn't want me to be influenced by people that wasn't a Christian and living a godly lifestyle. Many of her church friends had granddaughters about my age, who also showed an interest in me.

I accepted their names and phone numbers, and I gave them one of my applications and I added them to my 'list', but I never called them, some of them would ask for a date but I turned them down because it would have been a disrespect to my girlfriend.

The neighbors knew me as a child, and they showed a genuine concern for me. They also knew the 'bad boys' in the neighborhood that they knew that my grandmother wouldn't have approved of me having them over or having any kind of association with them. They weren't bad boys who got in trouble a lot, they just didn't go to church. My grandmother was what some might call, "old fashion", she believed that Saints and sinners had nothing in common. I often heard her quote the Scripture, *"come out from them, and be ye separate."* Therefore, she didn't want me hanging out with any of the boys that didn't go to church. She also had the mindset that, "because they weren't living a Christian lifestyle that they were prone to get into trouble, and if I hung out with them, they would lead me into trouble and sin as well." She used to say, "evil communications corrupts good manners."

On school days one of my next-door neighbors, who was a very close friend to my grandmother would call me every morning to make sure that I was up and ready for school. And if she saw the lights on in my house late at night, she would call me to remind me that, "I should be in bed so that I could be up early to get ready for school." She knew that my grandmother made me go to bed at ten o'clock on school nights, and since I had the phone number changed and I didn't give it out, she would send one of her kids over to make sure that I was up.

I realized that I had made a mistake by having the phone number changed because several of her friends who called me, systematically showed up unannounced to check on me and to see who I was keeping company with. They knew that I had stopped going to church and on Sundays, they would make it their business to invite me to attend church with them and their families as well.

Oftentimes, especially on Saturday nights I would stay at the rooming house above the pool hall and come up with an excuse as to why I didn't attend church with them. With that, they would remind me that, "I wasn't living up to my grandmother's expectations of me." It was like having a dozen grandparents watching over me all the time. There was a group of four who called themselves, "The Prayer Warriors", they would go to the hospitals, nursing homes and to people homes who was sick and shut-in praying for them. At the request of my grandmother, they added me to their mission and prayer list.

I had classmates, mostly girls who wanted to hang out, skip school and stay at my house. Some of them offered to stay with me, and to cook and clean the house for me. I turned them down because of my nosey neighbors who constantly checked in on me, to see if I allowed any girl to spend the night. After my house parties were over, I made sure that everyone would help clean up and I made sure that they got home safely. If I was too 'toasted' to drive, I would send them home in a taxi. I respected my girlfriend, and I didn't cheat on her in our relationship. Therefore, I didn't take any of the girls up on their offer to be my live-in girlfriend nor my housekeeper.

I told them that my grandmother had taught me how to take care of myself. She had taught me how to cook and clean the house, she even taught me how to wash and iron my own clothes, how to mend them, and how to sew buttons on my shirts. She had told me that she was teaching me how to take care of myself, "just in case that I marry a wife who either wouldn't do it for me or didn't know how." Later in life I found out that my grandmother was a very wise woman.

My grandmother and most of her friends and the elderly neighbors were very judgmental, they didn't believe in cohabitation before marriage. They believed that a man and a woman shouldn't be sharing a home and a bed unless they were married. There were several couples in the neighborhood that wasn't married but they lived together. My grandmother once asked a young man that lived with his girlfriend, "Why doesn't he marry her?" He responded, "why should I buy a cow when I can get free milk?" Most of the Christian elders labored them, 'fornicators', and said that "they were living in sin." I didn't want that label to be applied to me, so I didn't take any of the girls up on their offer to live with me, nor did I let any of them spend the night nor stay for extended periods of times.

My neighborhood guardians also knew that my grandmother had warned me about conniving and seductive women and girls who wouldn't have my best interest at heart, that, they were just 'gold diggers' who would try to get impregnated by me just to have a financially secured lifestyle. She had told me, "Because of my financial status many women and girls would be pursuing me, trying to develop a relationship with me." She was right again because there were single young adult females in the neighborhood who also wanted to stay with me, and to be my housekeeper. I politely thanked them for their offer, and I turned them down as well. I told them that my grandmother had taught me everything that I needed to know as to taking care of myself.

A single young lady who showed an interest in me and was about eight years older than I was, and the mother of three small children stopped by to visit one night. She brought me a three-layer chocolate cake. I don't know how she knew that chocolate was my favorite cake, but I accepted it and I thanked her for it. I invited her in, and I took the cake into the kitchen, poured me a glass of milk and I cut me a big slice of it, and I offered her some. She said, "no thanks sweetheart, it's for you." I knew what she was up to, but because it was my favorite cake, I accepted it anyway.

I went against my grandmother's advice; she had warned me of an old saying that "the best way to a man's heart is through his stomach." And she had told me, "Not to be quick in eating every woman's cooking, that an evil women would put voodoo in a man's food to control him."

And she also told me, "Never let a woman cut my hair." I think she got that one from Samson and Delilah. But after studying the Scriptures for myself, I found out that Delilah didn't cut Samson's hair, instead, she called for "a man" who came in and cut his hair while he was asleep upon her lap (Judges 16:19). However, I learned a lesson from that passage of Scripture; that I should be careful of who's lap that I lay my head on. Therefore, I turned down the single young mothers, the church girls and my female classmates on their offer to be my housekeeper.

The young lady told me, "When I finish the cake that she had dessert for me." I knew what she was referring to, but I pretended that I wasn't listening. When I had finished eating, she unbuttoned her shirt and suggested that we go into the bedroom so she could, "give me my dessert." Still playing the 'dummy role', I told her that my grandmother didn't allow me to eat in my room and especially in bed. I changed the subject and I told her that I didn't need a housekeeper, that my grandmother taught me how to take care of myself, that she taught me how to do it all.

She said, "I'm not talking about food, I'm the dessert, I want you to make love to me." She pulled her shirt over her shoulders exposing her bare breast and said, "I can give you what your grandmother couldn't." I told her, "No doubt", but my grandmother had warned me about women and girls who were just looking for financial security, and that I should be aware of them. And I told her that my grandmother also advised me to protect myself by not having a "one night stand", nor a "long term sexual relationship" with any of them. I told her that she was the very type that I was warned about, and I told her, "I appreciate the cake, and thanks for the peek show."

She got upset and she seemed highly offended; and she slammed the door on her way out of the house. Once again, my grandmother was right, she had told me to date "Christian girls" my own age that didn't have any kids, because the older ones, especially those with children had, "been around the block" and that I wouldn't be a good soulmate for them. She also explained to me that the fathers of those children would want to, and had a right to visit their kids, and that I had to allow them the time, which most likely would put a strain on my relationship with the mother. I knew that my grandmother was right again, because there was a single young lady in the neighborhood whose boyfriend and the father of her three children was incarcerated. She allowed her new boyfriend to move in with her and her kids, and after about two years the kids father was released from prison, and he came back home. The new live-in boyfriend had fathered a child with her as well, and he had to move out. And there was a lot of contention going on between the three of them regarding child support and visitation rights.

My grandmother would stress the fact that a father should be in the home and involved in his children's lives. She never said it, but I think she was disappointed in my father because he was her only son, and he was never there for us. I never heard her mention that he sent her any money for the support of his nine children.

She told her friend that, "he dropped us off with her after our mother passed and went on with his life." She also told her that, "she really didn't need the money, but the decent and proper thing for him to do was to offer her something in support of his own children." She said, "I've got a surprise for the (Expletive), he thinks he will get my possessions when I'm gone, but I'm leaving everything to Ray-Ray."

My grandmother always told me stories from the Bible about people who lied, connived and committed murder just to get what they wanted. She told me about King David, that he had gotten a married woman pregnant, and he concocted a scheme to blame the pregnancy on the woman's husband. But the husband refused to go home and sleep with his wife while his army friends were on duty. Instead, he stayed in the camp with them, and that King David set the man up to be killed to cover up his own sin.

She also told me about Joseph and Potiphar's wife, how she tried to get him to sleep with her, but he kept refusing her advances. And that one day she caught him off-guard and alone, grabbed him by his clothing trying to seduce him; and that he broke away from her and ran out of the house so fast that he left his coat behind. And the wife lied and said that Joseph tried to rape her, and he ended up spending years in prison for something that he didn't do. She told me to read the story in Genesis 39 so that I would know how to avoid flirtatious women and girls.

She encouraged me to read my Bible daily, she told me that the Bible is our 'roadmap of life', and whatever problem or situation that I would have in life, that the Bible has an answer for it. She gave me a Topical Bible and told me to read it, and whatever problem or situation that I might have, that I could find the answers or the solutions to them in the Topical Bible. And it will show me where to find the Scriptures which would give me the answers to my problems and situations in the Holy Bible. She also told me to "read and obey" the Books of Psalm, Proverbs and Ecclesiastes, that they will guide me and keep me on the right path in life. I was really fascinated by the wisdom of life in the Book of Proverbs, which I read more than any other book in the Bible. I think I loved it so much because of a father's words of wisdom that he passed on to his son.

I didn't have a father or grandfather around to advise me, and to make me aware of the facts of life that I, as a young man will have to face in my lifetime. I always respected the wisdom of my elders, especially the men. I used to go to my grandmother's friend that sold me the car for advice, but he passed on about seven months after selling me the car. There were men at church that I could confide in, but they would question me as to why I wasn't attending church anymore, so I stopped going to them for advice. There was a Christian male teacher at school that I would go to for advice, but he and his wife was killed in an automobile accident on their way home from the school's championship basketball playoff game.

I would talk to the older men at the pool hall, but their wisdom and advice was of the world and not godly wisdom, which was what I need most, therefore, I relied heavily on the Bible for wisdom and instructions.

The day before my grandmother passed, she called me into her bedroom and lectured me about her wishes and expectations for me. The prayer warriors, hearing that she was sick and homebound came by to visit and to pray for her. She asked them to uphold me in their prayers, that she didn't want me to get trapped by any of the women and girls in the neighborhood, especially "that Jezebel." And she asked them to make sure that I stay away from "Jezebel." That wasn't the girl's real name but that was the nickname that the elders in the neighborhood called her. I once asked my grandmother, "Why did they call her by that name?" She said, "Jezebel was a woman in the Bible that used her beauty, charm and influence over men to get what she wanted." And she advised me to stay away from her, that she was a "little [expletive]"; and she wasn't good enough for me, and that I deserve better. She had told me that she better not get a report from any of her friends nor the neighbors that I was seen with her or at her house. She told me that I should be aware of beautiful, cunning and flirtatious women and girls.

I knew that she was right about this girl, she was attractive and very beautiful, she had long pretty hair, and a beautiful shapely body, and strange, but beautiful multi-color eyes that seem to hypnotize you if you stare into them. I used to shoot marbles as a kid, I had two identical ones that I kept in a small glass jar in my bedroom, and I labored them 'Jezebel's eyes' because they reminded me of the color of her eyes. One day my grandmother, on one of her routine bedroom checks to make sure that I didn't have any hidden adult magazines: she saw the jar with Jezebel's name on it and she question me about it, she thought that I had an attraction for her. But I told her that the marbles reminded me of her eyes. She again warned me to stay away from her and she reminded me that Jezebel was very promiscuous, that she would have sex with three to five boys at one time, at her house when her parents were away or at one of the boy's houses. She said that a person that sexually active would most likely catch a disease.

She specifically mentioned gonorrhea and syphilis and she told me that, "if I come up with any one of them, that she would know that I had been with Jezebel." This was one of my grandmother's 'tactics' of controlling me, she always used fear to keep me in line and out of what she called, "bad company." She could read me like an opened book, if I seemed to be nervous while I was around her, she would question me about my demeanor. I oftentimes ended up confessing my wrong doings because if she found out that I had did anything that she didn't know about and if I didn't confess them, she would add to my punishment.

Knowing Jezebel's reputation and the warnings from my grandmother's advice, I avoided her like a plague. Late one evening my grandmother had sent me to the neighborhood grocery store, which was owned by an elderly couple, they were friends of hers, I had to pass by Jezebel's house to get home. I stopped and chatted with a couple of boys from school that was also at the store. It had gotten dark by the time I got home from the store. Jezebel was standing in the glass storm door of her house, and she had what appeared to be a thin white curtain rapped around her beautiful, sexy and shapely body.

As far as I could see inside of the house, it was dark, and it seemed that she had a spotlight shining on her which produced a radiant glow over her very attractive body. She called out to me in a very sexual and suggestive voice and said, *"Hey Ray Baby, Come Here."* I remembered that my grandmother had told me that the devil can transform and present himself as an angel of light. I knew that she was probably watching me as she always did when I had to go pass Jezebel's house, so I ran home as fast as I could. When I got home, I told my grandmother why I was late, and I told her about Jezebel just in case she or one of the neighbors saw me talking to her and assumed that I was at her house.

My grandmother believed everything that her friends told her. I often got disciplined for things that I didn't do. They sometimes would report to her that I was at certain places doing things that I wasn't supposed to. But luckily for me, one of her friends called her one day and told her that she saw me with a group of boys "throwing rocks at a drunk man." She asked her, "when did it happen?" The lady said, "they're doing it right now and Ray-Ray is with them", but I was in my room doing my homework and my grandmother knew it. I told her about all the times that I'd gotten punished because of false reports that she had gotten from her friends and the neighbors. And if I tried to defend myself by telling her that the reports weren't true, then she would add to the discipline. She would say, "I was calling her friends and the neighbors a lie!" If she half-way believed me, she would justify the punishments by saying, "In that case, this is for the things that you'd gotten away with." It was a no-win situation, so to make things easier on myself, I learned to accept whatever discipline that she doled out without trying to defend myself.

There were times when the reports on me was true, but there were also times when they were wrong. I learned how to keep a straight face in her presence so that I wouldn't end up telling on myself, and I made sure that she never found out the difference. From that point on she stopped believing every report that she got on me. If she did get a report from any of them, she would ask, "what color shirt did I have on?" I had wised up, she had made me a red and white checkered shirt that I really didn't like, but I wore it from home whenever I had plans to go where I wasn't supposed to be. I told her that "it was my favorite shirt because she made it for me." But I had several shirts at a friend's house, and I would stop by and change shirts whenever I wanted to be with my girlfriend who didn't live in my neighborhood or with any of my friends or the boys that she didn't want me to be with. Apparently, she had been watching me more than I realized.

After her passing I found a pair of binoculars in the drawer of a nightstand that she kept by the window. I'm glad that she never found out about me changing shirts and that most of the reports that she had gotten on me were indeed true. Jezebel knew that my grandmother didn't want me to associate with her, but she wouldn't give up and I didn't give in to her advances. She attended my grandmother's funeral and brought a sympathy card by late that night. I didn't open the door for her, I lied and told her that I had company, that my girlfriend was there and to put it in the mailbox and I would get it later.

The next morning, I got the card and a note that she had put in the envelope. In it she told me how greatly she admired me, and she wanted to be my girlfriend. She described all the illicit sexual things that she wanted to do to me. From that I knew for sure that she wasn't the right girl for me, and that my grandmother and the neighbors was right about her all along. I was able to avoid her for several days after that, when I saw her, she asked me "did I read her note?" I told her "Yes", "that It was abhorrent and as a Christian, I would never let her perform those sex acts on me." However, that didn't stop her, she was very consistent, and she still flirted with me every chance that she got, in the neighborhood and at school as well.

She often would come to my house ringing the doorbell and knocking on the door, but I never did let her in, and if I was outside and saw her coming my way, I would go inside just to avoid having a conversation with her. I could imagine how Joseph felt in his resistance to Potiphar's wife. However, unlike Joseph, I made sure that she didn't catch me alone with my guard down. But late one rainy night she knocked on my door claiming that her parents had put her out of the house and that she didn't have anywhere to go. I let her in because it was storming outside, and she was soaking wet. My grandmother kept a boot mat in the hallway near the door, I didn't want her to track mud on my floor and carpeting. I asked her to take her wet and muddy shoes off and put them on the mat, and to wait in the hallway while I go and get her a towel so she could dry herself off.

As she was drying herself off, she asked me, "Why I always avoided her? That, other boys would pay attention to her, and no one had ever turned her down." I told her, "That was her problem, that she used her beauty and sexuality in the wrong way and because of her reputation, no decent guy would want her as a steady girlfriend." I told her what I had heard that the boys thought of her, that, "she was just a sex object", and none of them would have her to be their girlfriend. And I asked her, "had any of them ever offered to take her out to a movie, the skating rink, or any other public place?" She said, "No" I told her, "Now you know why." She said that she really liked me and that she would stop having sex with other boys if she could have me.

She then said that she wanted to get out of her wet clothes so that she wouldn't catch a cold. Immediately my mind led me to Proverbs Chapter 7 and I wanted to put her out of the house and back out into the rain.

But for some reason, looking at her beautiful shapely wet body; I had compassion for her. Instead of putting her out as I knew that I should have done, I let her stay; intentionally long enough for her to dry herself off and the rain to stop. I was going to let her use my grandmother's umbrella that she kept in the hallway near the boot mat if the rain didn't subside. I took a bathroom break while she was still drying herself off, but she wasn't in the hallway when I came out of the bathroom. She had gone into my bedroom disrobed and got into my bed and asked me to lie down with her. Immediately my mind led me to Potiphar's wife, and I told her "NO" because I had a girlfriend, and I would never cheat on her.

She threw off the bed sheets exposing her beautiful, fully naked body. She said, "look at all of this beauty, it's for you; does it change your mind?" As beautiful and tempting as she was, I still refused her, and I told her to "get out of my bed and out of my house!" She got up and put her arms around me, and asked me to hold her, she said that she need warmth and affection. It took every ounce of my strength to resist her. She was even more beautiful naked and much harder to resist than when she was fully clothed. And because of her hypnotic eyes, I made sure that I didn't make direct eye contact with her. I think she chose that rainy night just to gain my sympathy and to get me to open the door and let her in. She did everything within her power to get me to give in unto her. She even tried to do the things to me that she had described in her note.

I felt my manliness, from the closeness of our body contact, it was as though our bodies had become magnetized. Since I had ignored the warning from Proverbs Chapter 7 and didn't put her out of the house, another Scripture came to my mind, *"yield not to temptation."* Not only that, but I could hear the warnings from my grandmother telling me to stay away from her and other seductive women and girls like her. I also heard the voices of the prayer warriors praying for me, "LORD GOD ALMIGHTY, PLEASE GIVE HIM THE POWER TO RESIST JEZEBEL, SO HE DON'T GET CAUGHT IN A TRAP SET UP BY SATAN."

The feelings and the temptations that I was getting from our body contact was very strong, so strong that I literally had to push her away from me. I pushed her away so hard that both of us stumbled and fell to the floor. She acted very strange, uttered a sinister groan as though she was desperate for sex. She got on top of me and tried to unzip my pants as I was down on the floor. Her strange, but beautiful eyes seemed to gleam, and I felt myself getting weaker as I made eye contact with her. I closed my eyes as we wrestled around on the floor. I was able to get both feet in her chest area and I pushed her away from me with both feet as hard as I could! She flew about six feet across the room into the wall. She hit the wall so hard that the force from her body put a dent in the plastered wall. I got up, ran into the bathroom and locked the door. She kept pounding on the bathroom door begging for me to come out and make love to her, but I didn't open the door.

She asked, "Why was I fearful of her?" And she said, "if I make love to her, all of my fear would go away." I told her that she had an evil spirit in her and to leave my house and never to come back! It seemed that about an hour had past when I finally came out of the bathroom. I came out only after I didn't hear her in the house. I looked under my bed and in the closet for her. I looked throughout the whole house, in every room, under every bed and in every closet to make sure that she was gone and that nothing was missing. Her wet clothes that she had on was gone, therefore, I knew that she had left.

I had left the key to my reserved room at the pool hall, and it was closed so I couldn't go to my hide out. I drove to a friend's house and spent the rest of the night there. I'm glad that I had slowed down in my drinking because the vibes and the temptations that I got from our body contact was so strong, that I may not have had the strength to resist her if I'd had a drink. It was only by the Grace of God, through the remembrance of Scriptures, the warnings of my grandmother, the concerns and prayers of my guardians and the prayer warriors that I was able to resist her temptations and advances.

I was also able to resist her because of her reputation at school and in the neighborhood. I had heard what other girls had said about her, that she had gotten pregnant and had a miscarriage and that she was pregnant again, and she wasn't sure who the father of the child was. Therefore, I knew that she was just seeking financial security because I had money, a car, and a house. In the past when I felt my resistance to her advances was getting low, I stayed at a friend's house or in my room over the pool hall just to avoid her.

But someone found out that I was staying with my friend and the room and reported it to the neighbors. They started coming by his house and the pool hall inquiring about me, so I had to give them up. I asked another one of my friend's parents if I could rent a room with the family? I told them about Jezebel and what she was trying to do. His mother understood and said that she knew of Jezebel's reputation and that my friend wasn't allowed to have anything to do with her either. She said that she heard from her two daughters that Jezebel was pregnant, and that she only showed an interest in him after he had gotten a job.

I had the freedom to hangout, to come and go as I pleased but my life was not the "bed of roses" that I had imagined nor hoped for. I had everything that I needed and everything that most people would desire, a mortgage free, three-bedroom house, a car and money in the bank. And I could have afforded anything that I wanted, yet I was miserable. I had no peace and not much privacy. Oftentimes whenever my car was parked at home someone would stop by to see me or wanting to pray for me. Because of this, I often would park my car somewhere else, and I would take a bus or a taxi to where I wanted to go. Wherever my car was parked, and someone would see it, they would report it to the neighbors and soon they'll come knocking on the people's door asking about me. Some of the kids from the neighborhood had become *spies* for their parents. Whenever I was missing for several days and the '*spy kids*' would see me or my car, they would report it to their parents and soon a group of people, sometimes up to about eight, would show up asking about me. For this reason, I abruptly stop going to the playground and buying refreshments for the kids. I knew that they were just following the instructions of their parents, but I felt that they were traitors, and I distant myself from many of them.

Most times, I would park my car and leave it not knowing the people that lived in the house. I once parked it and ran to catch a bus, I fell asleep on the bus and when I woke up, I saw another bus coming; I boarded it, and I rode a trip on it as well. I rode at least seven busses that day throughout the city giving myself time and space from everyone. And when I decided to go home, I had forgotten where I had parked my car, it took me about three hours to find it. After that experience I would park my car late at night in my girlfriend's neighborhood and I would sneak back home.

Oftentimes I would be at home for several days before I came out of the house. I painted the windows black in my rear bedroom and I put up dark curtains so that the light wouldn't be seen. It was my way of isolating myself from everyone so that I could relax and be at peace. I had become somewhat of a recluse in my own house.

My financial blessing had become more of a curse to me. My problem was avoiding Jezebel and hearing the constant nagging and the visitations from my grandmother's friends, the neighbors and the prayer warriors. They would all remind me that I wasn't living up to her expectations of me. The prayer warriors were dedicated to their mission, they were as consistent as the religious sect that walk the streets daily, rain or shine, going from house to house trying to get people into their religion. They often showed up unexpectedly wanting to pray for me and reminding me of the promise that they had made to my grandmother; the wishes that she had for me, and my commitment to God.

Once they audaciously came to my school asking about me and wanting to know if I was still attending school. Even when they weren't around, I could hear their voices and lectures, especially when I was about to do something that I knew that wasn't right or didn't meet their approval. Once I was tempted to commit a crime so that I would go to jail just to get away from them. But I ruled out that thought because I knew that they would come to the jail and visit me, and that I couldn't run and hide from them if I was confined.

Because of the pressure that was put on me from my guardian neighbors and the advances of Jezebel, I stayed away from church in my teenage and young adult years. Because of this, my spirit man just wasn't satisfied. Something within me kept prodding me to give up my worldly lifestyle and start back going to church. In a sense, I felt like the prodigal son that I read about in the Bible. Although I didn't get broke and hit rock bottom as he did, but I wasn't ready to give up my freestyle life.

My problem was that I didn't have much of what I wanted nor desired, because everyone was constantly in my face advising me, wanting to pray for me, and reminding me of my grandmother's expectations of me. Up to about two years after her passing some of her friends from church would stop by to check on me and invite me to church asking, "Why wasn't I attending church anymore?"

They also would remind me that I wasn't living up to her expectations of me, and that I had become a disappointment to her memory. With people watching me and lecturing me about my life became a thorn in my flesh. I just couldn't take it anymore, hearing the same things from the same people caused me to have anxiety and sleep insomnia, and I felt that I had to get away from them all. Someone found out that I was staying with my friend's family and the prayer warriors started showing up at their house wanting to pray for me. I didn't want to put the family through what I was going through, I didn't want everybody coming by looking for me all hours of the day and night.

My friend's family wasn't religious people that attended church as most of the neighbors and my grandmother's friends did. But they were good people and knowing how hypocritical most of the elders in the community were; I can understand why they didn't go to church. They didn't put any unnecessary pressure on me, and they didn't annoy me as everyone else did. They accepted me as part of the family, and I felt at home and at peace while I was there. They were a quiet and poised family, they never asked to borrow money as some of the neighbors did. My friend had two sisters, they both showed an interest in me, but I didn't make any advances towards neither of them. I told them that I had a girlfriend and as 'pretty' as they were, that it would be hard for me to choose one of them over the other. Therefore, I'd rather regard them as my 'half-sisters' and not as a girlfriend.

They were very pretty girls and they carried themselves in a respectful manner, they were the type that I would have pursued if I didn't have a steady girlfriend. But I knew that if I had developed a relationship with one of them that it would become a problem with the other one and I told them so. I didn't want to sow discord among the family; therefore, I treated my friend as a brother and his sisters as my own. The four of us would often go to the movies and the skating rink, and when the Cotton Carnival and the State Fair came to town, we would attend them as well. We did everything that normal brothers and sisters did, and I would pay for whatever the expenses were. And when their birthdays came around, I made sure that I got them whatever they wanted or whatever I thought they needed. I didn't mind the cost because I really enjoyed their company and our time together; we had a brother and sisters relationship that was void within my own family.

Because of this, out of appreciation, whenever I saw a need in the family, I would buy the things that they needed because I knew that their parents wouldn't ask for help. I bought birthdays and Christmas gifts for their parents as well.

My friend's dad had a minimum wage job, he was a handy man with many labor skills. Their landlord was an elderly man that owned several rental properties. For a reduction in rent, my friend's dad would make repairs on the properties, and he would do work for other people and businesses as well to ensure that the family's needs were met. Their refrigerator once quit working and my friend's dad spent several days in his spare time trying to fix it.

His parents twenty fifth year wedding anniversary was coming up, I wanted to do something that the whole family could benefit from. So, I went to Sears and Roebuck, and I bought them a brand-new refrigerator, it only cost me $195.00. Somehow Jezebel found out that I was staying at my friend's house, she started pursuing him as well, but I think she was trying to make me jealous. She came by so often that his mother told her to, "stay away from her house and from her son." Jezebel asked her, "Why?" His mother told her, "Because of your reputation." She also warned her that, "she was living a dangerous lifestyle by having sex with so many boys." My friend knew one of her sex partners and he avoided her as well, he didn't want his name and reputation to be tarnished by having any association with her.

But Jezebel was very persistent, despite the warnings and the 'cold shoulders' that she received she still didn't stop trying to develop a relationship with him. I didn't want the family to be burden with my problems, I didn't want a mob of people coming by their house looking for me, so I went back home.

A job opening occurred within his employment in West Memphis, Arkansas, which is six miles from Memphis. His mother advised him to put in a transfer, "to avoid Jezebel's advances" which he did, and he was accepted. She thought that because of her beauty and charm that he wouldn't have the strength to resist her as I did. So, he moved out of his parent's house and was renting a two-bedroom apartment, but he only had a few items of furniture that his mother had given him. All that he had was his bed and the sofa bed that I slept on when I stayed at his house, a small kitchen table with two chairs and a hot plate to cook on; he used a thirty-gallon metal wash tub with a block of dry ice in it for refrigeration.

I told him that I would furnish the whole apartment and pay the monthly rent of one hundred ten dollars if he would let me stay for a while, that I was desperate for peace and tranquility. He gladly accepted my offer, and we went to a thrift store where I spent about five hundred dollars on used furniture to furnish the whole apartment. I bought everything, two complete bedroom sets, living room furniture, a stove, refrigerator and a kitchen table with four chairs. I even bought two television sets, one for the living room and one for my bedroom. And we agreed that he would pay the utilities which averaged about thirty-five to forty dollars a month. And by this, he could help his family so that his dad wouldn't have to work so many jobs.

My friend had a cousin that worked on the same job, I paid him and one of his friends to paint the whole apartment.

I went through all that trouble and expenses just to have freedom and a peace of mind. It was very well worth it, and it was the most peaceful time that I had after my grandmother's passing. However, now looking back on my life, I'm glad that her friends, the neighbors, and the prayer warriors didn't give up on me. I now understand the meaning of the proverb, "It takes a whole village to raise a child."

Furthermore, I can truly understand why many rich people are so miserable; if you're not living up to God's standards all the money, fame, and worldly goods that one may have cannot satisfy the soul of a man. Jesus said, *"...a man's life consisteth not in the abundance of the things which he posesseth."* It was true in my case, I had inherited a three-bedroom mortgage free house valued at about

$20,000.00 and over $45,000.00 cash, as well as the ten thousand dollars that I received from my grandmother's friend, but I was spiritually miserable. I'm glad that I didn't let my fortune ruin my life. As King Solomon so eloquently said it, *"Vanity of vanities, all is vanity."*

I lived with my friend at the apartment for about eight months, and I would briefly stop by my house late at night twice a week to check on things and to get my mail. One night one of the prayer warriors saw the lights on in my house, she rounded up the rest of them and they rushed over asking questions about where I'd been, that they were worried and concerned about me, and that they had been constantly praying for me.

Out of respect, I didn't tell them the whole story, that I was tired of them, and everyone else, trying to run and dictate my life. I just told them about Jezebel, and that I had to get away from her and her advances. I told them how she had gotten into my bed and the illicit sexual things that she tried to do to me. And that it was getting harder for me to resist her, and I needed some time and space to avoid her advances and temptations. Then I thanked them for their prayers and supplications for me, to my surprise they understood me. They praise God even more for giving me the mind, heart, will and strength to say "NO" to sin.

Unfortunately, it backfired on me, it made them feel that God had answered their prayers concerning me, and it made them stop by and pray for me more often than before. After the word had gotten out that I was back home, soon things were back to normal again. This time it was worse because many of my grandmother's friends would stop by to visit and invite me to church and Sunday dinner with their families.

One of the prayer warriors had a spare bedroom, her son was deployed to Vietnam, and she said I could stay at her house, and she offered his bedroom to me. She was as strict on house rules as my grandmother, and I knew that by accepting her offer that my freedom and my freestyle life would be compromised. Her son had told me that he was thinking about moving out or going into the military to get away from his mother's "iron rule." I knew that she wouldn't have treated me any differently, so I thanked her for her kindness, but I turned down her offer.

The elders and the neighbors used my absence as an excuse to check on me and to see who I was keeping company with. And there were single young women in the neighborhood which I believe had ulterior motives for being nice to me. Most of them had children and they would stop by to see me as well. Some of them brought me food, some offered to cook for me, and some of them invited me over for dinner with their families. There also was a thirty-four-year-old widower with four children, whose husband was killed in the Vietnam war.

She said that she had heard that I was alone with no one to look after me. She brought me a banana pudding, I thanked her for it, and I told her that I have more food than I could eat, and I suggested that she keep it for her children. In our conversation she said to me, "I've been thinking about remarrying; since you live in this big house all alone, maybe we can get to know each other, and see where our relationship will take us." I showed her my notebook with all the names and phone numbers that I had collected over the years, and I told her, "You will have a long wait." I also told her that I wasn't ready to settle down, that my girlfriend and I had plans of getting married after she finishes college and medical school. I told her that because she was almost twice my age, that I didn't think it would work out; and I didn't want to lead her on, nor did I want to get involved in an unwanted relationship. Therefore, I plainly told her "No thanks."

Again, I had no peace and not much privacy. I spent most of my time at the apartment in West Memphis, because they had found out where my friend lived and about the room in the boarding house over the pool hall which I had to give it up. I didn't want anyone to be burden by any of my 'guardians' because they were very consistent, they never gave up on me. Whenever they would hear of my whereabouts or see my car parked, they would stop by to check on me. Many times, I wished that they would "get a life" and leave mine alone, but out of respect, I never mustered up enough courage to tell them that.

Overall, I think they had my best interest at heart, but it was an overkill. It seemed that they were more concerned about me and my whereabouts than their own kids. Many times, I thought about asking them, "if I could pay them to leave me alone." My friend had an on-the-job injury and his mother wanted him back home so that she could look after him because, she couldn't afford the commute to be there when he needed her. We agreed to let his married cousin that had three children rent the apartment. He had painted the apartment for us, and I had a good relationship with him, but I didn't want to share the apartment with his family, so I went back home again.

But I still didn't start going back to church. I kept telling myself that I should do so, and maybe, people would stop troubling me about my life. One of my grandmother's usher friends from church who knew how much money she had left me asked, "What would it profit a man to gain the whole world and lose his own soul?"

That was a wake-up call for me, the deep tone of her voice, with that passage of Scripture hit me like a ton of bricks! However, it took a serious automobile accident to bring me back to my senses and start back going to church and to fulfill my Christian duties and commitment to God. To me, it seemed as though God was giving me an ultimatum: to return unto Him or die in my sins. Through my experiences, I fully understood what my grandmother was trying to teach me by having me to read the same passage of Scripture twice daily that; someday I would stop going to church and since God is not willing that any should perish, that the Spirit of God would eventually lead me back into the household of faith.

As she used to say, "I would understand it better, by and by", I now understand. I've also come to realize that we have guardian angels watching over us. They may not always be angelic being, but they could very well be someone in the neighborhood who cares about us, and constantly praying for us. As it is written: *"The prayers of the righteous availeth much."*

After this, I realized that I had caused most of my problems by simply not attending church and living the Christian lifestyle that my grandmother and everyone else expected of me. Since the elders in the neighborhood was very judgmental, I didn't want to be labored a 'hypocrite' by going to church and still living a freestyle life, so I stopped going to church. Later, I realized that I had inadvertently put fun, pleasure and freedom above worshiping and serving God.

Jezebel heard that I had come back home, one night she came by with her child and she wanted me to see him. She said that I would be a 'perfect father' for her son. She pursued me just as she always did, but now with her little child in tow. She would ask to borrow money so she could get things for her son. I told her, "NO", that that was her baby's daddy's responsibility. She said that she wasn't sure who the father was and no one [of her sex partners] took responsibility. I suggested, "before she goes to bed with them, that she should take up a collection from all of them to buy the things that her child needed. And since they had the pleasure of getting him, that they should help support him."

She brushed off that suggestion and she said," that would make her a prostitute." I told her, "She was doing it anyway, and that she should benefit from it, at least for the sake of her child." Then I told her, [sarcastically] "justify it as, trading what you got for what you and your child need." I didn't let her use her child as an excuse to gain my sympathy. I also told her, "If her sex partners didn't chip in to help her, then she should stop giving herself to them." I don't know if she took my advice or not. I didn't ask her about her business, I stayed out of it, just as I wished everyone would have stayed out of mine.

I also told her what my grandmother used to tell my sisters, "You laid down to get them, now lay down to take care of them." My grandmother wasn't that nice about it, she used the expletive

("F") word. She made sure that people didn't use her kindness for weakness just to get what they wanted from her. Sometimes young females from the neighborhood would come to her to borrow money to get things for their children, she would advise them to, "get it from the child's father or go on welfare." She used to tell me that people, especially females would try any and everything, sometimes shirking in their own responsibilities to gain my sympathy and that I should be aware of that. Once again, she was right about Jezebel. Although she may have liked me as she claimed, but her overall goal was for financial security for her and her son.

By this time, my youngest sister and her husband had divorced. She wrote asking about how things were going at home? She said that she had called but the phone number was changed to a private number. She didn't know that our grandmother had passed. I told her if she come back home that I would give her the house because I wanted to leave town. Within two weeks she was back home with her four children. I gave her the house with everything in it and $3,000.00 cash and I moved to Milwaukee, Wisconsin. It was my way of permanently getting away from the constant nagging of my grandmother's friends, the neighbors, the prayer warriors and most of all, the influences and advances of Jezebel.

I loaded my car with my clothing and personal belongings, and I stopped at the neighborhood grocery store to buy snacks for my trip and to say "goodbye" to the owners who were nice, elderly people and friends to my grandmother. They didn't get in my business as everybody else did, therefore, I looked up to them as my 'adopted grandparents'. I affectionately called them, 'grandma and grandpa'.

As I was leaving the store, Jezebel happened to be passing by with her child, she saw my car was packed with my belongings. She asked me, "Was I going on a trip?" I told her "Yes" and that "I won't be coming back." We had a brief conversation, as a matter of fact, I talked to her longer on that day on a personal level than I ever had. I was so busy running from and avoiding her that we had never engaged in a real conversation. She told me that she really liked me and that she did everything within her power to get me to like her as well. She admitted that she knew that I was a Christian, and that she didn't approach me as a 'Christian lady' should, and that she now realize that she had been lewd in her advances which drove me away from her.

She said, "now she has matured and is a mother, and she was trying to be a good mother to her son; and she didn't want her reputation to follow her as her child grew up." She said that "all she needed was a real man in her life that would be a good example and role model for her son to follow after." I could relate to that because I didn't have a father figure in my life, but I wasn't persuaded by it. I was touched by her confession, but I didn't let it deter me.

I ended up telling her how beautiful she was and that I almost gave in to her that rainy night when she had gotten into my bed. I apologized to her for how I had to push her away from me.

She said that she wasn't hurt physically, but she was emotionally hurt because she truly and sincerely loves me. I told her, "If she wasn't the type of person that she was that there may have been a chance that we could have had a meaningful relationship." She apologized again and said that "It could still happen, that we could get to know each other and see where our relationship would take us." I told her "NO", that I had given the house to my sister and my mind was made up, and I was following through with it and I was going on with my life, and I suggested that she do the same.

However, I confessed to her that the older I became the harder it was for me to resist her. That it was easier when we were teenagers, and that, being a young man now and understanding adulthood, that I may not be able to resist her as I did in the past. So, I felt that my best solution to get away from her and my "guardian neighbors" was to leave town. As I was talking to her, I felt myself empathizing with her and I realized how she charmed her sex partners. It was very hard to resist her, anyone without a strong conviction wouldn't have been able to say 'No' to her.

I made sure that I didn't have direct eye contact with her because it seemed that she always got what she wanted with her cunning, hypnotic eyes. Some of the elders believed that "she had sold her soul to Satan" just to get what she wanted in life. She said that "Everyone deserves a second chance, and she was trying very hard to change." I told her, "According to the Bible, human nature doesn't change, even if she does become a Christian, that eventually she would get weak and fall back into sin." She said, "God forgives sins", and asked me, "why won't I forgive her?" I told her that I wasn't mad at her, "that she had a right to live her life as she pleased, and to do the things that she enjoyed, but it should be done in a Christian manner."

I told her, "I'm not God, and my human nature wouldn't allow me to love and forgive as God does." I had one hundred and twenty-three dollars in my shirt pocket, I put it in her hand and kissed her on the forehead and told her "Goodbye." She smiled and reached out to embrace me, but I gently pushed her hands away. She looked sadden and very disappointed, and asked me, "Would I send for her?" I told her, "No", that, "this is probably the last time that we would ever see each other." She asked me, "Where was I going?" I lied and told her that I was going to Chicago, Illinois that my girlfriend has a cousin there, and she was coming up to be with me, and we had talked about living together.

She then suggested, "Since we won't be seeing each other again, we should check into a motel and make it memorable." I shook my head "No", got into my car and I drove off. As I was pulling away, I looked through the rear-view mirror to see her reaction, she was crying, and she seemed very hurt; she clutched her stomach and her knees buckled as she was holding herself up by a light pole. I tried to reason within myself, "maybe she's really serious and can change her ways, and maybe she really does care for me."

As I turned the corner, I saw people running towards her direction, I assumed that she had fallen to the ground. One mind told me to "turn around go back and see about her", and another mind told me to "keep driving." I kept driving because I knew that the feelings that I really had for her deep down inside would have prevented me from leaving town. I also knew that if I had turned around that it would have been a 'let down' to my grandmother, the neighbors, her church friends, and the prayer warriors. And all their time, energy and prayers for me would have been in vain. And I would have been a disappointment to them all. I didn't want that decision to haunt me for the rest of my life, therefore, I figured that I had more to lose than to gain, so I kept on driving.

On my trip to Wisconsin, I thought about Jezebel a lot. My mind went back to earlier years when I kept the jar in my bedroom with the marbles in it that resembled her eyes. Many nights I would go to bed fantasizing of having a sexual relationship with her. Sometimes I would wake up the next morning and my bedsheets would be wet. I remembered watching a horror movie once where a woman was asleep and thought she was dreaming, but when she woke up, the devil was having sexual intercourse with her.

One night my grandmother heard groaning in my bedroom, she came into my room to see what was going on. She woke me up and asked, "who was that in my room?" I told her, "No one, that I was alone." She said, "somebody was in here with you, they vanished when I turned the light on!" I told her that I had went to bed thinking about Jezebel, and I dreamed that she came into my room and got in bed with me. She threw the bed sheet from me, and my manhood was at full attention and my sheets were wet! She said, Jezebel has an evil spirit in her and that she may have transformed herself into my room and got in bed with me! She said, "if a person desire having sex with anyone other than their spouse, that person has committed adultery in their heart and in my case, I was guilty of fornication." She told me to get up and read Matthew 5:28 and 1 Corinthians 6:18 and to go and take a bath.

She took the jar with the marbles in it that I had labored, 'Jezebel's eyes' from the bookshelf that was attached to the headboard of my bed, and they were gleaming, as though they were alive! She took the jar and flushed the marbles down the toilet, and she broke the jar. It was about 3 A.M., she immediately called the prayer warriors and told them what she had witnessed, and she told them my confession, and asked them to come over and pray for me.

Within an hour they rushed over and anointed me with what they said was 'Holy Oil' and they denounced the sexual demon in the Name of Jesus. They mention the demon by name, but I don't remember what the name was, but it wasn't a name that I'd ever heard for a human being. I never had another 'wet dream' about her after that, and it made me wonder; "Had Jezebel, somehow, actually came into my room and had sex with me?" And the two miscarriages that she had, "Were they the result of my imaginary sexual encounters with her?"

I also wondered how my life would be had we connected. But I reasoned within myself that it would never have worked, because she desired more sexual attention than I probably was able to give her. It was evident by the many sex partners that she had and as often as they, 'got together' that I was no soulmate for her.

Also, I remembered that my grandmother had told me that Adam put a generational curse on his descendants with one bad choice. And that sin entered the world because of his disobedience to God, and mankind is still suffering from pain, sickness and death, all because of the one bad choice that Adam made. With that I reasoned that I made the right decision by not turning back.

I didn't want to be "another Adam." I envisioned my daughters or granddaughters might inherit the spirit of Jezebel. I didn't want to put a curse on my descendants, which was even more reason that I kept on driving. I never contacted anyone, not even my sister, my girlfriend, nor my best friends after moving to Milwaukee, Wisconsin. I didn't want the word of my whereabouts to get out and have Jezebel nor anyone else coming to Milwaukee seeking me, by doing so, it would have negated my whole purpose for leaving town.

I returned home about seven years later to have the house officially put in my sister's name. She wasn't home when I got in town, so I drove around visiting friends and the people that I was close to. I found out that many of my 'guardians' had passed on. I was amazed that they died so quickly after I left town. I assumed that their sole purpose in life was to watch over me, and since I wasn't around, that they had no more purpose to live.

I went to the neighborhood grocery store to say "Hello" to 'grandma' and 'grandpa' and to see if they were still alive. I knew by this time they should be nearing ninety years old. Their two sons were running the store, I was told that 'grandpa' suffered a massive heart attack during a strong-armed robbery at the store and he had passed away. And 'grandma' was so distraught by it, that she suffered a seizure during the attack, and went into a coma. And after two weeks she woke up, but she had a severe case of Alzheimer's, and that her condition was so bad that she couldn't recognize nor remember anyone.

The only person that she could remember was grandpa, she constantly called out to him, and that she would often leave home going looking for him. They said that they had to make sure that the doors were locked to keep her from wandering off. I was told that one night, they were at the store conducting an inventory and somehow, grandma wandered out of the house going looking for grandpa and she was struck and killed by a freight train.

I went to my hang out at the pool hall on Beale Street to say "Hello" to my friend and his dad. The pool hall had closed and gone out of business, and the whole building was boarded up.

The barber shop had moved down the street, and the owner told me that "about four years ago, there was an armed robbery at the pool hall and my friend, his father and two other people were killed, and that the family sold the building and relocated somewhere in Kentucky." He told me that the same people were responsible for the robbery at the grocery store which caused grandpa's death, he said that it all happened three weeks apart.

I drove to my friend's house, the one that I shared the apartment with; their house had been torn down and was now a vacant lot. I learned that he and his mother had died of smoke inhalation in a fire. I was told that he came home intoxicated late one night and tried to cook, he left a skillet on the stove and went to bed, and the house caught fire. And it spread so quickly that he and his mother was overcome by the smoke, and they couldn't get out of the house. His dad and his two sisters were the only survivors, and after their tragic lost they moved to Nashville, Tennessee.

Hearing this really saddened me, because I considered them as, my "adopted family", we shared a bond as brothers and sisters that I never experienced in my own siblings. I couldn't remember my girlfriend's phone number, so I went to her house to see how she and her family was doing. Her mother said that she waited for me to contact her for over a year after I left town; that she never heard from me, and there were reports that I was killed in an automobile accident in Nashville, and that she had gotten married to a college sweetheart. That they both have ambitions to become medical doctors, and through grants and scholarships, they are attending medical school in South Carolina. And after their upcoming graduation she and her husband have plans to return home and open a medical clinic in the neighborhood.

My ex-girlfriend just happened to call her mother while I was there. I apologized to her for my absence, and I told her why I abruptly left town. She said that Jezebel had spread rumors in the neighborhood that I was coming back to town and that we were going to stay in my house. She said that she knew better because of all the trouble that I went through just to avoid her. She said a friend of ours was traveling through Nashville and happened to come across a local newspaper which reported my accident; and it had a picture of me in the hospital where the doctors thought that I wasn't going to recover.

She said that word had gotten out around the neighborhood that I was killed in the accident; that she never heard from me, and she had accepted it because I never got in touch with her, so she decided to go on with her life. She said she and a high school and college classmate started dating and eventually, they fell in love and got married.

She said, "hold on, I have someone who would like to say 'Hello' to you." She gave the phone to her husband which happened to be a friend of mine from ninth grade. He was a straight- A student, very smart and I thought very highly of him. He was a decent guy, and even in high school I could tell that he would be successful in whatever career that he chose. He once tutored me in my science class preparing me for a test. With his help I got a B + grade, it was the highest grade that I got that school year. I told him how much I appreciated him in helping me pass the test. I gave them my blessings and I told him that I believe they would be a perfect couple because they are comparable, very smart and have the same dreams, ambitions and goals; and that I wanted to support them in their effort. I told him that I would leave a five thousand dollars cashier's check with her mother to help them get started on their plans. I felt really bad that I had allowed myself to be disconnected from my friends and those whom I was close to. After hearing that everyone thought I was dead, I reasoned that was why so many of the elders and my neighborhood guardians had passed on so quickly after I left town.

I was told that Jezebel and her ten-year-old son had also died. I went to her house to visit her parents and to offer my condolences to the family. They told me that Jezebel had started back having unprotected sex with her friends, and one of them had been tested positive for STD and he didn't tell her. And that they all had contracted the disease, and the guys and her child had died from it. But no one knew for sure how the child got it. Her mother told me she thinks it was spread to him through her because, "she always shared her sodas with him, that they drank from the same bottle."

She said as her health was failing her, she would often talk in her sleep, calling out to me and apologizing that she wasn't the right one for me. She said that Jezebel left a suicide note requesting that no one should see her dead body, and she wanted to be cremated because she didn't look like the same person. She said that she understood why she made the request, "because she had lost all of her beauty, her long pretty hair had gotten thin and had mostly fallen out, her teeth had protruded out of her mouth; her multi-colored eyes had turned black, 'as black as tar', and to look into them was like 'looking into a black hole', and that, they had sunken into her head."

She also said that "her looks was so frightening that she wore dark sunglasses all the time; her shapely body had become nothing but skin and bones, and that she had become so weak, that she couldn't stand up nor walk." I was told that she and her son stayed in her room and in bed all the time; that she didn't want any visitors because she didn't want anyone outside of the family to see her in her condition. And that, "she was so devastated by the disease, her looks, and the sickness of her son; that she took all of her meds at once, and she died in her sleep while holding her dead son in her arms."

Her dad said, she looked as though a curse had been put upon her, and that he had heard the rumors that she sold her soul to the devil. He said, "she looked like a zombie from a horror movie." And, some nights strange noise could be heard in her bedroom, and that, she requested, "no one was to come into her room after dark, when her company was there." I asked him, "Her company?" He said, "yes", that they believe she was being visited by her deceased sex partners.

And she would request that her son be taken out of her room and the family would sometimes have to leave the house "for about an hour or so" when things got too noisy in her room. He said, "the noise stopped after she died and that for a long time there was an eerie feeling coming out of her room, and that, he thought about putting up a wall to seal it off from the rest of the house." He said that he decided to put a pad lock on her door because everyone was reluctant to go into her room.

Her brother told me that her life would have been different if I had shown her affections and allowed her to be a part of my life. But he knew how she was, and that he understood why I didn't have anything to do with her. He also confirmed that she was "trying to change her ways" and was looking for a decent man to be a father to her child; but he didn't think that she could be faithful to one man. He said that she caught the disease when she had started back having unprotected sex with her partners. That they had been "doing it" for so long, even in their pre-teens; and it had become "a part of their lives, and the cause of their deaths."

Her mother told me that she left a small package for me if I ever came back to town, and it's locked up in her room. She asked her husband to unlock her door and get it for me. I told him, "NO", to leave it, that I didn't want it. I told the family about the marbles that resembled her eyes and the experience that I had with them. I didn't want to "resurrect her" by accepting anything that she left for me; most likely it would have been another pair of marbles or some other personal item of hers.

I'm glad that the family didn't blame me for her demise. However, oftentimes I wondered: "had I'd lived the Christian lifestyle that everyone expected of me; could I have made a difference in her life as well? Perhaps, if I hadn't been so busy avoiding her and the neighbors and becoming a committed Christian and shared my faith with her; and encouraged her to repent of her sins, and to be saved: maybe, just maybe things would have been different for the both of us? Only God knows.

I now try to share the gospel with everyone. I passes out tracts to everyone that I meet, this is the message that I give them.

THIS MESSAGE IS FOR YOU...*JESUS LOVES YOU:*

But if you die without knowing Him as your personal Savior, you will spend eternity in Hell! Question: What if you were to die today, where will your soul spend eternity?

The answer: Heaven or Hell-*They're your only choices!*

You are going to die someday. *"It is appointed unto men once to die, but after this the judgment"* (Heb.9:27). At your physical death, your soul goes immediately to Heaven or Hell. While funeral arrangements are being made for the deceased, the soul is already transported into eternity!

Bible proof: Read Luke 16:22,23

The beggar died, (saved) *and was carried by the angels into Abraham's bosom,* (i .e. R.I.P.) *the rich man died also* (unsaved) *and was buried. And in hell he lifted up his eyes being in torments"* (in hell's fire). This passage of Scripture proves that there is life after death. The body dies but the soul lives on FOREVER!

Ezekiel 33:11, *"Say unto them* (the unsaved) *as I live said the Lord God, I have no pleasure in the death of the wicked...turn ye...from your evil way; for why will you die?"* Note: God is talking about the Spiritual death of the unsaved soul, which will be separated from Him and His mercy FOREVER! (Read Rev. 20:11-14).

Note: This is a desperate plea from God Himself, that people be saved from His judgment and wrath which is to come upon this sinful world. Jesus Christ is our only Savior, He is the only one qualified to get you into the presence of God. *"I am the way, the truth, and the life: no man cometh unto the Father but by me"* (John 14:6).

Since you know that you're going to die someday, you should ask, "What must I do to be saved?" You must confess your sins to God, repent and believe in His Son Jesus Christ (Please read and follow the instructions of Romans 10:9,10).

How I came to know the Truth about the timing of the Rapture of the Church:

The Pre-Tribulation Rapture doctrine was taught at this church and believed by seemingly every member, including the chairman of the deacon board who was very knowledgeable of the Bible. He could quote Scriptures word by word, if you ask him where to find a particular passage of Scripture, he could give you the exact Scripture text and verse. He even knew how many books are in the Bible, how many chapters and verses each book contains and he could name each Book of the Bible in order from Genesis to Revelation. I was really impressed by his vast knowledge of the Bible, I viewed him as a walking, talking, human Bible. I very much wanted to be like him in his wisdom, knowledge and understanding of the Bible.

In my thirst for it, I read many books on how to understand God's Word. I desired a closer walk with God hoping that He would see my sincerity and implant a portion of that wisdom, knowledge and understanding in me as well. However, in my Bible studies I found out that the deacon's vast knowledge of the Bible wasn't God given, but rather, it was learned! I ran across one of those study Bibles that had that information in it.

Many of the members of the church would ask the deacon questions about the Bible rather than going to the pastor. For the members that did confide in the pastor and sought his counsel, if he couldn't give them what he thought, was a satisfactory answer, he would advise them to, "ask the deacon." This led to pride on the deacon's part. I later found out that the deacon wanted to present himself as the most knowledgeable person in the church, even above that of the pastor. I was somewhat disappointed in the deacon, but I still admired him greatly for his ability to retain such vast knowledge of the Bible.

I still wanted to know as much as I could about the Bible. Due to my respect for the pastor and my disappointment in the deacon, I didn't go to neither one of them for any questions related to the Bible. Since I had spent so much money on Bibles and study books, I started studying the Bible on my own. That's when I Learned the truth about the Rapture of the Church. In my own way, I was in competition with the deacon. I'd learned that he didn't like competition; one night in Bible study I was able to show him that, "although he basically knew the whole Bible from memory, but if he doesn't 'Rightly Divide' it, it becomes in the eyesight of God; false teachings.

He seemed to have gotten offended and asked me to "clarify myself", in which I was glad that he did because I was prepared and eager to do just that. I told him, "there are sixty- six books in the Bible, thirty nine in the Old Testament and twenty seven in the New Testament. Nowhere in the Bible can one find a single passage of Scripture that teaches the Pre-tribulation Rapture of the Church, and that, he like many Bible commentators, Christian book writers and theologians will take a passage of Scripture out of context and use it to teach the Pre-Tribulation Rapture Doctrine." I reminded him that he, and other "Pre-Trib" Rapture teachers uses 1Thess. 4:13-18 to justify their false view of the Rapture of the Church. He said, "That's the very passage of Scripture that proves the imminent return of Jesus and the Rapture of the Church!"

I asked him to read it, [knowing that he was going to read, 'over it' and add his own interpretations to it as he usually does]. He read it and just like he always did; he read 'over' the Scripture and he explained the doctrinal view of it just as I knew that he would do.

Then I said, "before a building is erected, the foundation must first be laid; tonight, I'm going to lay the foundation then we will build upon it." I took them to Acts 8:26-31 where Philip was sent by God to explain the Scriptures to the Ethiopian eunuch who was reading the book of Isiah as he was traveling along on his journey. Philip climbed aboard his chariot asked him, *"Understandest thou what thou readest."* The man replied, *"How can I, except some man should guide me?* (vs. 30, 31). Then I said, "the deacon just read 1 Thess. 4:13-18 and told you that that passage of Scripture proves the imminent return of Christ and the Rapture of the Church: now he's going to understand exactly what the Bible says."

I lectured the class on how misinformed saints uses that passage of Scripture to teach that "false doctrine", and that, "if they would just read and explain it as it is written without 'twisting the Scriptures' to make them say what they want them to say, then, they would learn the Truth about the timing of the Rapture of the Church!"

The deacon made an off -the- wall comment that, "he was studying the Bible long before my mother was breast feeding me." I didn't respond to his comment, but I told him, according to the Bible, the passage of Scripture that you just read said, *"The dead in Christ shall rise "first", "then", 'afterwards', we will be caught up* [RAPTURED] *to meet the Lord in the air."*

Then I sarcastically asked him, "which part of *'first'* and *'then'* that he didn't understand?" I said, "God is the same yesterday, today and forever, He changes not, neither does His Word; and that I truly believe that judgment is going to begin at the House of God." And that God will judge those false teachers who have trampled over His Holy Word and mislead others astray through their false beliefs." Then I said, "forsake of an argument, let's let the Word of God, speak for God."

I then reminded him of a passage of Scripture in Isaiah 11:6, where it is recorded that, [in the Millennium Reign of Christ], *"a little child shall lead them."* I asked for a child to stand and read the same passage of Scripture. A mother with a little girl about eight years old nudged her to read it. The child raised her hand to read, and I acknowledged her, the mother had turned to the passage of Scripture and handed her a Bible and showed her where to read.

It just happened that she was given a NIV version of the Bible. After the child stood up and read it, I asked her to re-read verses 16 and 17. She stood up again and read, *"For the Lord himself will come down from heaven, with a loud command, with the voice of the archangel and with the trumpet call of God, and the dead in Christ will rise first, After that, we who are still alive and are left will be caught up together with them in the clouds to meet the Lord in the air."*

I commended the child on a job well done and then I asked her, "What did you learn from the Scripture that you just read, did it say that Jesus was coming 'first' or did it say that we will be caught up to meet him 'first'?" She rightly replied that "Jesus was coming 'first', 'after that' we will be caught up to meet him and the angels in the air." I then explained to the class that the Resurrection of the dead, that died in Christ will precede the Rapture of the Church! Which will be the First Resurrection.

Then I said, "I'm amazed that people can quote the Bible word for word, yet, because they're blinded by religious doctrines, they fail to understand the plain teachings of the Bible!" I quoted 2 Timothy 3:16, 17 *"All scripture is given by inspiration of God, and is profitable for doctrine, for reproof, for correction, for instruction in righteousness: That the man of God may be perfect,* [in teaching God's Word] *thoroughly furnished* [equipped] *unto all good works."* Then I said, "People transgress the teachings of God through their traditions and that, they have made the Word of God of none effect by their traditional teachings, ideologies and doctrines."

The deacon sensed that I was speaking directly to him, he became furious, he got up out of his seat and walked over to me and stood there for a few seconds. I made direct eye contact with him; I saw an evil and hatred spirit in his eyes that I'd never seen in him before. I was a little bit frightened by his looks and actions, I thought he was going to punch me in the face. My mind got to wondering, "what should I do if he does hit me, shall I defend myself or, turn the other cheek?"

Most likely I would have turned the other cheek because he was old enough to be my grandfather, I was taught to respect my elders even if they were wrong. I'm glad that he didn't punch me; but instead, he said that "he had never seen it in that fashion." Personally, I believe that if we weren't in church that he would have punched me in my face!

After Bible Study was over the child's mother came up to congratulate me on my presentation of the Truth. She said that she had her doubts about the "Rapture teachings" but she didn't question it because she didn't want to cause a confusion in the church. She said that she bought a 'Plain English' Bible so that it will explain the Holy Bible to her because, "they always take the King James Bible and make it say what they want it to say." And that she thought the deacon was going hit me, because he didn't like to be challenged, she said that "he viewed a challenge as threat to his ego, intelligence and most of all a sign of disrespect." That was the last time that I sat down when teaching the Bible.

I never told the deacon about the books that I had purchased, I wanted him to know that *"God is no respecter of persons"* and that God could educate others in the church and in His Word as well. It was through this experience and in my Bible studies whereas I learned that: There is no Pre-Tribulation Rapture of the Church. But before I learned this truth, I was following the lead of the pastor, the deacon and their wives who were Sunday School teachers; and there were other teachers in the church as well.

Up to that point, I had not heard anyone who taught anything contrary of the Pre-Tribulation Rapture of the Church. So, assuming that it was true; I jumped on the Pre-Tribulation Rapture Doctrine bandwagon and started telling people, "Jesus could come back at any moment and Rapture the Church, and that, no one knows the day nor the hour that He would return; therefore, they should be ready, and that, if they weren't saved, that they would be 'left behind' and be thrown into the lake of fire on judgment day."

As you may recall, someone wrote a book entitled, "88 Reasons Why the Rapture Will Be In 1988." Since the pastor taught us this 'myth', this 'theory' this 'false doctrine' and the very knowledgeable deacon in the word along with seemly, every member of the church believed the same thing. Not only that, but we would fellowship with other churches of the same denomination; every one of those pastors would talk about the Saints being Raptured out of the world. Some would say, "this is Jesus' way of separating the sheep from the goats." I was gullible enough to believe that it was true. I swallowed that false doctrine hook, line and sinker. I even purchased a hundred of those booklets and went on a witnessing campaign trying to save the world with them.

I started telling people to, "get ready because the church could be Raptured out of the world at any moment and the sinners will be 'left behind' where they will go into the Tribulation Period and they will be cast into hell until judgment Day and after that, they would be cast into the lake of fire where their body and soul will burn FOREVER!" I even carried a small New Testament Bible with me, and I would let them read Revelation 20:11-15 as proof. However, I should have read Chapter 22:18,19 myself! I've since repented of my false teaching after learning the Truth about the timing of the Rapture of the Church.

One day during lunchtime at work I witness to a co-worker of mine who didn't even belong to, nor did he attend any church. I told him that, "Jesus could come and Rapture the Church at any time and that he should be ready because no man knows the day or the hour when it will occur." He told me not to believe that (expletive), that the church will go through the whole seven (7) years of the Tribulation Period and then the Rapture would come. He asked me, "How is God's judgment going to begin at the House of God if the church is already Raptured up to heaven?"

It made sense to me, but I dismissed it, I didn't put his opinion above that of which I'd heard and had been taught in church. I later found out that he had been 'church hurt' because of the false doctrine that he'd been taught, it was a church of the same denomination that I had joined.

But I was so convinced into my false belief that I was willing to bet my whole paycheck as well as my life savings [about $38,000.00] that the Rapture would happen in that year. My assumption was, the church won't be here, and I can't take the money with me anyway so why not bet on it? My co-worker told me to keep my money because I would need it in 1989 and the years to come. Low and behold, 1988 came and went and the church is still here! That false doctrine went out over thirty years ago and the church is still here!

Not only that, but I was so convinced in my false learning that I mailed my tenants a certified letter with instructions written on it that it should not be opened until rent day 1989. In it I had drafted a notarized document giving my house to the tenants if I failed to collect the rent for January 1989.

As you know there has been many date setters as to when some believed that the Rapture would occur in a certain year, apparently, they had forgotten the passage of Scriptures that said, *"No one knows the day nor the hour* of the Rapture and Christ's return."* They were all wrong in their date settings because the church is still here.

On January 2, 1989, when we had returned to work from the holidays my co-worker and others mocked us Christians because we weren't 'RAPTURED' in 1988. Some even joked, "perhaps you guys were the ones that was left behind!" There were other believers of different denominations that also believed in the Pre-Tribulation Rapture. We all became a laughingstock among the un-churched and non- believers alike.

They often joked and poked fun at us saying, "I thought you guys would be gone up in the Rapture! Some joked asking, "Where is the promise of His coming?" etc. One of my co-workers had asked me, "could he have my car after I'm gone?" On our return to work he joined the mockers and said he wished that I would have been 'Raptured' "because he really needs a nice car." Another co-worker had asked for my truck, boat, and fishing gear, he also joined the jokesters saying, "now I'll have to bank fish because you didn't leave me your boat." Another co-worker had asked if "he could have my cabin up North after I'm gone?"

My friend asked me, "Aren't you glad that I didn't take you up on your bet?" I never told him 'Yes', but I was glad that he didn't take me up on it. Most likely I would have paid it or made a compromise because I'm a man of my word and I've never reneged on a promise. Whenever a believer would miss time from work someone would make a joke of it saying, "I thought you were 'Raptured' and left your brothers and sisters behind." They really laid it on the pastor, whenever one of those mockers saw him with one of his members together, they would say, "If the blind leads the blind, both will fall into a ditch."

This ridicule went on often, almost daily, it had gotten to the point that the pastor would eat lunch in his car just to avoid them. We stopped inviting our unsaved and the un-churched co-workers to visit the church. The pastor figured that they wouldn't come anyway; and he probably was right, most of them was bold enough to tell him to his face that they didn't want to attend any church where the Bible wasn't taught!

The joking and the ridicule were constantly in our faces, it had gotten to the point that the pastor just couldn't take it anymore and he took an early retirement. He said that the Lord wanted him to devote more time into building up the church. Personally, I think it was because of the ridicule that he had to face daily. I believe a man of lesser faith would have committed suicide.

My tenants also seemed somewhat disappointed that I wasn't RAPTURED because they didn't get a free house! Being respectful but disappointed they questioned the churches doctrine and teachings. Their ten-year-old daughter asked, "Is this the same church that you kept inviting us to visit?" I was hurt, ashamed and embarrassed hearing that coming from an innocent child. I've never felt so embarrassed in my whole life; because of this I let them stay rent free for January and February of 1989. I never did invite them to the church again, even after I started my own ministry.

However, I encouraged them to get to know Jesus Christ as their Lord and Personal Savior. They said that they were believers, that they had repented from their sins and accepted Jesus Christ as their Lord and Savior according to Romans 10:9,10; but they didn't go to church to worship anymore. I was told that they had a pastor in the family who also taught the Pre-tribulation Rapture of the Church and that, "his church would be Raptured in 1988." They said that they would only go to his church for funerals and family reunions but not to worship because, "they felt like something was wrong with his teaching." I truly believe that *"judgment is going to begin at the House of God"* so that God will judge the false teachers who have trampled over His Word and led others astray through their false beliefs. They have made the Word of God of *"none effect"* through their false doctrines and teachings.

One day I mustered up enough Holy Ghost boldness and asked the pastor, "why would he teach us this 'doctrine' if it wasn't true"? And that I thought he had direct communication with God because he always told us that we should have a certain time and place to go and pray. He advised us to "go into our prayer closet and pray to God." He confessed that he really didn't personally study the Scriptures relating to the Rapture, that he was following the teachings and beliefs of that denomination. I was vexed in my spirit, but I didn't stop going to church as my co-worker friend did. I had learned not to give up on the Lord, because there is One God, One Lord and One Savior, Jesus Christ the Righteous of God, so where else could I go?

I knew that the problem was not with God and His Word. But rather, it was with man's *"lack of understanding"* of the Word of God. This taught me that man's religious doctrines will blind us from the truth of the Bible. In the end I still respected the pastor's position and authority, however, I stopped taking in everything that he taught unless I studied it first. From that experience I learned to study the Bible for myself, (2 Timothy 2:15) that's how I came to learn the Truth about the timing of the Rapture of the Church.

CHAPTER

The Resurrection was not on a Sunday Morning:

After that experience I kept my Bible opened and I would write down every passage of Scripture that the pastor would refer to whenever he was in the pulpit preaching or teaching. I also purchased a small tape recorder, and I would record every sermon that he preached. It became a habit, and I also recorded visiting speakers and every service that the church was invited to. Many sincere and well-meaning believers believes that Jesus was Crucified on a Friday and Rose three days later, on a Sunday Morning.

This is another falsehood that's being taught in many churches and believed by most Saints today. They are sincere in their beliefs but since that belief doesn't line up with Scriptures that makes them- sincerely wrong! The pastor also believed and taught the Sunday Morning Resurrection of Christ. I had really mustered up Holy Ghost boldness and I wasn't afraid to question anything that was taught that wasn't in accordance with the 'Rightly Divided' Word of God.

I didn't spare the punches, one night in Bible study I had to correct his misunderstanding of the timing of the death, burial, and the day of the Resurrection of Christ as well. I could feel some animosity from the deacon after our last encounter, however, I didn't allow it to hinder me from speaking the Truth. In my explaining that the Resurrection was not on a Sunday Morning. I said, "First of all, anyone who isn't deceived or blinded by religious teachings and doctrines and who can count from one to three will know that one cannot get three (3) days and three (3) nights, a period of seventy (72) two hours by counting from Friday to Sunday!"

The pastor said, "the Jews used a different time and calendar than ours, therefore, the hours really didn't add up to seventy (72) two hours as we would count it." I then reminded him of what Jesus said in John 11:9. I asked him to read it, he read, *"Jesus answered, Are there not twelve hours in the day? If any man walk in the day, he stumbleth not, because he seeth the light of the world."* I explained to him and the class that according to Jesus, a day is *twelve hours* long no matter what time zone or calendar is used. I told him that, in this sinful generation that man in his finite wisdom has attempted to change days into night by coming up with daylight savings time, therefore, the sun may not shine for a complete twelve (12) hours but it's still part of a day.

Then I said to him, "let's do the math." I asked, "12 hours of daylight x's 3 equals 36, doesn't it?" The pastor and the deacon replied, "Yes!" And 12 hours of darkness x's 3 also equals 36, doesn't it? They again said "Yes."

And then I asked 36+36= 72, doesn't it? They confirmed that the math was correct, the deacon became silent and started flipping pages in his Bible and dropped out of the conversation. The pastor still couldn't explain the difference. I then took him to the prophecy of Daniel (9:24-27) and had him to read it. He did, but he didn't fully grasp what the Scriptures taught.

I didn't want to confuse him with Bible prophecy because I knew that he didn't fully understand it, so I asked him simple questions from what he had just read. I asked him, "from verse 24, who did God send to make reconciliations for sin and to bring in everlasting righteousness?" He replied, "Jesus."

Then I asked, "Who is the Messiah and Prince? [of Peace]. He rightly answered, "Jesus." From verse 26 I asked him, "What does it mean that Messiah be cut off." He answered, "Jesus was to be killed."

I then drove my point home and asked him, "According to Scripture then, on what part of the week would Jesus be killed?" He rightly said, "in the midst of the week." Then I asked him, "What is the middle day of the week?" He replied, "Wednesday." Then I asked, "According to Scripture then, what day of the week would Jesus be killed on." He amazingly replied, "Wednesday!"

After this I explained to the class that when God created the world He called the days into existence, He started with the evening first, He said, *"the evening and the morning was the first day; the evening and the morning was the second day"* etc. I then explained that Jesus was Crucified and Buried on a Wednesday; and He was in the grave Wednesday night [12 hours], all day Thursday [12 hours.] (Day 1), Thursday night [12 hours], all day Friday [12 hours], (Day 2); Friday night [12 hours], and all-day Saturday [12 hours] (Day 3); which was the Sabbath, a total of [72 hours].

I then took him to the Gospel of Mark (16:9) and had him to read it as well and then I asked, "Exactly what did Mark pen, did he say, *Jesus 'Rose'* on the first day of the week when the women arrived at the grave site to anoint His body or did, he say Jesus *'was Risen'* when they arrived to anoint His body"? He confirmed that Jesus had *already Risen* when the women arrived at the tomb which was outside of the city. I then went on to explain that the Jews were under the Law, and they strictly kept the Sabbath Day travel law, [Sabbath Day's journey, about 3/4 of a mile] therefore, there were no eyewitnesses to the Resurrection and that the women arrived at the tomb as soon as the [Saturday's] Sabbath had passed.

I also explained to him a fact that many believers overlook in trying to teach the Death, Burial and Resurrection of Christ. That there were two [2] Holy or High days in Jesus' Passion Week, the Passover [which was on a Thursday and the Sabbath which has always been Saturday]. The first Holy [High] Day was the Passover (Luke 22:1; Ref. Exodus 12th chapter). Under the Law, the Jews weren't allowed to work on a Sabbath Day (Exodus 35:1-3), therefore, they had to do their servile work on the day before a high day which was called, the *"Day of Preparation."*

Jesus, our Sacrificial Lamb was Crucified and Buried on the Preparation Day *[Wednesday]* for Thursday's Passover, *Friday* was the Preparation Day for Saturday's Sabbath, Therefore, Jesus could not have died on a Friday and Rose three days later, on a Sunday Morning!

I also explained that the modern-day church breaks the fourth Commandment every week because of man's lack of understanding of God's Word. God said, *"Remember the Sabbath day to keep it holy."* Jesus, who was God in the flesh, kept the Sabbath and so did the Apostle Paul and the early church (ref Luke 4:16). Paul urged the Christians believers to, "imitate him as he imitated Christ" [worshipping on the Sabbath] (1 Cor. 11:1). Also, Paul preached to the Jews as well as to the Gentiles on the Sabbath Day (Acts 13:42). Because of animosities between the two groups, this brought opposition from many of the Jews because the Gentiles eagerly and readily received the Gospel. They even rosed up opposition and persecution against Paul and Barnabas who were Jews themselves; and they were expelled from the region by the religious authorities (vs. 44-50).

How did Sunday Worship fasten itself into modern day Worship Service?

I'm glad you asked. Again, it's because people 'read over' the Scriptures instead of "rightly dividing" them. Many Saints have misunderstood 1Corinthians 16:1-2. In this passage of Scripture, Paul was not calling for a Sunday worship on the first day of the week, instead he was calling for the Corinthian church to, "gather supplies" for needy Galatian brethren! It was to be done on the first day of the week, when the Sabbath had passed because if the supplies had been gathered on the Sabbath it would be in violation of the Sabbath Law because it would have been considered work.

Let's look at another, 'misunderstood' passage of Scripture? In Acts 20:7 we read that the disciples came together, "on the first day of the week" not for worship service but for a fellowship meal i. e. "the breaking of bread." I'm sure that prayers were offered up, but the purpose of the meeting wasn't calling for a change from Saturday to Sunday worship service.

Also consider, Mary Magdalene went to Jesus' tomb on Sunday morning, *"after the Sabbath had passed"* (Mark 16:1; John 20:1-2) and found it empty. It was empty because Jesus had risen at least twelve hours before she and the other women arrived to anoint His body to give Him a proper burial. As I've already explained, Jesus was crucified on a Wednesday and was laid in the tomb at sundown; and He rose three days later at sundown on the Sabbath fulfilling the sign of Jonah (Matthew 12:40).

Furthermore, consider that Jesus said that He, "the Son of man" is, "Lord of the Sabbath" and that, "the Sabbath was made for man, and not man for the Sabbath! (Mark 2:27, 28).

Easter is a Pagan Festival:

I went on and explained to the class that Easter is a pagan custom and festival that the world was celebrating during the time of Christ's Resurrection. I asked, have you ever stopped and ask yourself, "What does decorating, and hiding colored eggs have to do with the Crucifixion and the Resurrection of our Lord and Savior Jesus Christ?" I told them the answer, absolutely nothing!

Then I asked, "Why do you believe the things that you believe and do the things that you do? The chances are you never stopped to ask yourself that question. You have been taught since childhood to accept Easter as the chief of the Christian holidays. You have supposed it is part of the true Christian religion to observe "Lent", "Holy Week" and "Good Friday", to have colored Easter eggs, to dress up and go to church Easter Sunday- perhaps to attend an Easter Sunrise Service!

I then said, because of the "sheep" instinct in humans, we follow traditions and most of us believe and do things that are not true. Most of us do a lot of things that are wrong, supposing these things are right, or even sacred! I told the class that this custom was a celebration of the pagan goddess, Ishtar, a sexual, fertility goddess represented by rabbits and chickens which reproduces fast.

According to Jesus, there will be no sex in heaven (Matthew 22:30) so why would we honor a sex goddess here on earth and associate it with the Resurrection of Christ? I then said, "I'll tell you why, it's because of man's religious doctrines and teachings!" God told His people to, "Be holy because He is Holy", so then I asked, "How does a sexual festival honors our Holy God?" The only time sex is pleasing in the eyesight of God is when we are married, united in Holy matrimony.

I ask the class if they celebrated Easter. Everyone raised their hands, by this time the deacon was coming back from a restroom break, and he overheard the question, he shouted; "Of course we do, it honors the Resurrection of our Lord!" I told him that he was out of the sanctuary, and he missed that part of the lesson, but for his benefit, I will explain again that, "Easter is a pagan practice celebrated by pagan people long before Christ was born!" It predates Christianity, with customs involving rabbits, colored eggs and fresh hot baked bread with sunrise services. And that, these were ancient fertility rites celebrating spring and honoring ancient pagan gods and goddesses. I then sarcastically asked the class, "Who's blood paid for your redemption from sin, was it the rabbit's, the chicken's that laid the egg, or the Blood of Jesus?"

Ishtar, a pagan goddess:

I asked the class, "What is the meaning of the name "Easter"? You have been led to suppose the word means "Resurrection of Christ." For 1600 years the western world has been taught that Christ rose from the dead on a Sunday morning, but as I've already explained, the resurrection was not on a Sunday morning, it is one of the *old wives" fables* the Apostle Paul warned young pastor Timothy to expect and be aware of (1 Timothy 4:7). A transliteration of this passage of scripture will reveal that Paul was telling Timothy to, "avoid profane and fabricated myths" and exercise himself to be godly. These false doctrines called "myths" are described by God as "profane" because they promote ungodliness and are "fabricated" because they come from man's imagination rather than the "rightly divided" Word of Truth. The name "Easter" which is merely the slightly change English spelling of the name of an ancient Assyrian and Babylonian goddess Ishtar, it comes to us from old Teutonic mythology.

The Phoenician name of this goddess was Astarte, a Syro-Phoenician goddess of love and fruitfulness. She was a consort of Baal, the sun god, whose worship is denounced by the Almighty in the Bible as the most abominable of all pagan idolatry. Ancient Israel made offerings and burned incense unto him (2 Kings 23:5). If you look up the word "Easter" in Webster's dictionary, you will find it clearly reveals the pagan origin of the name.

I went on the explain that "Easter", is derived from an ancient goddess A*starte,* which is another slightly spelling of the word which refers to, *"dawn in the east"* and that we got our translation from the Babylonian *"Ishtar",* also known as Ashtaroth, the *"queen of heaven."* I asked for someone to go to the churches library and bring me a volume of an encyclopedia with the word 'Easter' in it. The little girl who volunteered to read ask her mother could she go. She returned about ten minutes later, I asked her to give it to the deacon which she did; then I said, "God wants us to prove all things", I asked the deacon would he look up the word 'Easter' and to read it to the class? He did so and it basically confirmed the same thing that I had taught.

I told the class that worshipping and honoring false gods was an abomination to our Holy God, that God commanded the children of Israel not to participate in nor practice the religions of the people in the land that He had overthrown and given to His people. I asked the deacon to read Deuteronomy 12:29-32, I told him that I know that he knows the Scripture by heart but for the benefit of the class, that I would like for it to be read. He stood up to read, I asked him to read the subject of the Scripture, he read:

'Warning against idolatry'

"When the Lord thy God shall cut off the nations from before thee, whither thou goest to possess them, and thou succeedest them, and dwellest in their land; Take heed to thyself that thou be not snared by following them, after that they be destroyed from before thee; and that thou inquire not after their gods saying, How did these nations serve their gods? even so will I do likewise. Thou shalt not do so unto the Lord thy God: for every abomination to the Lord, which he hated, have they done unto their gods; for even their sons and their daughters they have burnt in the fire to their gods. What thing soever I command you, observe and to do it: thou shalt not add thereto, nor diminish from it."

I thanked the deacon for the reading, and I explained to the class that God does not accept such worship even if it's meant to honor Him. I asked the deacon to read Amos 5:21 which he did, he read that God said, *"I hate, I despise your feast days and I will not smell* [savor] *in your solemn* [sacred] *assemblies."* I told the class, "In Isiah 1:10-15 God called for a repentance of such abominations of His people in their religious practices unto Him." He said, *"Bring no more vain oblations; the new moons and sabbaths, the calling of assemblies,* [including Good Friday, Sunrise Services, which signifies the worship of Baal, an ancient *Canaanite* sun-god] *I cannot away* [endure] *with; it is iniquity, even the solemn meetings. Your new moons and your appointed feasts my soul hateth: they are a trouble unto me; I am weary to bear them. And when ye spread forth your hands, I will hide mine eyes from you: yea, when you make many prayers, I will not hear..."* (vs. 12-15). I explained Deut. 12:31 that at one time the children of Israel were sacrificing their own children to Molech, an Ammonite pagan god (ref. Lev. 18:21).

Easter, pagan Sunrise Services:

I asked, "so you think Easter Sunrise services are beautiful"? You need to read Ezekiel 8:15-18, you will learn that God was showing the prophet the sins of His people in a vision-a prophecy that is relevant for today! Ezekiel was shown in a vision idol worship among professing people of God.

"Then said he to me, Hast thou seen this, O son of man? turn thee yet again, and thou shalt see greater abominations than these. And he brought me into the inner court of the LORD's house, and behold, at the door of the temple of the Lord, between the porch and the alter, were about five and twenty men, with their backs towards the temple of the LORD, and their faces toward the east; and they worshiped the sun towards the east [sun-god Baal] *Then he said unto me, Hast thou seen this, O son of man? Is it a light* [trivial] *thing to the house of Judah that they commit the abominations which they commit here? for they have filled the land with violence and have returned to provoke me to anger: and, lo, they put the branch to their nose. Therefore, will I also deal in fury: my eye shall not spare, neither will I have pity: and though they cry in mine ears with a loud voice, yet will I not hear them."*

Then I asked, "Did you understand what this most "abominable" thing is"? Those people turned their backs to God, by turning their backs towards the temple, and they faced the east and worshipped the sunrise! It is the identical thing millions of professing Christians are doing every Easter Sunday Morning with the sunrise service-standing with their faces towards the east, as the sun is rising, in a service of worship which honors the sun-god Baal and his mythical idolatrous consort Ishtar. God gave ten commandments for us to follow, His third one He said, *"Thou shalt have no other gods before me."* We are to worship the Creator, not His creation, (Romans 1:25) therefore, we are forbitten to worship the sun, moon, stars, etc. (Deu. 17: 1-5). I told the class that following the signs of the Zodiac is also an abomination to God because people are following their horoscopes instead of allowing God to lead them!

The Word of God says, *"In all thy ways, acknowledge Him and He will direct our paths."* Therefore, following our Zodiac signs and calling up phone lines, which God calls, "soothsaying" to have our fortune told is a lack of faith to allow our Creator to lead us. It's a good thing that we are under grace rather than the law, if we were under the law then many professing Christians would be stoned to death for their idolatrous worship. Thank God for a "better covenant."

All Western nations have been deceived into thinking that Easter honors Christ, they have dropped, or not known the origin of pagan festivals that has fastened itself in modern day churches. Easter celebrations are not a memorial of Christ's resurrection, but rather, it is in commemoration of the counterfeit "savior" and mediator Baal, the pagan sun-god of ancient Israel, named after the mythical Ishtar, his wife, who became the idolatrous "queen of heaven." This is not Christian; it is pagan to the core! Yet millions are deceived into observing this form of heathen idolatry, under the delusion they are honoring Jesus Christ the Son of God!

This is Bible Truth; Easter does not honor Christ! Yet, many Christians are like blind sheep, they will follow their Spiritual blind leaders which have been led to believe in and to observe this pagan custom. *"The times of this ignorance God winked at; but now commandeth all men everywhere to repent: Because he hath appointed a day, in which he will judge the world in righteousness by that man whom he hath ordained; wherefore he hath given assurance unto all men, in that he hath raised him from the dead"* (Acts 17:30, 31).

I again told the class; "surely, Christ was risen from the dead, but the Resurrection was not on an 'Easter' Sunday Mornings. He rosed on a Sabbath [Saturday] and on the first day of the week [Sunday Morning] Jesus had already risen from the grave when Mary Magdalene and the other women arrived at the tomb to anoint His body" (Mark 16:1, 2).

Dyed eggs:

I explained this pagan custom with a question. I asked, "Do you know that dyed Easter eggs were also figured in the ancient Babylonian mystery rites just as they are in Easter observance today"? Yes, these are pagan too! Eggs were sacred to many ancient civilizations and formed an integral part of the religious ceremonies in Egypt and in the Orient, the priests and the ceremonials bore an egg as the sacred emblem of their idolatrous order. Eggs were hung up in the Egyptian temples as a symbol of "generative life", proceeding from the mouth of the great [false] god of Egypt. The mystic egg of Babylon, hatching the Venus Ishtar, was believed to have fallen from heaven into the Euphrates River, thus embracing the term, "queen of heaven." It was believed that Easter, or spring was the "season of birth, terrestrial and celestial."

So why do people who believe themselves to be Christian's dye eggs at Easter? Do they suppose the Bible ordained, or commands heathen customs? There is no word of it in the New Testament.

Paul said, *"Be ye followers of me, even as I also am of Christ"* (1 Cor. 11:1). Christ certainly did not start it, neither did any of the apostles nor any Christians of the early church. Then why should you do it today? I asked, "why follow heathenism and try to convince yourself you are a Christian"? God calls such things "ABOMINATION"!

How Easter Crept into the Church:

I also explained that; parents of the latter-day churches thinks that this pagan festival honors Christ, they saw the fun and appeal that it brought to their children in conducting Easter egg hunts and the bright colors that comes along with it. Those children grew up and taught their children as they were taught, eventually this pagan practice injected itself into professing Christian religion.

I then shared my personal experience with the class, I told them. "My grandmother made sure that I had new clothes to wear to church on Easter Sunday. She would spend hours boiling eggs on Saturday night and I would help her color and decorate them for the Easter egg hunt." Parents would take their eggs to church, and we would have three o'clock Easter services where most of the children would recite speeches and afterwards the children would go outside and hunt Easter eggs."

In the back of my mind I often wondered, "What does this have to do with the Resurrection of Christ." I remembered that Moses, on the night before the children of Israel left Egypt on their journey to the promise land instructed them to put blood over their doorpost so that the angel of death would "Passover" their homes if the blood was presence, but I couldn't recall a single passage of Scripture where Jesus, His disciples nor the early church called for nor practiced it.

I was afraid to ask my grandmother, she was the type that didn't liked to be questioned. If she told you that the sky was green, it would be better to agree with her than to disagree. So, I accepted it, but I was skeptical of the practice. It was fun to me as a child, some of the eggs were plastic with cash money hidden in them. When I was about ten years old, I found a 'prize egg' one with a five-dollar bill hidden in it. I showed it to my grandmother, and she told me to, "give it to a poor child because I didn't need the money." As I grew older and started learning the Bible, I came to realize that this practice wasn't done nor taught in the New Testament church. I came to realize that it was a pagan festival and not supported by Scriptures, that, it was a great deception.

At the age of ten, I still believed in Santa Claus, however I often wondered, "how could one fat guy go to every home up and down chimneys all around the world and leave presents for every child on the same night"? I dismissed it because as a child I was taught, "God is everywhere, all the time living in the hearts of every person." I compared Santa Claus as a miracle worker, that he, just like God can be everywhere performing His miracle as well. I found out the truth of the Santa Claus myth on my eleventh Christmas.

My grandmother knew that I wanted a bicycle for Christmas, she bought it several weeks earlier, and hid it in her closet and told me to stay out of her bedroom. I thought this was strange of her because I had to clean up the whole house every day before school. I didn't question her because it was less work for me to do. My cousin told me that she had gotten me a bicycle for Christmas and hid it in her bedroom.

One day there was an automobile accident in the neighborhood, my grandmother was outside looking on which gave me the opportunity to see for myself. Sure enough, the bicycle was there in her closet. I was glad to get it and I acted surprised and excited Christmas morning when she told me, "Santa had brought me a bike because I had been a good boy."

I was glad to get the bike, but somewhat disappointed in the Santa Claus myth. I realized that I should have followed my own suspicion knowing that it was impossible for one man to deliver presents to every child everywhere at the same time. I promised myself, "If I ever have children, I will teach them the truth, I will teach them the Bible and not religion nor religious festivals that people ascribe to God."

Christmas, a pagan festival:

I shared my experience with the class whereas learned at an early age that Christmas is a pagan holiday. I suppose that's why some religions don't recognize nor celebrates it. After that Christmas and the thrill of the holidays was over, I started reading the Bible for myself and see what it said about Christmas and celebrating Jesus' birthday. I couldn't find a single passage of Scripture where the early church and the apostles celebrated nor commanded it. I went through my grandmother's Bibles and study books that she had looking for a book with the word 'Christmas' in it, I found none.

I remember a sermon that I heard where the pastor said that "Jesus was hung on a tree." So, I started looking up the word 'tree' and I found one in Jerimiah 10:1-6. I learned that it was comparing God with idols, where people would go out into the forest, cut down a tree, take it home and decorate it.

My grandmother used to keep Christmas cards from her friends and neighbors, I went through them, and I found some with Jesus lying in a manger and the wise men bringing presents to Him. After studying the Scriptures, I learned that the wise men weren't present when Jesus was born.

I read that when Jesus was born there was a decree issued that all people had to go to their hometown to pay their taxes. Mary was pregnant with Jesus and Joseph didn't want to leave town and leave her alone, so he took her with him, and while they were in Bethlehem, Jesus was born (Luke 2:1-7). I learned from vs 8-20 that the wise men aren't mentioned to be present when Jesus was in the stable lying in the manger.

I also learned that Mary and Joseph had moved into a house and Jesus was a small child, probably two-three years old when the wise men brought Him gifts (Matt. 2:1-23). I also questioned, the timing of Jesus' birth. The Bible says that the shepherds were watching over their flocks the night that Jesus was born. Therefore, I knew that December 25th wasn't His birthday because no one would have their cattle and sheep out in an open field in the dead of winter because the ground would be frozen, and most likely snow covered. My grandmother had told me that they always corralled their animals before winter set in.

I also learned that the Jews traveled in caravans when they had to go to Jerusalem for their yearly festivals (Luke 2:41-52). God would not have His people traveling long distances in the dead of winter to pay taxes. This again proves that December 25th isn't Jesus' birthday. I read a historian's account of Jesus' birthday, it said that "Jesus probably was born around September 29th because the Jews corralled their flocks around of before October 15th."

Then I said to the class; two facts must be firmly fixed in mind to understand this great deception.

First, Jesus and the apostles foretold, not a universal widespread popular growth of the New Testament Church, but rather a "falling away" from the Truth on the part of the great majority. Prophesying a popular, universal falling away from the faith once delivered to the Thessalonians Paul stated, *"The mystery of iniquity doth already work."* Paul wrote his letter to the church only some 20 years after the church began.

He referred to the very "Chaldean Mysteries" of which Easter and Christmas were two chief festivals! The deacon had excused himself to use the telephone, on his return he only heard part of the lecture. He interrupted, pointed his finger at me and said, "What's wrong with this guy? Christmas honors the birth of Christ, our Savior!" I responded by saying, "If those are your thoughts, then you don't know what God told His prophet Jeremiah. God told Jeremiah to warn His people of their heathen pagan customs, they would go out into the forest, cut down a tree and take it home and decorate it with silver and gold. I asked the little girl to read Jeremiah 10:1-6.

The deacon said, "I know the Scripture." I told him, "Sure you do, you know the whole Bible by heart, but you lack understanding of its teachings." Then I said, "for the sake of those that don't know the Bible by heart, I would rather have it read." The little girl stood up and read the Scripture: *"Hear what the Lord says to you, people of Israel. This is what the Lord says: "Do not learn the ways of the nations or be terrified by signs in the heavens, though the nations are terrified by them. For the practices of the people are worthless; they cut a tree out of the forest, and a craftsman shapes it with his chisel They adorn it with silver and gold, they fasten it with hammer and nails so it will not totter. Like a scarecrow in a cucumber field, their idols cannot speak; they must be carried because they cannot walk. Do not fear them: they can do no harm nor can they do any good."*

I told the deacon, "You know the Bible inside and out, where can I find a passage of Scripture that teaches us to celebrate Easter and Christmas? Show me a passage of Scripture where Paul instructed us to celebrate Jesus' birthday? I explained, "This heathen practice of cutting and decorating trees was celebrated at least seven hundred years before Christ was born, therefore, it doesn't honor His birthday!" I told the class, "You don't have to answer this question, but how many of you, during the holiday season goes out and buy a tree, bring it home and decorate it with electric lights and put presents under it for your family, friends and loved ones?"

Then I asked the deacon, "Does he buy Christmas presents for his children or grandchildren?" He said, "of course I do." I then asked him," did Santa Claus deliver them, or did he buy and plant them under the Christmas tree himself?" Then I said, 'there is nothing new under the sun' "today- we have the convenience of electricity, instead of gold and silver-colored decorations, but the concept and the traditions are the same and God, our heavenly Father hates it!"

Secondly, although Jesus said, "the gates of hell would never prevail against His church", yet it is prophesied in the New Testament to be the "little flock" never as a great, large popular universal church (Luke 12:32). This is a fact that the Christian community doesn't realize today. Most Christian churches and believers are following practices that was handed down to them by their parents and their church leaders, they blindly celebrate Easter and Christmas thinking it honors Christ!

But if one would, "search the Scriptures" they won't find one that supports the Easter tradition of decorating and hiding eggs. I can't find one Scripture that tells us to have Easter eggs hunts! Jesus didn't institute it and the disciples didn't follow the tradition. Had it been a Spiritual event, I'm sure the Apostle Paul would have encouraged the church to continue it!

Again, nothing illustrates this very fact more vividly than the actual history of the injecting of Easter into the Western church. I said, anyone who wants to, "prove all things" can research this information from the *Encyclopedia Britannica* (11th edition, vol. V 111, pages 828-829); "There is no indication of the observance of the Easter festival in the New Testament, or in the writing of the Apostolic Fathers...The first Christians [the original true church] continued to observe the Jewish [God's] festivals, though in a new spirit, as commemorations of events which those festivals had foreshadow.

I told the class-

True Christians kept the Passover:

The New Testament reveals that Jesus, the apostles, and the New Testament church, both Jewish and Gentile-born observed God's Sabbaths, and God's festivals-weekly and annually. But the false, and paganized church grew in numbers and political power.

Decrees were passed in the fourth century A.D. imposing the death sentence upon Christians found keeping God's Sabbath or God's festivals. Finally, in order to keep the true way of God, many Christians, [composing the true church] fled for their lives. But another large portion of the true Church of God, failing to flee, yet remaining true to God's truth, paid with their lives in martyrdom (Rev. 2:13; 6:9; 13:15; 17:6; 18:24). They loved obedience to God more than their lives! But throughout all generations, through every century, though persecuted, scattered, unrecognized by the world, many true Christians have kept alive the true Church of God-the church composed of those who have the Holy Spirit of God abiding in them. Thus, the Passover, with a new conception added to it, of Christ as the true Paschal Lamb and the *"first fruits from the dead"*, which the true church continued to observe.

Although the observance of Easter (which had crept into the church) was at a very early period in the practice of the Christian church, a serious difference as to the day of its observance soon arose between the Christians of Jewish and those of Gentile decent, which led to a long and bitter controversy.

What did Jesus Command?

The "communion", often called the "Lord's Supper" is the Passover-as the ordinance should more properly be called. Luke recognized the festival as, *"The day of unleavened bread"* (Luke 22:7). Let's examine the way Jesus observed and commanded us to keep the ordinance, because we can't be wrong if we follow His example. In Luke 22:14-20 we read, *"And when the hour was come, he* [Jesus] *sat down...And he took bread, and gave thanks, and brake it, and gave unto them, saying, This is my body which is given for you: this do in remembrance of me...Likewise also the cup after supper, saying. This cup is the new testament* (covenant) *in my blood which is shed for you."*

Notice, it was, *"when the hour was come,"* that Jesus introduced the unleavened bread and the wine. There was a definite time-a definite hour-when He held this ordinance as an example for us. Notice also, He commanded them to observe it- *"This do"!* And why? *"In remembrance of me."* Jesus instituted this New Testament way of keeping the Passover on that tragic night, the very eve of His death. In Matthew's account, the Bible shows that this ordinance was at the very time of the Passover, *"as they were eating"* (Matthew 26:2, 26). Jesus knew that His time had come. He is our Passover, sacrificed for us (1 Corinthians 5:7).

I looked directly at the deacon and said, "if you really want to do things God's way then we should be having communion at Easter and Christmas, instead of the pagan practices handed down through the church from generations to generations." This is what Jesus commanded, He said, *"Do this in remembrance of me."* The deacon got highly upset, excused himself from the class, he put on his coat and left!

My Holy Ghost boldness had really kicked in. I went on to explain: On observing the Passover, as on every practice, Jude exhorts *"that ye should contend earnestly for the faith which was once delivered to the saints"* (vs. 3). With the Jewish Christians, the fast ended on the 14th day of the month at evening, without regard to the day of the week. The Gentile Christians on the other hand, [that is, the beginning of the Roman church, now substituting pagan for true Christian doctrines] identified the first day of the week [Sunday] with the resurrection and kept the preceding Friday as the commemoration of the crucifixion, irrespective of the day of the month.

The Western churches [Catholic] kept Easter on the first day of the week, while the Eastern churches [containing most of those who remained as part of the true Christian church] followed the Jewish rule, that is observing Passover on the 14th of the first sacred month [Nisan: March-April] instead of the pagan Easter. The Passover had always been held on the eve of the 14th of God's first month, [Nisan] according to the Jew's Sacred calendar; the Passover was to be observed annually, along with the Days of Unleavened Bread. If one, does it too often, it becomes a ritual and it will lose its spirituality. *"Thou shalt therefore keep this ordinance in his season year to year"* (Exodus 13:10). Jesus set us an example (1 Peter 2:21), observing this ordinance at the same time once a year (Luke 2:42).

Suppose the Israelites in Egypt had observed this ordinance at some other time other than that sat by God? They would not have been saved when the death angel passed by that night! God does things on time; He has given us an exact time for this ordinance. Jesus instituted the New Testament symbols, *"when the hour was come."* Now that we know the pagan origin of the Easter celebration, let's clear away from it and the web of error that overshadows the truth about keeping the Passover, which is the memorial of Christ's death.

Two Churches-One False-One True:

Note: This is a two-fold prophecy, it relates to the Catholic Church which will be instrumental in the establishment of the New Holy Roman Empire and the United States of America as, "MYSTERY

BABYLON THE GREAT, THE MOTHER OF HARLOTS AND ABOMINATIONS OF THE EARTH."

In the New Testament prophecy two churches are described. One, the great and powerful and universal church, a part of the world, ruling in its politics over many nations, and united with the "Holy Roman Empire", it's brought to a concrete focus in the Book of Revelation chapter 17. This church is pictured with great pomp, ritual and display, decked in purple, scarlet and gold; proud, worldly and boastful. She is pictured as a universal deceiver-all Western nations spiritually drunk with her false doctrines, their spiritual perception so blurred by their paganized teachings and practices they are unable to clearly distinguish truth!

She boasts she is the true church, yet she is drunken with the blood of the Saints she has caused to be martyred. But how could she have deceived the whole world, as foretold in God's Word? One may think, "surely, the Protestant world isn't deceived!" Oh, yes, she is! Verse 5 says she is a mother church, her daughters are also churches who have fundamentally followed in pagan doctrines and practices. God is not willing that any should perish, therefore, He have called His Saints to, *"come out of her, my people, that ye be not partakers of her sins, and that ye receive not of her plagues. For her sins have reached unto heaven, and God hath remembered her iniquities"* (Rev. 18:4, 5).

They too, make themselves a part of this world, taking an active part in its politics-the very act which made a "harlot" out of their mother. The entire apostate family, and more than 400 daughters' denominations, all divided against each other and in confusion of doctrines, yet all united in the chief pagan doctrines and festivals-has the family name! They call themselves "Christians", but God calls them something else, He call them, "idolaters." Part of the religious "Babylonian" system that many of today's churches have fallen into.

"Babylon" means confusion! But *"God is not the author of confusion"* (1 Cor.14:33). God always names people and things by calling them what they are. And here are the identical ancient Babylonian Mysteries now wrapped in the false cloak labored "Christianity." Because of the different denominational views of the Bible, I decided to go non-denominational when I accepted my calling and established the church; that I may teach the Truth of God's Word from Genesis to Revelation.

I don't add to nor take away from the Holy Scriptures. Rev. 22:18, 19 says, *"If any man shall add unto these things, God shall add unto him the plagues that are written in this book: And if any man shall take away from the words of the book of this prophecy, God shall take away his part out of the book of life, and out of the holy city, And from the things which are written in this book."* That passage of Scripture alone warns me to teach the Truth of God's Word. Yes, the Truth might offend you, but I would rather offend you with Truth, rather than to offend God in error and erroneous teachings!

True Church-Small-Scattered:

Did the True church of God, of which Jesus Christ is the living, directing Head, become perverted, or did it merely apostatize into this mystical system? No! The "gates of hell" have never prevailed against the True church of God, and it never will! The True church has never fallen! It has never ceased! But the True church of God is pictured in prophecy as the "little flock." The New Testament describes this church as continually persecuted, despised by the large popular churches because it is not of this world or its politics, but has kept itself unspotted from the world. The True church has always kept the Commandments of God and the faith of Jesus.

During the coming Tribulation period, the devil through the Antichrist is going to persecute the True Saints of God because of our faith in Christ. Rev. 12:17, says, *"And the dragon* [Satan] *was wroth* [enraged] *with the woman* [Jewish believers, the nation of Israel] *and went to make war with the remnant of her seed* [Gentile believers, who was adopted into the family of God by Christ through the seed of Abraham] *which kept the commandments of God, and have the testimony of Jesus Christ."*

The True Church Has Kept God's Festivals, Not the Pagan Holidays:

The True church has been empowered with the Spirit of God. That church never became the great popular church as the world supposes. That church (faithful believers) has always existed, and it exists today. Then, where did it go? Where was it during the Middle Ages? Where is it today? I'm glad that you asked.

First, remember this church was never large, never politically powerful, or a world-known organization of men. It is a spiritual organism, not a political organization. It is composed of all whose hearts and lives have been changed by the Spirit of God, whether visibly together, of individually scattered. True believers from all denominations make up this True church. Jesus said in John 10:16, *"Other sheep I have which are not of this fold: them also I must bring, and they shall hear my voice; and there shall be one fold,* [flock] *and one shepherd."*

At the Rapture of the Church, which, according to Scripture will occur, *"Immediately after the Great Tribulation* (Matt. 24:29-31), and at the last trumpet (1 Cor. 15:51,52), Jesus is going to separate His sheep [true believers] from the goats [unfaithful and deceptive]. His sheep will be at His right hand and the goats on His left. He's going to say to His sheep, *"Come ye blessed of My Father, inherit the kingdom prepared for you from the foundation of the world"* (Matt. 25: 31-34).

Under the lash of continual persecution and opposition from the organized forces of this world, it is difficult for such a people to remain united and organized together. Daniel prophesied the true people of God would be scattered (Daniel 12:7). Ezekiel also foretold it in (Ezekiel 34:5-12). Jeremiah, as well (Jeremiah 23: 1, 2). Jesus foretold it in Matthew 26:31, *"... All ye shall be offended* [made to stumble] *because of me this night: for it is written, I WILL SMITE THE SHEPHERD, AND THE SHEEP OF THE FLOCK SHALL BE SCATTERED ABROAD."* The apostolic church was soon scattered by persecution (Acts 8:11).

Ignored by Most Histories:

You won't read much of this True Body of Christ in secular histories of this world. No, the world little notes, nor long remembers, the activities of this "little flock", hated and despised by the world, driven into the wilderness by persecution, always opposed, usually scattered.

Even in Paul's day, many among those attending at Antioch, at Jerusalem, Ephesus, Corinth, and other places began to apostatize and turn away from the truth. Divisions sprang up. Those individuals, unconverted or turned from God's Truth and way of life were no part of God's True church! John wrote, *"They went out from us, but they were not of us; for if they had been of us, they would no doubt have continued with us, but they went out, that they might be made manifest that they were not all of us"* (1 John 2:19).

This apostasy greatly increased, by the year A.D. 125 the majority in most churches, especially those Gentile-born, were continuing in many of their old pagan beliefs and practices, through professing to be Christian. Gradually, a smaller and smaller portion of the visible churches going by the name "Christians" remained truly yield to God and His Truth and allowed themselves to be led of His Spirit. After Constantine took virtual control of the visible, professing church in the early fourth century, this visible organization became almost wholly pagan, and began excommunicating all who held to the True Word of God.

Finally, it became necessary for real Christians, who, even as a scattered people, alone composed the True Christian church, to flee in order to truly worship God. Persecution had gotten so bad that many of the believers met in secret, they used the cross and fish symbols to alert the followers to their meeting places.

Once again, Easter, with its pagan practices doesn't honor Christ! Easter is only mentioned once in the Bible, it's found in Acts 12:4. The book of Acts was penned by Luke, a Gentile. Luke wrote two books of the Bible, the Gospel that bears his name and the Book of Acts. Luke wrote primary to Gentile believers, he was writing to another Gentile named Theophilus, (Acts 1:1) informing him of the persecution of the church and that Herod had killed the Apostle James and imprisoned Peter, and 'after Easter' he was intending to have Peter killed also. The Easter festival which the pagans celebrated coincided with the Passover, which was celebrated by the Christian church, and it was celebrated as *the days of unleavened bread"* (Acts 12:1-4).

As I've already explained Good Friday Crucifixion and Easter Sunday Resurrection tradition directly contradicts the Word of God! However, many professing Christians think Easter is the most sacred holiday of the year. But because of religious doctrine, people have overlooked this basic Bible Truth and assumed that Jesus was crucified and buried on a Friday. They have induced the Good Friday [church service] celebrations, but as the Scriptures has proven, Jesus was already in the grave on Friday because He was Crucified and Buried on a Wednesday. Remember that Jesus said, *"Think not* [don't think] *that I am come to destroy the law, or the prophets: I am come not to destroy, but to fulfill* (Matthew 5:17).

Through my research, I have discovered that doctrines of Jesus Christ our Savior have been drastically altered, watered down, and infused with pagan philosophy and religion. Most preachers deliver a "feel good" gospel every week to their congregation. They have become, "politically correct" they don't want to offend anyone; therefore, they don't condemn people that practice a lifestyle contrary to the teachings of the Bible. But God commanded His prophets and teachers to, *"Cry aloud, spare not, lift up thy voice like a trumpet, and show my people their transgressions"* (Isaiah 58:1), which is the sole purpose of this book. The pastor sensed that I was directing that statement to him because we had a practicing homosexual piano player and his partner, his "boyfriend" was one of the choir directors.

The pastor once confided in me that he knew that their open relationship was wrong when they started visiting the church. He said that they eventually joined the church, and that he was hoping that they would realize that their relationship was an abomination to God and that they would change. But he had allowed it to go on for so long, and that he wasn't sure how to address it, because he didn't want to offend them. He said, "I know that you don't mind 'shooting straight from the hip' in teaching the Bible. And he asked me, "how would I handle the situation if I was in his position?" I asked him if he was aware of, "the watchman's duty" as recorded in Ezekiel 33? He said yes, and he acknowledged that it was his responsibility as pastor to warn them of their abominable lifestyle, otherwise their blood would be on his hands at the Judgment Seat of Christ.

I said, "well then, you already know the answer." I gave him the same advice that Paul gave to young pastor Timothy in 2 Timothy 4: 2-4, *"Preach the word; be instant in season, out of season; reprove, rebuke, exhort with all longsuffering and doctrine. For the time will come when they will not endure sound doctrine; but after their own lust shall they heap to themselves teachers, having itching ears; And they shall turn away their ears from the truth, and shall be turned into fables."*

I told him, "Their *'itching ears'* was constantly being scratched because he didn't counsel them privately regarding their relationship." I don't know if he ever talked to them privately, but afterwards he started preaching against homosexuality, but they continued their relationship. The choir director was found to be HIV positive which turn into full blown AIDS: he died, and his 'boyfriend' went to another church.

In the interim the pastor stopped preaching the Friday to Sunday Morning Death, Burial and Resurrection of Christ, he started preaching it just as it is written; *"For as Jonah was three days and three nights in the whale's belly, so shall the Son of man be three days and three nights in the heart of the earth"* (Matthew 12:40). Sometimes, in his sermons he would say, "Jesus Rose after three days and three nights with ALL POWER! O DEATH, WHERE IS THY STING? O GRAVE, WHERE IS THY VICTORY?"

God has said that *"His Word would not return unto Him void, but it shall accomplish that which I please and that it shall prosper in the thing whereto I sent it"* (Isaiah 55:11). Sure enough, it did, from that time onward the pastor's preaching and teaching was in accordance with the Bible. However, there were times that he seemed not to understand certain passages of Scriptures; he would read them just as they were written without trying to explain them by adding his own interpretation to them, he had learned not to add to nor take away any words of the Bible (Rev. 22: 18,19). Many of today's pastors will let just about anyone come in and preach to or teach his flock, oftentimes, those teachings aren't in accordance with the 'Rightly Divided' Word of God. God is going to hold those pastors accountable on Judgment Day.

An example can be found in the churches at Pergamos and Thyatira, they were found guilty of allowing false teachers to influence the congregations (Rev. 2:12-20). Therefore, we should pattern ourselves after the church at Berea, those Saints didn't accept just anyone's doctrine or teachings; they *"searched the Scriptures daily, for themselves to prove whether the teachings they were hearing was true"* (Acts 17:11).

Jesus said to the seven churches in Asia Minor, *"He that hath an ear, let him hear what the Spirit saith unto the churches."* God, through His Holy Word, is still speaking to the churches today in the volume of His book, the Bible. Religion and religious doctrines can and will blind us from the Truth of God's Word. Again, nowhere in the Bible can one find a "Rightly Divided' passage of Scriptures that teaches that Jesus died on a Friday and Rose three days later, on a Sunday Morning! That false teaching comes from man's ideologies, doctrines, and the misunderstanding of the Bible.

Therefore, my Christian brothers and sisters, and especially you pastors; I would advise you that if you would commemorate the Resurrection of our Lord and Savior Jesus Christ, that you do it in the fashion that the Apostle Paul laid out to the Corinthian church. According the instructions that the Lord Jesus left for us concerning His last supper with His disciples in the upper room: Paul said, *"For I have received of the Lord that which I delivered unto you, That the Lord Jesus the same night in which he was betrayed took bread: And when he had given thanks, he brake it, and said, Take, eat: this is my body which is broken for you: this do in remembrance of me, After the same manner also he took the cup, when he had supped, saying, This is the new testament in my blood: this do ye as oft as ye drink it, in remembrance of me"* (1 Corinthians 11:23-25; Ref. Matt. 26:17-30).

Question: How did Jesus say that we should commemorate the resurrection? Did He say, "with painted eggs or with communion?" If we are to do things God's way, then the church should have communion to celebrate the Lord's Resurrection instead of "Easter eggs hunts!"

Halloween honors Satan, it's not a Christian event:

Not only does most Christian churches celebrate the pagan festival of Easter, but some believing parents also allow their children to celebrate Halloween. Do you know that Halloween is a celebration of the dead? Our God is a Living God, He is not dead, He's God of the living! Therefore, we, as Christians should not celebrate or glorify the work of Satan nor let our children participate in it.

God declares that He is a jealous God (Exodus 20:5). He doesn't want His children glorifying His adversary, the devil. However, many Christian families spends hundreds of dollars yearly on Halloween decorations, costumes and jack-o-lanterns and they allow their innocent children to go through the neighborhood masquerading as the dead or something spooky.

God also doesn't want us to deal in the occult, by reading and followings our horoscope, etc. We are to, *"walk by faith and not by sight."* Reading and following our Zodiac signs shows a lack of faith in Him to lead, guide, protect and provide for us. This is another reason that I believe that *"judgment is going to begin at the House of God."* Furthermore, mostly every television show on TV these days seem to glorify Satan and his agenda rather than that of our living God. Just turn on your TV set and count the number of shows (and commercials) that has some sort of homosexuality, mystical spells, witchcraft or the dead people walking in them. Many popular rock stars also glorify Satan with their music, satanic attire, etc.

But as soon as a Christian mention the Name, Jesus, people get offended and try to silence them (ref. John 5:43). But what happens when there's a tragedy or a mass shooting? They always call on the Christian Community for prayers and comfort. Oh, how hypocritical we have become as a nation of people! It doesn't surprise me because the Lord has already warned us that we will be hated for His Name's sake. Jesus went through great links warning us in the Gospels of the coming Tribulation and the Great Tribulation Period (Matt. 10:16-23; Mark 13:5-23; Luke 21:17). According to Jesus, this time of trouble and great distress will occur before the Rapture of the Church (Matt. 24: 29-31).

Again, the church must go through the whole seven (7) years of the tribulation period. I didn't learn this in church. I first heard it from a person, my friend and co-worker that didn't attend any church! And after studying the Scriptures for myself, I've come to realize that people of the world, whom most Christians has labored "sinners" will probably get into the kingdom of God before we do!

I'm often reminded of John 5:39 where Jesus said, *"Search the scriptures; for in them ye think ye have eternal life..."* Jesus was addressing His church, not the people of the world! Therefore, we are not to judge them just because they don't belong to nor attend church services.

Most of them may be more knowledgeable in the Word of God than we are. I'm also reminded of the thief on the cross, he didn't belong to any organized church, not baptized, nor paid tithes or giving offerings. But at the last minute he confessed his sins and accepted Christ as his Savior.

If a person has breath in their bodies, they have an opportunity to be saved, however, I wouldn't advise nor lead a person to wait until they are faced with death, it can come suddenly and unexpectedly. I tell people that hadn't accepted Christ as their Lord and Savior that they'll playing Russian roulette with their soul by putting off a confession in Christ.

The Mission of the Church:

The church has a mission and a mandate to evangelize the world. If the unsaved and the ungodly are going to hear the Gospel of our Lord and Savior, Jesus Christ, it must come from us, the Christian community, His Body of baptized believers. As followers of Christ, we have a mission and a co-mission to win souls for Him (Matt. 28:19, 20). If the world is going to be saved, the Gospel must come from believers (the Christian community). Those who have trusted Christ for our eternal salvation.

We weren't saved to glory in, *"the joy of our salvation"* but rather to share the "Good News" with others, we are to "occupy" until the Lord returns (Luke 19:13). The church is called to be, *"The salt of the earth"* and the *"light of the world"* (Matt. 5:13,14). The Bible instructs us to, *"Let the redeemed of the Lord say so"* (Ps 107:2). In this troubled world only the Word of God have the answers; God said, *"If my people which are called by my name, shall humble themselves, and pray, and seek my face, and turn from their wicked ways; then will I hear from heaven, and I will forgive their sin, and I will heal their land* (2 Chronicles 7:14).

Did you understand what God said? A paraphrase version of what He said is, "If My people" (the church) would honor Him and obey His laws and ordinances that, He would heal the land! Then and only then can we be the *"salt and light"* to the world that we are called to be.

Our world is sick with sin and God is sick of our sins! Our government won't teach you the way of righteousness because many of our politicians doesn't know it themselves. Many are calling for, "separation of church and state." How dumb can people get? When one separates themselves from God, failure is at their door! Anyone that's foolish enough to separate themselves from their creator should have sense enough to realize their doom and destruction.

Unfortunately, many of God's people believes that same malarkey. We are supposed to be the *"salt of the earth and the light of the world"* but many 'church folks' have adopted the world's view and abandoned the righteousness of God and gone the way of Cain. Many will have you to believe that "there are many roads one can take to get into the kingdom of God" but that isn't what Jesus taught. He said, *"I am the way, the truth, and the life: no man cometh unto the Father, but by me"* (John 14:6). That "other way" leads to destruction. It's one of Satan's, (who Jesus rightly called), *"The father of lies"* strategies that will cause spiritual deception and the damnation of your soul if you ignore the Truth of God's Word!

Remember the Words of our Lord and Savior, that, *"The thief* [Satan] *cometh not, but for to steal, and to kill, and to destroy:* [your life and soul] *I am come that they might have life, and that they might have it more abundantly"* (John 10:10). Therefore, we must remain faithful and steadfast in our beliefs and use of the Bible, which is the Words of God as our foundation in our witnessing, instructions and teachings.

The Bible is our foundation, everyone has one in their homes, if not, they can get one. Therefore, we should use it in instructing and delivering the way of the Truth. Why? Because we will be opposed by the unsaved and by some 'so called' "Saints" of different denominations as well. But by them reading the instructions for themselves they will know that we're not giving out our own opinions, but rather, the written Word of God. And if they reject sound doctrine, then they have rejected Christ our Savior and God our creator (John 12:44-50) [Emphasis mine].

By giving them Scriptures rather than our own opinions, we would have tried to fulfill our mandate. Jesus said in Matthew 10:14; [which was written primarily to the Jews] Mark 6:11; [which was written to believers under Roman rulership] and Luke 9:5 [which was written to Gentile believers] to, *"shake the dust off of our feet* [if they didn't receive us or our testimony of Him] *as we depart from them.* He said, *" It will be more tolerable for the land of Sodom and Gomorrah on judgment day than for those that rejected Him"* [Emphasis mine]. Jesus didn't shed His Precious Blood for that generation, but He has done it for us, therefore the judgment of God will be more intensive for those who turns a deft ear to the Word of God. *"He that hath an ear, let him hear what the Spirit saith unto the churches."*

The Churches Misunderstanding of The New Birth:

The term "Born Again" is one of the most used and misunderstood passage of Scriptures among many in the Body of Christ. You have heard many Saints say that they have been "Born Again" or "you must be Born Again." If you're a Christian, I'm sure that you have been saying it too. If you ask most Saints, "What does it mean to be "Born Again?" most of them would not be able to give a clear understanding of what the Bible say that it means.

Because of it, many unsaved people don't want anything to do with the church nor many "so called" Christians, they view us as "hypocrites" because our walk does not line up with our talk!

Once I was about an hour early for an appointment to have my vehicle serviced, I decided to stop in a diner near the auto shop and have a cup of coffee and read the morning newspaper just to kill a little time. There was a gentleman sitting in a booth, he was looking troubled and very despondent. I wanted to strike up a conversation with him to see if I could be some encouragement by sharing the Gospel with him. I was thinking of a way to approach him, just to open a conversation.

As I observed him to see if he was lacking anything that may prompt me to approach him, I couldn't figure out a single thing to start a conversation with him. He didn't seem to be lacking anything, he was causally and neatly dressed, and he didn't touch the food that he had ordered; therefore, I knew that he wasn't hungry nor homeless.

He had been watching and texting on his cellular phone for several minutes, and in his deep thoughts, he uttered a profanity and hit the table as hard as he could. That was my cue to start a conversation with him and to see if I could offer him a word of comfort. He made a phone call and after several minutes of overhearing his profanities to whomever he was talking to; I went over to him and introduced myself, informing him that I am a pastor, and that I perceive that he is troubled about something. And I asked if I could be of a service to him. He replied, "get away from me preacher, I don't want to hear anything you hypocrites have to say!" I was somewhat offended, but I didn't respond to his comment. Instead, I apologized for my intrusion, went back to the lunch counter and paid my bill.

On my way out of the door, he called out to me and motioned for me to come over. He apologized for his comment, and he asked if he could ask me a question. I said, "Yes sir, and if I can't answer it, the Bible can." He asked me, "Why do church folks always talking about being "Born Again" yet they're still sinning?" He said, "I thought you people have stop sinning, you all say, y'all cannot sin because you're Born Again." Then he said, "Some 'church folks' that I know personally are living in more sin than people who doesn't even go to church." "That's why I've labored Christians to be a bunch of hypocrites because they say one thing, but they always seem to do the opposite."

I asked him was there a particular reason that he asked the question. He said "yes", and he showed me a cellular phone video of a woman that he said was his wife and a man that he said was a preacher, her pastor, coming out of a motel. He said a friend recorded it for him because his friend knew that he wouldn't believe it without proof; because he trusted her, and he thought she was faithful to him. I had to go to great links to explain the difference between our "New Birth" and our "Conversion."

I told him "As long as we live in our flesh bodies that we will sin, and that we're not 'Born Again' until we die; because flesh and blood, our human bodies cannot go into the presence of God." I asked him, "had he ever sinned?" He replied, "yes, everybody has." I then asked him, had he committed adultery since he's been married? He said, "No" that he's been faithful in his marriage. I then asked him has he ever desired a sexual relationship with another woman since he's been married? He replied, "Well, yes in a way." He said, "There was a co-worker that I had a relationship with for several years before I got married, but I broke off the relationship, but she continued to flirt with me, I enjoyed the attention because I remembered the intimacy and the good times that we used to have. But I never had sex with her after I got married."

He said that he thought about it and wanted to, but he was faithful to his vows. I told him, "According to the Bible, because you desired a sexual encounter with her, you have committed adultery with her in your heart." He asked, "How could that be possible? I didn't have another sexual encounter with her after my marriage." I quoted Matt. 5:28 to him and I explained to him that, as long as we live in our flesh bodies on this earth that we will sin, whether it's by co-mission or by omission.

I told him that it was good that he didn't break his vows, God will honor that, but he still committed sin. That he had committed, "sin by desire", because he desired to take his 'ex' to bed and because of this, he had "sinned in his heart." And I also told him that it doesn't excuse his wife's infidelity, but because of "the lust of the flesh" that we sometimes get weak in our human nature, and if we don't allow the Holy Spirit to constrain us, then we will sin.

He asked, "What do you mean by conversion?" I've never heard a Christian use that term, they always talk about a new birth." I had to go through great links to explain the difference of our Conversion and our New Birth to him. I also told him that the pastor should have known better; that God is going to hold him accountable for his actions. I pulled out my pocket size New Testament Bible and I read and explained Luke 12:46 to him and I told him that the judgment of God is going to be greater for the pastor because he took advantage of her in her weakness and vulnerability.

I explained to him that we are "converted" in the flesh, where we will continue to sin while we live in our flesh bodies on this earth. Because we are all human beings and the difference between a Saint and a sinner is that we don't "practice sin" as the sinner does; but sometimes we fall into sin if we don't allow the Word of God to rule supreme in our lives. Then I asked him, "was there a problem in their relationship that would cause his wife to seek pleasure outside of their marriage?" He said, "Probably so, about two years ago I and a friend were victims of an armed robbery, and in my resistance; I was shot in the groin and my performance in the bedroom hasn't been the same since."

I told him that most likely that was the problem, and I suggested that he talk it over with his wife, perhaps the two of them could work out something together if they still wanted to salvage their marriage. I then answered his question and I explained to him that the only time that we "cannot sin" is when we die; because then, and only then, can we be "Born Again." Born into Eternal Life where we, "cannot sin" because we are Born of God, [Spiritually].

I opened my newspaper to the obituary section and showed him several death notices of the deceased that was described as, "Born into Eternal Life." I explained to him when we die a physical death, we get our glorified bodies in heaven, there we *cannot sin because we are born of God."* I read and explained to him First, Second and Third John, after that, he had a clear understanding of the meaning of the "New Birth" and what it means to be "Born Again."

I also explained to him that most church folks are biblically illiterate when it comes to the knowledge of the Bible. I told him how religion blinds us of the True teaching of the Bible. He said, "if that's the case, most church folks don't know the Bible either." I agreed and I took him to John 3: 1-4 and I gave him the example of

Nicodemus, a religious teacher in Israel. He was teaching others, yet he didn't understand the meaning of the New Birth himself, he thought a person had to go back into their mother's womb and be reborn. In verses 5-13 Jesus had to explain the New Birth to teacher, Nicodemus.

He said, *"Except a man be born of the water and of the Spirit, he cannot enter into the kingdom of God."* I explained to him, to be born *"of the water"* is a physical birth when one is born into the earthly realm, and *"of the Spirit"* is when a person dies and is "Born Again", this time into eternal life. I also told him that Jesus was "God in the flesh" yet He himself, didn't return to heaven until after His physical death (John 1:1-14). The Bible declares Jesus as, *"The first- born among many brethren"* (Romans 8:29).

In verses 6 & 7 Jesus explained to Nicodemus the difference of our physical and Spiritual birth. He said, *"That which is born of the flesh is flesh; and that which is born of the Spirit is spirit."* In other words, Jesus was teaching that a person is flesh before they become saved, and that person will remain flesh after they're saved; but that same person doesn't get their glorified body until they die a physical death. In verse 8 Jesus gives an example of our Spiritual birth, that it is invisible just like the wind. No one can see the wind with the naked eye; so, will we be when we get our Spiritual bodies. No human being can see into the Spiritual Realm unless God opens their spiritual eyes. I didn't have the Old Testament Bible with me, but I wrote down Numbers 22:21-33 and 2 Kings 6: 16, 17 and suggested that he read them when he gets home.

The man thanked me for presenting a clear understanding of the Bible to him, and he asked me, "could he and his family visit my church?" I told him that they were welcome to come, but I clarified that the Church belongs to God, Jesus Christ is the Head of the Church and I'm just the overseer. I suggested that they would attend our Wednesday night's Bible study where we would have time to answer or explain any questions that they might have about life or the Bible. I had to reschedule my automobile appointment, but I didn't mind because I had shared the Gospel with the man.

About two weeks later he brought his wife and eight more people to our Bible study, he introduced them as his in-laws, neighbors, and friends. And he asked me to explain the New Birth to them as well. I told them that, "I like to lay a foundation before I build upon it." Then I asked, "How many of them was saved?" Most of them said that they believe in God, but they weren't sure what I meant about "being saved." I explained to them the meaning of salvation, and I told them that Jesus Christ is our Only Savior.

I read and explained John 3:16- 17 to them. I also read and explained Romans 10: 9, 10 to them and I told them that this confession of faith is the only way that anyone can be saved, and only saved people can get into the kingdom of God. I took them to Rev. 20: 11-15 and explained the eternal state of unbelievers and those that opposed God or did not accept the Only One, Jesus Christ, that could secure their eternal residence in heaven. I was led to give them the plan of salvation as laid out in Romans 10:9, 10. They all repented of their sins, and they accepted Jesus Christ as their Lord and personal Savior.

After that I started the class by saying: "Tonight You will Learn the Truth About the New Birth, you will also learn the differences between one's Conversion and the New Birth." I explain to them the same things that I had told the gentleman. And I read and explained to them the following Scriptures.

Scriptures on our conversion:

Ps. 51:13 *"...and sinners shall be converted unto thee."*
Matt.13:15 *"...with their heart and should be converted."*
Matt. 18:3 *"I say unto you. Except ye be* [become] *converted."*
Mark 4:12 *"...lest at any time they should be converted."*
Luke 22:32 *"...and when thou art converted, strengthen thy brethren."*
John 12:40 *"...with their heart, and be converted."*
Acts 3:19 *"Repent ye therefore, and be converted."*

I told the class: "All of these Scriptures addresses people who are alive: they're calling for a change of heart." I also gave them the example of the conversion of Saul, (the Apostle Paul) on the road to Damascus, where he was on his way to persecute Christians (Acts 9:1-9). Paul was converted on his way to do evil; he was not "Born Again."

Paul never used that term to identify believers, he always talked-about, "the old man" (before we came to Christ in faith, and the "new man" after we confessed a hope in Christ (Romans 6:6; Eph. 4:22-24; Col. 3:9, 10). When Paul talked about our new birth, he Said, "...knowing that, whilst we are at home in the body, [living in our earthly-human bodies] we are absent from the Lord...We are confident, I say, and willing rather to be absent from the body, and to be present with the Lord [In the kingdom of God where we will be born into eternity] (2 Cor. 5:6-8).

I reiterated the conversation that Jesus had with Nicodemus. He said, "That which is born of the flesh is flesh... I told them, "You just accepted Jesus Christ as your Lord and personal Savior, you were flesh before your confession, and you are still flesh"... and that which is born of the Spirit is spirit." I also told them, "Your New Birth is eternal or everlasting. Although it is promised to us now, but we cannot inherit it until we die and leave this world. Jesus died so that we can inherit eternal life, therefore, when you die a physical death, you will inherit your glorified body because, 'flesh and blood', your human body, cannot enter into the kingdom of God."

Then I read and explained fully to them the following Scriptures:

Scriptures on our New Birth:

1 Peter 1:23 "Being born again, not of the corruptible seed [flesh]..."

1 Cor.15:53 "For this corruptible [our fleshly bodies] must put on incorruption [Spiritual bodies].

John 1:13 "Which were born, not of blood, nor of the will of the flesh..."

1 John 3:9 *"Whosoever is born of God doeth not commit sin...he cannot sin because he is born of God."*

I reiterated, "When a saved person dies and goes into the presence of God, he / she *"cannot sin"* anymore because they're where God is; nothing that defiles will enter into the kingdom of God" (Rev. 21:27). And from 1 John 2:29 I read, *"Everyone that doeth righteousness is born of Him"* [when they pass from physical death into eternal life]. They all had a clear understanding of the teachings and they all joined the church that night. Most of them became faithful and devoted members. Through those ten, and in the span of six months, seventeen more of their friends and family members was added to the church. The man became a trustee of the church, and his wife joined the choir. Oh, what a difference the "rightly divided' Word of God will accomplish!

I make sure that I give an invitation to accept Christ as their Lord and Personal Savior to visitors of the church. I make it plain that, "today is the day of salvation." Why today" because tomorrow isn't promised to us. I let them know that they might be involved in an automobile accident or hit by a stray bullet on their way home, or while they're out for dinner after church, that they might choke on their meal, and if they die unsaved, they will wake up in hell.

I always give the example of the rich man and Lazarus as described by Jesus in the 16th Chapter of Luke. My wife used to tell me that, "I scare people with that passage of scripture." I would tell her that, "that's part of the purpose of the Bible, if we can put the fear of God in them and the reality of a sudden death, then, they will make room for Christ." I don't believe in 'sugar coating' God's Word, I let them know that death is ever present as we walk our daily journey on this earth.

Most people, especially youth and young adults think they have a lot of time and that they'll give their life unto the Lord as they grow older. But I let them know that death doesn't discriminate, they're never to young to die. And by putting off Christ is giving space to the devil, allowing him to keep them in sin, because the devil knows that one day their life will end, and if they die unsaved that he will have their eternal soul! I remind people the devil is come to steal, kill and destroy but Jesus came to give them eternal life, but they must accept it. And if they die without making a confession in Christ, that they would have automatically chosen hell over heaven.

Events to Occur Before the Rapture:

The persecution of the church precedes the Rapture:

Jesus warned us of the coming persecution during the Tribulation period. As I have already stated, many well-meaning but deceived pastors, teachers and Bible scholars will tell you that, "the church will be Raptured before the Tribulation period begins." Question: Who are you going to believe, the Word of God, our Heavenly Father or the words of your false prophets and teachers? May I remind you that it is written, *"Let God be true and every man a lie"* (Romans 3:4).

Many may wonder, "Why would God allow His people to be persecuted?" I'll tell you why, it's because God doesn't want us to become complacent, He wants us out of our comfort zone. He doesn't want us to sit back in our easy chairs, meet Him once a week in praise and worship while unsaved souls are hell bound. He wants us to fulfill our commission that Jesus laid out for us in Matthew 28:19, 20. Jesus told us to, *"Go ye therefore, and teach all nations, baptizing them in the Name of the Father, and the Son, and the Holy Ghost."*

"God is the same, yesterday, today and forever", He allowed the early church to experience persecution so that His Word would be spread abroad. In the early church people were being saved daily, thousands were added to the church, but God was not satisfied, this didn't fulfill His purpose that Gentiles would have the Gospel preached to them as well, He is no respecter of persons.

After Jesus was resurrected, He told His disciples to tarry [wait] in Jerusalem until the Day of Pentecost so that they would be endured [clothe with God's enablement] with the Holy Ghost so that they will be able to withstand the coming persecutions of that day [time] (Luke 24:44-49).

A walk through the Book of Acts shows us five (5) steps of persecution that the early church had to go through after they had received the Gift of the Holy Ghost.

- Acts 4:1 - Peter and John were threatened by the Sadducees [religious leaders] for healing a lame man and preaching the Gospel (Ch. 3:1-11).
- They were arrested for preaching the Gospel (Ch. 4:3).
- They were further threatened and warned not to preach or teach in the Name of Jesus (vs. 13-18).
- They were imprisoned but liberated by God (5:17-32).
- Stephen was arrested and killed for his faith and testimony of Christ (6:8-15; 7:54-58).

The End Time persecution of the church will be basically the same; we will be warned not to evangelize our faith in Christ. Under tremendous pressure, some will, "deny" Him, some will be imprisoned even put to death for their cause and conviction (Matt. 24:9-12; Rev. 2:8-3:22).

The Day of the Lord:

What is the Day of the Lord? Many ill-informed believers thinks that the Day of the Lord is when Jesus Christ returns to Rapture the Church and set up His Millennium Reign. They are wrong and seriously mistaken! The Day of the Lord will not be a "HALLELUJAH" happy time. But rather, the Day of the Lord is Judgment Day! So, you don't believe me? Let's see what the Word of

God says about it. Remember that *"All scripture is given by inspiration of God, and is profitable for doctrine, for reproof, for correction, for instruction in righteousness: That the man of God may be perfect, thoroughly furnished* [equipped in teaching the Rightly Divided Word of God] *unto all good works"* (2 Timothy 3:16, 17).

With that said, the Bible says, *"Woe unto you that desire the Day of the Lord! To what end is it for you? The Day of the Lord is darkness and not light"* (Amos 5:18). God's prophet Joel pinned, *"Alas for the day! For the Day of the Lord is at hand, and as a destruction from the Almighty shall it come"* (Joel 1:15). And from Joel 2:1, 2 we read where the Word of God says, *"Blow ye the trumpet* [for warning] *in Zion, and sound an alarm in my holy mountain: let all the inhabitants of the land tremble: for the Day of the Lord cometh, for it is nigh at hand; A day of darkness and gloominess, a day of clouds and of thick darkness, as the morning spread upon the mountains: a great people and a strong; there hath not ever been like, neither shall be any more after it, even in the years of many generations."*

Also, Joel 2:11 says, *"And the Lord shall utter his voice before his army for his camp is very great: for he is strong that executeth his word: for the Day of the LORD is great and very terrible; and who can abide* [endure] *it?"* From Joel 2:31 we read, *"The sun shall be turned into darkness, and the moon into blood, before the great and terrible Day of the Lord come."* Isn't this what Jesus prophesied in Matthew 24:25?

Furthermore, from the message God gave His prophet Joel regarding His Judgment of the nations: we read in Joel 3:13-16 where God said, *"Put ye in the sickle, for the harvest is ripe: come, get you down; for the press* [winepress of judgment] *is full, the vats overflow; for the wickedness is great. Multitudes, multitudes in the valley of decision: for the Day of the LORD is near in the valley of decision. The sun and the moon shall be darkened, and the stars shall withdraw their shinning* [ref. Rev. 14:15]. *The LORD also shall roar out of Zion, and utter his voice from Jerusalem; and the heavens and earth shall shake: but the LORD will be the hope* [shelter] *for his people, and the strength* [a stronghold] *of the children of Israel."* Did you understand what the Word of God has just proven? This passage of Scripture along has proven that There is No Pre-Tribulation Rapture of the Church!

From Isaiah 13: 6-13 we read; *"Howl ye: for the Day of the LORD is at hand; it shall come as a destruction from the Almighty. Therefore shall all hands be faint,* [fall limp] *and every man's heart shall melt: And they shall be afraid: pains and sorrows shall take hold of them; they shall be in pain as a woman that travaileth:* [in labor pains] *they shall be amazed one at another; their face shall be as flames. Behold, the Day of the LORD cometh, cruel both with wrath and fierce anger, to lay the land desolate: and shall destroy the sinners out of it. For the stars of heaven and the constellations thereof shall not give their light to shine. And I will punish the world for their evil, and the wicked for their iniquity; and I will cause the arrogancy of the proud to cease, and will lay low the haughtiness of the terrible* [tyrants]. *I will make man more precious* [rare] *as fine gold: even a man than the golden wedge of Ophir. Therefore I will shake the heavens, and the earth shall remove out of their place, in the wrath of the LORD of hosts, and in the day of his fierce anger."* As you just learned, the Day of the Lord, will be a time of trouble and wrath from the Almighty upon His rebellious creation.

Furthermore, many have misunderstood Jesus' conversation with Martha, the sister of Lazarus whom the Lord raised from the dead. Martha believed in the resurrection of the body at the last day, (John 11:21-27) she was not looking forward to the "Day of the Lord" which is Judgment Day! As one can plainly see from these passages of Scriptures, the Day of the LORD is not the Rapture of the Church nor Jesus' Second Coming to set up His Millennium Reign here on earth. But rather, it's God's Judgment on the nations and on people who turned a deft ear to His Word!

From Rev. 6:15-17 [at the opening of the 6th seal vs. 12] we read, *"And the kings of the earth, and the great men, and the rich men, and the chief captains, and the mighty men, and every bondman* [those placed under servitude during the Tribulation Period] *and every free man, hid themselves in the dens* [caves] *and in the rocks of the mountains; A said unto the mountains and the rocks, Fall on us, and hide us from the face of him that sitteth on the throne, and from the wrath of the Lamb, For the great day of his wrath is come; and who shall be able to stand?"*

6

World War III will occur before the Rapture of the Church:

Revelation Chapter 9

Man is capable of self- destruction:

In the Book of Revelation, we read of the opposition of Christ and His Saints. The church will experience a time of great turmoil, distress and suffering. Some of it will be because of Satan's opposition to Christ (and us, His followers) and some of it will be caused by mankind ourselves. In our finite wisdom, man has created enough weapons of mass destruction that we probably have enough nuclear weapons that can destroy the world ten times over.

With the rise of technology, someone can push a button and send nuclear missiles anywhere on the globe. Nations have already stockpiled more than enough weaponry to annihilate all human life from the face of the earth. What if, some disgruntled leader decides to attack another nation? That nation is going to respond with nukes of their own, their allies on both sides will most likely join the fight and come to their rescue and attack the enemies of their enemy, which will create a domino effect and before you know it, the whole world would be at war!

Personally, I believe this is how World War III will begin. According to the Bible a war is coming that is going to kill 1/3 of the world's population. One of every three people on earth will die! (Rev. 9:15-18). This war must be a nuclear war because a third of the world's population [about 2 billion people] can't be killed at once with conventional weapons. Zechariah prophesied the destruction of the nations that will fight against Jerusalem, he said, *"Their flesh shall consume [decay] away while they stand upon their feet, and their eyes shall consume away in their holes,* [eye sockets] *and their tongues shall consume away in their mouth* (Zechariah 14: 12).

Again, this passage of Scripture, no doubt relates to nuclear weaponry because the heat from a nuclear blast is so intense that it will melt the flesh off a person's body before it can fall to the ground. God is going to intervene to keep man from destroying himself. Jesus foresaw this coming war which will follow on the heels of the Tribulation period. He said, *"Except those days be shortened...no flesh will be saved, but for the elects* [the churches] *sake those days shall be shortened"* (Matt. 24:23).

When will this war start? No one knows nor can they predict the day when this event will occur, but it will be after Satan and two hundred million of his locusts like demons, the size of horses will be released from the bottomless pit to wage war against mankind (Rev. 9: 1-21). Remember, the book of Revelation is not written in chronology order, but Revelation Chapter 9 gives us an insight of this coming event, it describes the first two woes-of trumpets five and six.

The fifth trumpet brings a five-month period of torment on the unbelievers of the earth.

Vs. 1-3 *"And the fifth angel sounded, and I saw a star* [angel, which had fallen] *fall from heaven unto the earth; and to him was given the key of the bottomless pit. And he opened the bottomless pit;* [shaft to the abyss] *and there arose a smoke out of the pit, as a smoke of a great furnace; and the sun and the air were darkened by reason of the smoke of the pit....And there came out of the smoke locust upon the earth:* [locust like demons, the size of horses v. 7] *and unto them was given power, as the scorpions of the earth have power."*

The bottomless pit is the abyss, the abode of evil spirits or demons (cf. Luke 8:31). The *key* represents authority. *Smoke* from the pit represents fires below. John saw, "locust-like creatures come out of the smoke." In the Old Testament, *Locusts* are symbols of destruction (cf. Ex. 10:1-20; Deut. 28:42; 1 Kings 8:37; Ps. 78:46; Joel 1:2-2:11). Like *scorpions* they can hurt people. Note: This isn't a human army, but rather, it will be demonic, demons from hell that's going to wage war on mankind!

Vs. 4-6 *"And it was commanded them that they should not hurt the grass of the earth, neither any green thing, neither any tree; but only those men* [mankind] *which have not the seal of God on their foreheads* (cf. Rev. 7:2,3). This is further proof that the church is still on earth and the Rapture of the Church hasn't taken place yet...*And to them,* [the locust-like demons] *it was given that should not kill them, but that they should be tormented five months: and their torment was as the torment of a scorpion, when he striketh a man. And in those days shall men seek death, and shall not find it; and shall desire to die, and death shall flee from them."*

These locust-like demons, the size of horses will not harm vegetation as normal locust would, but rather only those who does not belong to God. They are not allowed to kill anyone at this point, they only torment unbelievers for five months. The pain will be like that of a scorpion's sting. The torment will be so great that people will desire to die, but part of the judgment of God will be that one cannot die to escape it (therefore, "Who shall be able to stand"?).

Vs 7-10 *"And the shapes of the locusts were like unto horses prepared unto battle; and on their heads were as it were crowns like gold, and their faces were as the faces of men...And they had hair as the hair of women, and their teeth were as the teeth of lions...And they had breastplates, as it were breastplates of iron; and the sound of their wings was as the sound of chariots of many horses running to battle...And they had tails like unto scorpions, and there were stings in their tails; and their power* [authority] *was to hurt men five months."*

The description of the locust-like demons indicates that they were given physical form to manifest their destruction and torment. *Horses* show their warlike character. Their *crowns* depict them as conquerors. Human *faces* show intelligence. Their feminine *hair* and their *teeth* as a lion depict a fierce look, they will be destructive and hurtful. *Breastplates of iron* make them indestructible. *Wings* symbolize their swiftness, the *stings* in their tails give them power to hurt.

Vs. 11,12 *"And they had a king over them,* [Satan] *which is the angel of the bottomless pit, whose name in the Hebrew tongue is Abaddon,* [Destruction] *but in the Greek tongue had his name Apollyon* [Destroyer]...*One woe is past, and, behold, there comes two more woes hereafter. "Two more woes are still coming"* As the end approaches, the intensity and severity of the trumpet judgment increases dramatically.

Vs. 13-15 *"And the sixth angel sounded, and I heard a voice from the four horns of the golden alter which is before God, saying to the six angel which had the trumpet, loose* [release] *the four angels which are bound in* [at] *the great river Euphrates....And the four angels were loosed, which were prepared for an* [the] *hour, and a day, and a month, and a year, for to slay the third part of men."*

The six trumpet results in the death of a third of the world's population, [more than two billion people will die!]. The *four* bound *angels* are fallen angels or demons who have been bound by God. They are loosed for the purpose of leading an army and killing a "third" of the world's population. They appear to oversee the horde of demonic horsemen who will accomplish the massacre (vs.16-19). This leads me to believe that the Euphrates River is one of the "gates (plural) of hell" that Jesus spoke of in Matt.16:18. I also believe the Bermuda Triangle is another one of the "gates of hell." I believe this because of the violent weather conditions and the reports of "strange disappearances" of ships and aircrafts in that area.

We know that there will be "twelve gates" leading into the new Jerusalem (Rev. 21:12), therefore, there may be as many as twelve gates (globally) leading into hell [emphasis mine]. The Euphrates River was the northeastern boundary of both the Roman Empire and the promised kingdom of Israel (cf. Gen. 1:18; Deut. 11:24; Josh. 1:4; Is. 8:5-8).

Vs. 16-19 *"And the number of the army of the horsemen were two hundred thousand thousand:* [two hundred million] *and I heard the number of them...And thus I saw the horses in the vision, and them that sat on them, having breastplates of fire* [fiery red] *and of jacinth,* [hyacinth blue] *and brimstone:* [sulfur yellow] *and the heads of the horses were as the heads of lions; and out of their mouths issued fire and smoke and brimstone* [burning sulfur]*...By these three was the third part of men killed, by the fire, and by the smoke, and by the brimstone, which issued out of their mouth...For their power were in their mouth, and in their tails: for their tails were like unto serpents, and had heads, and with them they do hurt."*

John had no time to count the vast number of the demonic army of horsemen that was released from the bottomless pit, but he *"heard"* the number of them, it was an army of two hundred million. The *heads of lions* symbolize cruelty and destruction. The *fire, smoke and brimstone* are three separate plagues, which together kill a *third* of mankind. The demons of the fifth trumpet do not kill, but these demon riders do kill. Their *power* to kill is in their *mouth*, from which comes the "fire", "smoke" and "brimstone."

Their *tails* have heads like *serpents,* with the power to hurt people. This sixth trumpet, combined with the fourth seal (6:8), reduces the population of the earth to one half of its pre-tribulation level.

Vs. 20-21 *"And the rest of the men* [mankind] *which were not killed by these plagues yet repented not of the works of their hands, that they should not worship devils* [demons] *and idols of gold, and silver, and brass, and stone, and of wood: which neither can see, nor hear, nor walk: Neither repented they of their murders, nor of their sorceries, nor of their fornications, nor of their thefts."*

By this point in the Tribulation period, most surviving unbelievers will have permanently made up their minds concerning Christ. They will refuse to repent, even under this terrible judgment. Their religious activities will involve *worship* of *idols* and demons (devils), and *sorceries* or witchcraft, (with the use of magic potions). Apparently, some will compromise and worship the demons to escape the pain and death that they have the power to do over mankind. Idolatry is in fact the worship of demons (cf. 1 Cor. 10:20).

Three of the four sins in verse 21 are specifically prohibited in the Ten Commandments (cf. Ex. 20:3-17). For *"sorceries,"* compare Rev. 18:23; 21:8; 22:15; and Galatians 5:20. With the invading armies that will come up against the nation of Israel in the last days which will lead up to World War III and the releasing of the two hundred million demons from the bottomless pit, some nations will feel that they are outnumbered, and they will use their nuclear arsenals to eradicate the threat.

The Nation of Israel has already expressed using the "Sampson Option" if it must. We all know what Sampson did in his desperation when his enemies had subdued him, he brought down the whole house on himself and his enemies as well (Judges 16:23-30).

Nations will deploy their nukes in an attempt of destroying their enemies, and the invading demonic forces, but by deploying their nuclear weapons, it will result in killing themselves as well!

Again, Jesus prophesied, *"Except those days should be shortened, there should no flesh be saved: but for the elect's* [chosen ones, the church] *sake those days shall be shortened"* (Matthew 24:22). Further proof that: THERE IS NO PRE-TRIBULATION RAPTURE OF THE CHURCH!

There are many terrorist groups who have expressed their hatred for the United States, some have labeled us, "The Great Satan" and they would love to get their hands on such weaponry. They don't fear death, they will kill themselves and as many innocent people as they can just to satisfy their cause, which is their religious ideologies. You often read and hear of suicide bombers in the Middle East blowing themselves up and killing as many others as they can.

There has already been mass shooting in churches around the country. What if, a suicidal bomber walks into a Christian Church here in the United States and set off an attack? Don't you think that that kind of malice will affect church attendance? I wouldn't be surprised if someone would do just that.

Jesus warned us in the Gospels that, *"There will be wars and rumors of wars...Nations shall rise against nations...kingdom against kingdom...And because iniquity shall abound, the love of many shall wax* [grow] *cold"* (Matt. 24: 4-28). Not only that but Jesus foresaw religious denominations fighting against one another and children will be having their parents to be put to death (Mark 13: 13). Apparently, this will occur before the Rapture of the Church.

How can 'church folks' turn against one another and rebellious children having their parents put to death if the church is already 'Raptured' up to heaven? Please don't let anyone deceive you by telling you that the church will escape the Tribulation Period in the Rapture when Jesus plainly said, *"He will send His angels to gather* [Rapture] *the church Immediately after the* [Great] *Tribulation"* (Matthew 24:29-31).

The Apostle Paul said that the church will be caught up [Raptured] at the sounding of the last (7th) trumpet (1 Cor. 15:51,52). These are the two main passages of Scriptures that the

'Pre-Tribulation' believers either overlook or outright reject just to push their false beliefs! But the devil is a lie! The 'elect' [average church folks] will be deceived, but the "very elect" [true believers] will know the truth and we won't be deceived by the impostor, i.e. the Antichrist when he sat himself up in the, yet to be rebuilt Temple in Jerusalem claiming to be God. Oh, he will be a god alright, the false one, the one that the whole world will wonder after (Rev. 13:11-18).

The four (4) horsemen of the Apocalypse must ride first, before the Rapture according to Rev. 6:1-8. During this time of great turmoil and distress, the seven seals [events] must be broken [in occurrence to God's judgment] and the seven vials [of God's wrath] must be poured out upon the earth and the seven trumpets [as warnings] must sound before the Rapture. All these events will run concurrently doing those times.

Remember that the Book of Revelation is not written in chronological order, therefore, for one to understand it they must see things as John saw them; with two or more events happening at the same time, they must view each event from a different angel and perspective but ending with the same conclusion. Otherwise, the Book of Revelation may seem confusing and contradictory to the average reader of the Bible. During this time of trouble, the 144,000 Jews, a selected group 12,000 from each of the twelve tribes of Israel and the Gentile church which consist of an innumerable number will be sealed by God [for protection] here on earth during the seven years of the Tribulation Period (Rev. 7:1-9).

Remember, Jesus said, *"Immediately after the Tribulation, that he will send His angels to gather* [Rapture] *the church!* (Matthew 24:29-31). Paul said, *"I would not have you ignorant, brethren, concerning them which are asleep,* [has died] *that you sorrow not ...For the Lord Himself shall descend from heaven with a shout, and the dead in Christ shall rise first* (1st Resurrection). *Then* (simultaneously) *we which are alive and remain shall be caught up together with them..."* [at the

Rapture of the Church] (1 Thess.4:13-17). Remember that John saw the church, *"coming out" of the Great Tribulation* (Rev. 7:13-14).

Again, the seven seals [events] must be broken; the seven vials [of God's Wrath] must be poured out upon the earth and the seven trumpets [as warnings] must sound first. The seals, [the unleashing of End Times events] the Bowls [of God's Wrath] and the sounding of the trumpets [as warnings] will run concurrently doing those times.

Also, consider the fact that Jesus explained the End Times events in His Olivet Discourse (Matt. 24; Mark 13 and Luke 21). As much as you have read thus far in this book; and if you still believe in the false doctrine of the Pre-Tribulation Rapture of the Church: and you don't believe that the church will have to go through the seven years of the Tribulation Period then; I suggest that you stop here and read the following chapters of Scriptures?

In the Book of Daniel, read Chapters 11 and 12 first in their entirety before you finish reading this book. By doing so, you will familiarize yourself with the events which the Bible says that will occur before the Rapture of the Church.

Also, again as you read those passages of Scriptures, keep in mind that John was given two visions-a heavenly view as well as an earthly view of events which again, will run concurrently. By 'Rightly Dividing' the Word of Truth it will make End Times Bible Prophecy less confusing and it will broaden your understanding of the Book of Revelation. Again, the Book of Revelation is not written in chronological order, neither is this one; but when you are finished with it you will have learned as I did that, there is No Pre-Tribulation Rapture of the Church!

In my learning the Truth of God's Word, if I ran across a passage of Scripture that seems to contradict another Scripture, I would compare and study both passages and I would 'Rightly Divide' them to keep them in perspective and in context.

By doing so, I learned, who was doing the talking, to whom was the message given, and the time frame that it applied to. This self-learned method has taught me to keep things in perspective, by doing so, I am now able to distinguish truth from error.

Again, my mind goes back to several passages of Scripture, Isiah 58:1 where the Word of God tell His ministers, prophets, and teachers to: *"Cry aloud, spare not,* [don't hold back] *lift up thy voice like a trumpet, shew* [show / tell] *my people their transgression."* As Christians, these are our marching orders, if the world is going to learn the Truth, then it is up to us to tell them; how else will they learn? Jesus said, *"And this gospel of the kingdom shall be preached in all the world for a witness unto all nations; and then shall the end come"* (Matt. 24:14). Question: How will this passage of Scripture be fulfilled if the church is suddenly caught up [Raptured] out of the world?

Jesus said, *"Heaven and earth shall pass away, but my words shall not pass away"* (Matt. 24:35). Therefore, the sole purpose of this book is to warn God's people of the false deception that has crept into the churches. With the writing of this book, I personally consider myself as the voice that's, "Crying in the wilderness" because many of God's people have been deceived by their false preachers, teachers, Christian authors, and theologians. God has not called me to change the doctrines of any church, whether it's called by any denomination, sect, or a segment of His True church, but rather, He has called me to *"Teach His people the difference between the holy and the profane"* i.e. To teach them right from wrong (Ezekiel 44:23).

The Pre-Tribulation Rapture doctrine is "profane" to God because it goes against His Holy Scriptures. I've been called to warn His people to beware of Satan's deception. One would be wise to give heed to the written Word of God in order to avoid the catastrophe that will occur when Satan appears as the Antichrist. He's coming as the "deceiver" and he is going to [and already have] deceived many, but he will only deceive those that 'know of God'. Those that, *'Know God'* knows that there is a difference, and if you don't know that, then most likely you will be and have already been deceived! Satan will be convincing because he will give power to the

Antichrist, which will have the ability and power to call down fire from heaven! (Rev. 13:14).

As I've been warning you all alone, by now, you should consider the possibility that Satan might have already deceived you in believing his Pre-Tribulation Rapture Lie! This false doctrine has captured the minds and beliefs of most Christians today. Throughout this book, you will be given God's Truth, what you do with it is entirely up to you. It is your responsibility to accept it or reject it; there is no middle ground with God. Your eternal salvation just might hang in the balance. Right now, your soul is either saved or lost. And if you die an unsaved person; you will be like the rich man that died unsaved, you will wake up in hell where your eternal soul will be tormented FOREVER! (Luke 16:19-31).

Some people, even my wife sometimes get offended, when I talk about hell and the reality of it if a person dies unsaved. Jesus warns us about that terrible place of eternal punishment and damnation. As a matter of fact, Jesus taught more about hell than He did about the kingdom of God! You may ask, "why is that?" I would answer that question by stressing the fact that, Jesus loves us. He loves us so much that He gave His life as a ransom for us (Mark 20:45). Hell wasn't made for mankind but for the devil and his fallen comrades. Mankind will end up in that dreadful place of torment because people have and will reject the Only One that can save us. That One Savior is Jesus Christ Himself.

It is written of Jesus, "...*And being found in fashion* [appearance] *as a man, he humbled himself, and became obedient unto death, even the death of the cross. Wherefore God also hath highly exalted him, and given him a name which is above every name. That at the name of Jesus every knee should bow, of things in heaven, and things in earth, and things under the earth; And that every tongue should confess that Jesus Christ is Lord, to the glory of God the Father* (Philippians 2:8-11). Yes, Jesus warns us about hell because He loves us, and He doesn't want to see us thrown into the lake of fire on judgement Day!

He loves us so much that He gave His life for us. It is written, *"For God so loved the world,* [mankind] *that he gave his only begotten Son, that whosoever believeth in him should not perish, but have everlasting life. For God sent not his Son into the world to condemn the world; but that the world through him might be saved"* (John 3:16,17).

I've already stated that I'm not politically correct. That's why I teach the King James Version of the Bible. Many of today's translations of the Bible is a "watered down" version of the Holy Bible. Many of them diminishes the truth in their translation, but as truth barriers, for God and our Lord and Savior Jesus Christ, we're not to do that (Deu.12:32). Jesus wasn't politically correct neither, He called people and things just as they were (Matt. 23:23-36). I talk about things that Jesus talked about, and the things that the Bible warns us of. If we're really following His examples, then we shouldn't hold back the Truth of God's Word.

By holding back, it is suppressing God's Word and we'll be playing right into the hands of Satan by not presenting the Truth of God's Word to the unsaved. We are to warn them of the reality of their eternal damnation in the lake of fire. It's our duty to warn them otherwise, *"There blood will be on our hands"* (Ezekiel 33:1-7). The Bible calls Satan, *"the adversary"* and for good reasons, he opposes God in every aspect of his evil beings, he opposes us as well because we belong to God. God, our heavenly Father's intentions for us is to *know His Word* that we don't be deceived or fall into, *"the wiles of the devil."*

Satan attacks God's people immediately after they respond to the Gospel (Matthew 13:18-23). He is constantly on his job of standing against all who are called to be Christians.

His primary goal is to have you believe a lie, [about God and the Bible] that he might get you sidetracked from the Truth of God's Word. If you are influenced by anything other than the written Word of God, then most likely you're already living in deception. And, if you're not aware of that, then the chances are great that the enemy has already deceived you in a variety of ways. He has various ways of enticing the people of God.

The un-learned and the un-skilled in Scriptures will accept almost anything that comes out of the mouth of their pastors and teachers; believe me, I've experienced it myself. As I stated in the offset, I was a sincere and devoted believer but deceived by my denominational teachings and by my sincere, but wrong, religious teachers. They told me that there will be a Pre-Tribulation Rapture of the Church and that we won't be here on earth when the Antichrist will rise to power. I've learned that that teaching is a false doctrine, lies and deception from the enemy. Satan works through the church as a con man works through a crowd, he's gaining the attention of anyone who believes his lies!

Many popular and well-known TV evangelist, pastors, preachers, and Gospel book writers have deceived God's people with false and deceptive preaching and teaching. I won't name any of them, but if any of them tell you that the church will be raptured before the tribulation period, I would advise you to turn off the TV or change the channel. If you're sitting in a church and this false doctrine comes out of the mouth of any of them, I would advise you to get your coat and leave, go home and study the Word of God for yourself.

7

The Four Horseman of the Apocalypse:

The Seals

From Revelation Ch. 5:1-14, John described Jesus, as the Lamb of God and the only One qualified to open the Sealed Book given to Him by the angel of God. In Rev. 6:1, John sees Jesus opening the sealed book which he saw the four horsemen of the Apocalypse being loosed upon the earth. These horsemen must ride first, before the Rapture of the Church; they will be released in the opening of the first four seals (Rev. 6:1-8).

Seal # 1. The rider on the white horse is the Antichrist, the deceiver, the counterfeit Christ. He comes armed with a bow and seated upon a white horse (symbolizing war). Many well-meaning, but uninformed pastors, teachers and interpreters of the Bible erroneously ascribe this horseman as Jesus coming to "conquer the world and evangelize it." That belief is as far from the truth as the east is from the west! Jesus didn't come as a conqueror, but rather a Savior. When He returns [His Second Coming] He's coming back as a judge, defeating the Antichrist and overthrowing man's governments.

When Jesus Christ appears the second time, He will be riding upon the white horse of Revelation 19:11-14. Note: He is going to bring His Saints with Him [those that died in faith and those that will be Raptured at the seventh (7th) trumpet and on the 1,290th day, i.e., thirty (30) days after the Great Tribulation is over]. John said, *"I saw heaven open, and behold a white horse; and he that sat upon him was called Faithful and True, and in righteousness he doth judge and make war.... And he was clothed with a vesture dipped in blood: and his name is called The Word of God, And the armies which were in heaven followed him upon white horses, clothed in fine linen, white and clean."* Anyone who can read and understand plain English should have no problem in distinguishing the differences between these two riders.

The first rider is armed with a bow; he is given a crown and sets out to "conquer." The second one is [was] called, "Faithful and True", He will be clothed with a garment *"dipped in blood"* and His Name is called, *"The Word of God."* Jesus warned His disciples of this deception in Matt. 24:4-5. I believe that's the reason Thomas wanted to see the wounds on Jesus' body before he would accept the others testimony that the Lord had indeed risen. i.e., *"Prove all things"* (1 Thess. 5:21).

Many have labeled Thomas as a "doubter", but I see him as a good listener. He knew that the Lord's Words are True, therefore, he wanted proof because he remembered Jesus' warning that, *"Many would come in His Name deceiving many* (vs. 23-26). Thomas, by him seeing the wounds on the Lord's body was proof enough for him to accept their testimonies. If the churches of today had the spirit of Thomas, I believe that there would be far less false teachings in the church! Again, we need to pattern ourselves after the Berean Church, where those believers, *"search the Scriptures daily,"* [to see] whether those things [being taught] are so (Acts 17:11).

As I've stated, the Pre-Tribulation Rapture doctrine has been spread by word of mouth from the pulpits of unlearned pastors in today's churches, television preachers, teachers, pastors, and evangelist. This deception has been published in Christian books, magazines, and other publications. It's no wonder most of the whole world is living in deception. Only the "very elect" in Christ will survive it. *"He that hath an ear, let him hear what the Spirit saith unto the churches."*

Seal # 2. *"And when he had opened the second seal, I heard the second beast* [living creature] *say, Come and see. And there went out another horse that was red; and power was given to him that sat thereon to take peace from the earth, and that they should kill one another: and there was given unto him a great sword"* (Vs. 3,4).

The second seal brings forth the second horseman, mounted on a red horse [symbolizing bloodshed], he welds a great [giant] sword, and removes peace from the earth so that people begin to kill each other. Do you remember Jesus' Words of Matthew 24: 4-13?

Seal # 3. *"And when he had opened the third seal, I heard the third beast say, Come and see. And I beheld, and lo a black horse; and he that sat on him had a pair of balances in his hand. And I heard in the midst of the four beast say, A measure of wheat for a penny; and three measures of barley for a penny, and see thou hurt not the oil and the wine"* (Vs. 5 & 6).

This rider's horse is black; [symbolizing famine] he represents bad economic conditions, lack of food and intense hunger. The scales represent the extent of people's hunger which can be seen in the exorbitant prices for wheat and barley [an increase of grocery prices in our day].

Seal # 4. *"And when he had opened the fourth seal, I heard the voice of the fourth beast say, Come and see. And I looked, and behold a pale horse: and his name that sat on him was Death, and Hell followed with him. And power was given unto them over the fourth part of the earth, to kill with sword, and with hunger, and with death, and with the beast of the earth"* (Vs. 7 & 8).

This horseman rides a pale green horse, [symbolizing the color of death] and he was given power over a quarter of the earth [about one billion people] to kill with a variety of weapons, famines, pestilences, and wild beast. He represents the sickness and diseases, [pestilences, pandemics] that Jesus prophesied in Matthew 24:7. Jesus promised to protect His own, [those that keep the faith and doesn't deny Him]. He said, *"And except those days* [of the tribulation period] *be shortened, there shall no flesh be saved: but for the elect's* [true believers] *sake those days shall be shortened"* (Matthew 24:21-22).

Seal # 5. *"And when He had opened the fifth seal, I saw under the alter the souls of them that was slain for the word of God, and for the testimony which they held: And they cried with a loud voice, saying, How long, O Lord, holy and true, dost thou not judge and avenge our blood on them that dwell on the earth? And white robes was given unto every one of them; and it was said unto them, that they should rest yet for a little season, until their fellow servants also and their brethren, that should be killed as they were, should be fulfilled* (Vs. 9 -11).

This is the death and persecution of believers [martyrs] that will be killed during the tribulation period for their faith and testimony in Christ. Jesus promised us, *"If we loose our lives for His and the Gospel's sake that we will pick it up again"* (Mark 8:35). Oh, how I wish that there would be a Pre-Tribulation Rapture of the Church, if it were, then we would not have to experience these things (if they occur during our lifetime). Nevertheless Lord, "not my will, but let thy will be done."

The Bible says, *"All that will live godly in Christ Jesus shall suffer persecution"* (2 Timothy 3:12). Many have ignored this passage of Scripture and replaced it with "a feel- good doctrine of a Pre-Tribulation Rapture."

Seal # 6. *"And I beheld when he had opened the six seal, and lo, there was a great earthquake: and the sun became black as sackcloth of hair, and the moon became as blood;* [ref. Matt. 24:29] *and the stars of heaven fell unto the earth, even as a fig tree casteth her untimely figs, when she is shaken of a mighty wind* (Vs.12).

Death and persecution have been perpetuated against every Christian generation, it started with the birth of the early church (Acts 1:1-2:47; 5:17-32; 8:1-4), and it continues until this day. And it will get progressively worse until Christ returns to overthrow man's government and "The New World Order" that will be established by the Antichrist. Jesus Christ will overthrow it all and establish His earthly kingdom where there will be, *"no end."* Therefore, why does End Time believers [today's Saints and church leaders] come up with the conclusion that they will be 'Raptured' from it? I will tell you why; it's because of false doctrines that's being taught in most churches today!

I asked a pastor / acquaintance of mine, "Why does he still preach and teach the Pre-Tribulation Rapture doctrine after finding out the truth?" His reply was, "I don't want to put fear and doubt into my people, I've been teaching them ever since I started the church fifteen years ago." He assured me that I would never be invited to preach in 'his' church, he also told me, "Don't invite any of his members to my church?

I reminded him of Hosea 4:6; Ezekiel 33:1-9 and Luke 6:39. With that, he tried to use Luke 6:37 against me claiming that I was judging him. Not so, I told him, "God, in His Word, has already judged you and your sentencing will come at the Judgment Seat of Christ, that is, "IF" you are saved." I advised him to, "Swallow his pride and teach God's people the truth." I also reminded him of Matthew 7:21-23.

It is rightly said that "people will believe a lie before they believe the truth." The "lie" is the Pre-Tribulation Rapture of the Church. The truth is: THERE IS NO PRE-TRIBULATION RAPTURE OF THE CHURCH! Regarding the tribulation period, Jesus said, *"All these are the beginning of sorrow. Then shall they deliver you up to be afflicted,* [persecution and tribulation] *and shall kill you: and ye shall be hated of all nations for my name's sake"* (Matt. 10:16-23; 24:8,9; Rev. 2:9-11). Question: Does those passages of Scripture sound like a Pre-Tribulation Rapture to you? I think Not!

Another point to consider: Why would we [the church] need 'patience' (Luke 21:17-19; James 5:7-11) if the church won't be here on earth during the Tribulation period? I hope that you can see for yourself how your religious [false] teachers are misleading you, having you to believe in a false doctrine that will lead you straight to hell! Remember, Jesus has already warned us of religious deception that is coming upon the world before His return (Matt.24:6). John also warned us of false prophets that have, *"gone out into the world"* (1 John 4:1).

Believe me, it is going to get progressively worse before the return of Christ. "Deception" has the same end results, whether it's done out of, "the lack of knowledge" or by some other means. My pastor was a sincere and devoted man of God, yet he was wrong in his teachings. He was sincere, but he also was sincerely wrong! Only God knows how many souls was spared by my presenting the truth about the timing of the Rapture of the Church to the congregation.

By the same token, only God knows how many souls will be saved by the writing of this book. I take no glory, honor nor praise, I give it to God and Him alone through my Lord and Savior, Jesus Christ. My reward for teaching the Truth of God's Word is reserved for me in heaven (Matt. 16:27; Daniel 12:13).

The Tribulation period [if this generation is alive when it occurs] will be a testing of our faith. Daniel's faith was tested in the lion's den; the three Hebrew boys' faith was tested in the fiery furnace; Abraham's faith was tested when God instructed him to offer up his son Isaac for a sacrifice; and Job's faith was tested with the calamities that he endured. *"God is the same yesterday, today and forever"* therefore, the faith of the Saints who will be alive during the Tribulation period will be tested as well.

Unfortunately, many saints will lose heart during this time of great distress, and they will "deny" our Lord and Savior, Jesus Christ (read Matt.10:33; 2 Timothy 2:12; Rev. 2:13; 3:8). Read again where Jesus warned us of the persecution that His people will have to endure during the Tribulation period (Matt.10:16-23; Rev. 2:9, 10; 3:10-12).

I can't stress enough the warning of Christ to end time believers. Remember Jesus said, *"Whosoever therefore shall confess me before men, him will I confess before my Father which is in heaven. But whosoever shall deny me before men, him will I deny before my Father which is in heaven* (Matt.10:32,33*). "He that hath an ear, let him hear what the Spirit saith unto the churches"* (Rev.3:13). Question: How will these passages of Scriptures to be fulfilled if the church is suddenly taken out of the world, and, if- it has already gone up to heaven in a Pre-Tribulation Rapture?

Luke and John are in agreement here; we must have patience during the Tribulation period because we will not be "Raptured" from it! John foresaw the rise of the Antichrist, which will occur before the Rapture which I will explain more in depth later in this book, but first, again, I want to point out the fact that we must have "patience" during those troublesome times (Rev. 14:9-13).

Seal # 6. Vs.12-17. John saw a great earthquake (Matt. 24:7, 29-31; Joel 2:10, 31; 3:15). And unsaved people hiding in caves and under rocks of mountains saying, *"Fall on us, and hide us from the face of him that sitteth on the throne, and from the wrath of the Lamb; For the great day of his wrath* (the day of the Lord) *is come, and who shall be able to stand?*

Seal # 7. Ch. 8:1-5. At the opening of this seal, John saw silence in heaven about the space of half of an hour [for preparations of the seven warning trumpets]. Vs. 3 & 4, John said the prayers of the persecuted saints were heard by God.

Remember again, the number seven (7) in scripture represents completion. Jesus will return at the last seventh (7th) trumpet (1 Corinthians 15:51,52) to gather [Rapture] the church where we will go before His Judgment Seat to get our rewards and assignments in His Millennium Kingdom. Why do I believe this? I'm glad that you asked. Paul said, *"For we all* (the universal church) *must appear before the judgment seat of Christ; that everyone may receive the things done in his body, according to that he hath done, whether it be good or bad"* (2 Cor. 5:10; Ref. 1 Cor. 3:11-15).

When Christ return, (at His Second coming- Parousia) He will overthrow man's government (six thousand years of rule on earth) and the government of the Antichrist (his seven years reign) and set up His thousand years of Millennium Reign, where we will be kings and princes in His kingdom, which will have no end. We'll (the church) will even judge the angels that sinned which were expelled from heaven and cast into outer darkness (1 Corinthians 6: 1-3; Jude vs 6).

The Antichrist Will Appear
Before the Rapture:

The deceiver, the imposter, the impersonator of Christ, which the Bible calls, "the Antichrist" (2 John vs. 7), will set up his short kingdom before the Rapture of the Church. Jesus warns us of this deceptive figure in the Gospels of Matthew, Mark and Luke. The Gospel of Matthew was written primarily to the Jews, Jesus warned the Jewish believers who will be living in Jerusalem at this time to, *"Flee into the mountains"* i.e., "get out of the city" when they see the "ABOMINATION OF DESOLATION" prophesied by Daniel come to pass, (Matthew 24:15-20).

I'm sure everyone has heard of this devious and evil character that the Bible talk about. But who is the Antichrist? Who is that *"man of sin,* the *"son of perdition"* that the Bible warns us about? Many speculations have submerged as to who this dictator and world leader will be.

He has been ascribed to many past and present leaders from Adolph Hitler to a guy name Barack Hussein Obama. The Bible does not identify who the Antichrist will be, but Scriptures gives us many clues and characteristics to describe him. The world's stage is being set up to receive this evil character called "Antichrist." With "knowledge increasing" (Dan. 12:4) through the invention of the computer, nuclear weaponry, product bar codes on everything sold, food, clothing, furniture, appliances, etc. I can plainly see how one would not be able to, "buy or sell" during the Tribulation period (Rev. 13:11-18) without submitting to the rule and authority of the Antichrist.

I watch scientific movies to get a heads up on things that are sure to come in the very near future. Most people think that science fiction movies made in Hollywood are just for entertainment, but I have come to realize that they are telling us of things to come. Those movies have a hidden agenda that most people don't recognize. I once saw a movie that showed how parents would go to a generic supermarket to pick the race, sex, and hair color of their next child. I've heard from news reports that Russia is exploring this very same technology!

Several years ago, here in the United States, children have been born because of test tube babies, where doctors will plant the hormones of both parents in an incubator and produce a living child. Not only that, but animal hearts have been put into human bodies. Man is trying to play God!

God made sure that those scientific experimental humans didn't survive. "Knowledge" surely has increased as the Word of God said that it would. Also, there have been many movies made about mind control. The powers that be knows that if they can control a person's mind, they can control the population.

Man will someday, in the very near future become a chemically controlled machine during the reign of the Antichrist. *"There's nothing new under the sun."* Adolf Hitler wanted to create a superior race, he ran a fertilization farm, and he tried his diabolical scheme by eliminating those that were declared, "inferior" resulting in the Holocaust where six million Jews and many other races were exterminated under his tyrant control.

By the same token, the Antichrist will have a select group of people that he will delegate positions of authority to. In order to maintain their positions and authority they will have to receive implants in their bodies or brains to control them. If one renege on their agreement (with Satan) those implants would explode sending poison into their blood stream killing that person immediately!

Again, people view those movies as 'entertainment' but they are really showing and telling you, *"things which must surely come to pass."* And the church will still be here because: THERE IS NO PRE-TRIBULATION RAPTURE OF THE CHURCH!

Biblical names for the Antichrist:

- King of Assyria (Isaiah 10:12; 14:24, 25; Micah 5:5,6).
- King of Babylon (Isaiah 14:4). Ancient Babylon was located in Mesopotamia, modern day Iraq.
- Man of sin, the son of perdition (2 Thess. 2:3,4).
- The Beast (Rev. 13:5-8).

Characteristics of the Antichrist:

According to the Book of Daniel:

- He will come from ten kings [rulers] in the, yet to be restored Holy Roman Empire (Dan. 7: 7, 24).
- He will subdue three of those kings (Dan. 7: 8, 24).
- He is [will be] diverse [different] from the other rulers (Dan. 7:7, 19).
- His appearance is [will be] more impressive than his fellows (Dan. 7:20).
- He will make war with the Saints for 3 ½ years [i.e., 1,260 days of the Great Tribulation Period] and he will overcome them (Daniel 7: 21, 25).
- He will speak great words against God and blaspheme His name (Daniel 7:25).
- He will try to change times and laws (Daniel 7:25).

- He is a king of fierce countenance (Daniel 8:23).
- By peace he shall destroy many (Daniel 8:25).
- He shall come in peacefully and obtain the kingdom by flatteries (Daniel 11:21).
- He shall exalt and magnify himself above every god and shall speak marvelous [unusual] things against the God of gods (Daniel 11:36).
- He shall not regard the God of his fathers, nor the desire of women, nor any god: for he shall magnify himself above all (Daniel 11:37).
- He shall have power over the treasures of gold and of silver, and over all precious things of Egypt (Daniel 11:43).

Note: Daniel did not understand the things that was revealed to him, he asked God for more understanding, however, he was denied the revelation; instead, he was told, *"Go thy way Daniel: for the words are closed up and sealed until the time of the end* (Daniel 12:8,9). "The Time of the End" i.e. The end of man's six thousand years of rule on earth and the rise and fall of the Antichrist.

After which, Christ will overthrow the present world system and establish His Millennium which will, *"Be no end."*

The Bible says, *"For precept must be upon precept...Line upon line..."* (Isaiah 28:10). One can identify the Antichrist by comparing Scripture with Scripture. By comparing Daniel's prophecy in the Old Testament with the Revelation that God gave John we can identify the Antichrist so that his rise to power won't take us by surprise!

Daniel 7:7, 24	Revelation 13: 1; 17:12,13
Daniel saw- *"A fourth beast, dreadful and terrible, and strong exceedingly; and it had great iron teeth:...And the ten horns out of his kingdom are ten kings that shall arise...and he shall be diverse* [different] *from the first, and he shall subdue three kings."*	John saw- *"A beast rise out of the sea, having seven heads ten horns, and upon his horns ten crowns, and upon his heads the name of blasphemy...And the ten horns that I sawest are ten kings, which have received no kingdom as yet; but receive power as kings one hour with the beast."*

Facts Regarding the Antichrist:

He will come on the scene before the Rapture, the Apostle Paul warns believers:

- *"Let no man deceive you by any means: for that day,* [the Rapture of the Church] *shall not come except there be a falling away first, and that man of sin be revealed, the son of perdition..."*

He will set himself up in the yet to be rebuilt temple claiming to be God:

"...who opposeth and exaileth himself above all that is called God, or that is worshiped; so that he as God sitteth in the temple of God, showing himself that he is God" (2 Thess. 2: 3,4 ref Matt. 24:15).

He will be a world leader empowered by Satan:

- *"And the king shall do according to his will, and he shall exalt himself, and magnify himself above every god, and shall speak marvelous* [unusual] *things against the God of gods and shall prosper until the indignation be accomplished: for that that is determined shall be done"* (Daniel 11:36).

He will not respect the religion of his race nor any religious conviction:

- *"Neither shall he regard the God* [false gods] *of his fathers, nor the desire of women, nor regard any god: for he shall magnify himself above all"* (Daniel 11:37).

He will be wanted and accepted, not rejected:

- Those living during the Tribulation Period will look for a deliverer to deliver them from the troublesome times, a time of political, economic, moral, and religious deterioration. The Antichrist will arise to power [at the bidding of Satan] and offer a seven (7) years peace treaty between Israel and her enemies. The people will readily accept him and after 3 ½ years [of the Tribulation period] he will renege on his promise, the last 3 ½ years will result in the coming Great Tribulation (Matt. 24: 4- 21).

He will be appealing, not repulsive:

- With his charismatic appearance and soft speech, he will not be offensive in his conduct. He will not appear as a "Beast", instead, he will win people to him through miracle that he will be empowered by Satan to perform (Rev. 13:11-14).

He will come on the scene with great wisdom:

- Far beyond the wisdom of our modern-day leaders, the Antichrist will progress wisdom that will be extraordinary, he will use his, Satan given powers to gain support in which he will use it against God's people.

He will be a Gentile, not a Jew:

- From Daniel Chapter 7, we learn that the Antichrist will come from the divided Roman Empire, which is Gentile in origin.

The Scriptures tells us that the coming world dictator will rise to power out of the natural flow of events when the world will be at its height of troubles, mainly due to turmoil brought on by moral, economic, and religious indifferences. Those troublesome times will set the stage for Satan to put his insidious scheme for world dominance into motion.

This opportunity for Satan will occur before the Rapture and during the Tribulation Period where God's people will be, *"Hated of all nations* for the Lord's sake."(Matt. 24:9; Mark 13:13; Luke 21:17; John 15:21). His religious opposition to the church will not be a secret. He will speak out against the Most High, and persecute those who are Christians (v. 25a). As a political rival, he will abolish all previous laws and institute his own anti-God standards (v. 25b).

Rise of the Antichrist: (part 1)

Our Lord and Savior Jesus Christ, explained to us that the Antichrist will arrive on the scene before His return when He warned the End Time church about the, "ABOMINATION OF DESOLATION, spoken [prophesized] by Daniel" (Matthew 24:15). The Apostle Paul also warned us of this prophesied event as well in 2 Thess. 2:1-4. In Paul's day there was a dispute that rosed up in the church in Thessalonica, some believers thought the Lord had returned, others had questions about the Saints that had passed on. Paul settled the dispute and answered their questions as to when the Lord's Second Coming and the Rapture of the Church would occur.

Those unlearned Christian believers had heard that the Lord had already returned to rule over the nations (vs. 1-2). Paul informs them that this event will not occur until, *"the apostasy comes* [falling away of the faith in Christ] (1 Timothy 4:1-3; 2 Timothy 3: 1-5; 4: 3-4; 2 Peter 2: 3; 3-6) ....*and the man of sin is revealed, the son of destruction"* (v. 3).

During this time of heightened rebellion, the one who exemplify sin, will eventually have his day in God's court. His end is everlasting destruction [in the lake of fire]. Before the church is Raptured, the Antichrist will be revealed, he will oppose Christianity and all other religions as well and he will, *"exalt himself above every so-called god or object of worship; so that he as God will sit in the temple of God, showing himself that he is God"* (v. 4).

If you go back read and understand Daniel's seventh week, then you will learn that Daniel saw the revising of the Holy Roman Empire, but John, the revelator gives us a more complete revelation and understanding of the event in Revelation Chapters 13-17.

But first, before we go to the Book of Revelation let's see what John wrote to the church concerning the coming of the Antichrist, that "lawless one", that "deceiver" who will be sent on the scene from Satan, the "father of lies"; which will appear before the Rapture of the Church.

In 1 John 2:18 we read:

"Little children, it is the last time: [hour] *and as you have heard that antichrist shall come, even now are there many antichrists; whereby we know that it is the last time. they went out from us, but they were not of us; for if they had been of us, they would no doubt have continued with us: but they went out, that they might be made manifest that they were not all of us. But ye have an unction* [anointing] *from the Holy One, and ye know all things. I have not written unto you because ye know not the truth, but because you know it, and that no lie is of the*

truth. Who is a liar but he that denieth that Jesus is the Christ? He is antichrist, that denieth the Father and the Son. Whosoever denied the Son, the same hath not the Father: [but] he that acknowledgeth the Son hath the Father also."

So then, who is the Antichrist? He is the ultimate opponent of God, our Heavenly Father. He is against God, God's plans and God's people [the church]. The Antichrist has and will continue to sow discord among the Body of Christ, that he may further his diabolical agenda which is to divide and conquer the church [believers]. The devil has filled the minds of God's people with so much confusion in the churches that the unsaved doesn't want anything to do with the church. I've often heard unsaved people talk negatively against the church, many have labored us, "hypocrites" because they see or knows someone who claims to belong to Christ, yet they're still doing the things that the world is doing.

That's one reason that I stayed away from church so long in my teenage and young adult years. I knew that I wasn't ready to give up my life of fun and pleasure to start living the true Christian lifestyle where I would have to, *"come out from among them and be separate."* I thank God for His, Grace, Mercy and Patience that He has shown me and protected me throughout my wayward years. In my own experience I've come to realize that God is truly long-suffering and patient with His children.

Remember, the Apostle Paul warned us in 2 Thess. 2:1-5 that Satan is going to send his agent, the Antichrist on the scene and appoint him a place in the, yet to be rebuilt temple in Jerusalem to be worshiped as God. John wrote, *"Beloved, believe not every spirit, but try [test] the spirits whether they are of God: because many false prophets are gone out into the world. Hereby know ye the Spirit of God: Every spirit that confesseth that Jesus Christ is come in the flesh is of God: and every spirit that confesseth not that Jesus Christ is come in the flesh is not of God: and this is the spirit of antichrist, whereof ye have heard that it should come; and even now already is in the world. Ye are of God, little children, and have overcome them: because greater is he that is in you than he that is in the world"* (I John 4:1-4).

God's people will be hearing a lot of holy and religious sounding spirits that will not be coming from God, but rather from our adversary, the devil. Deception will be so strongly influenced and accepted among End Times believers that churches of different denominations will become so confused by doctrines and ideologies they will start fighting among themselves and start killing one another (Matt. 24:10).

That's why Jesus warned us in Mark 13:12 that, *"Brother shall betray the brother to death, and the father the son; and children shall rise up against their parents, and shall cause them to be put to death, And ye shall be hated of all men for my name's sake: but he that shall endure* [bare patiently] *unto the end* [of the Great Tribulation period] *the same shall be saved."*

Did you understand what Jesus said? He was not only addressing family feuds of family members of different denominations, but He was also warning us of things to come during the Tribulation period where divided church folks will attack and kill one another. During the Tribulation Period the Antichrist will pass laws that all Christian churches to be closed and any violators will be put to death. Do you remember the persecution that the early church had to endure? Those believers were scattered abroad, some was even killed [Stephen, in Acts 7:54-60; James, Acts 12:1-4] and they had underground churches where religious symbols [fish and a cross] were used to signal believers where they was meeting.

The Antichrist will issue decrees that family members report to the authorities anyone who violates his orders. Biological brothers of different denominations will report that his brother is a Christian and is secretly meeting with other Saints causing him to be put to death. Children will turn against their parents and report them to the authorities, and they will be put to death as well.

We have a prelude of that happening right now in our society, a disobedient child can report to the authorities that their parents are disciplining them, and social services will have the child removed from the home. Many times, those parents will be tried, convicted, and jailed. But during the Tribulation period those parents will be put to death, not because they disciplined their children but mainly, because they are Christians (ref. Acts 8:1-4; Daniel 6:1-13).

Remember also, it was the religious community [the chief priests] that accused Jesus, it was the religious community [the high priest] that condemned Him on trial and commanded that He be crucified. It was one of His own [Judas Iscariot] that betrayed Him; it was one of His disciples [Peter] that denied Him, but it was a sinner, [Pilate], that found no fault in Him and was willing to let him go. But it was the religious community, [the chief priest and the elders] who desired a sinner [Barabbas] to be released and Jesus to be put to death!

John explicitly told us how to avoid the doctrines, influences, and deception of the Antichrist, he told us to "test" [prove] the spirits to know for sure that the teachings and doctrines are from God. How does one 'test' teachings and doctrines? You test it to see if it lines up with the Bible, which is the Word of God [Isaiah 28:9,10; 1 Thess. 5:21; 2 Timothy 3:16]. If it doesn't, then it's not of God but rather from religious doctrines of the *spirit of the Antichrist!*

The spirit of the Antichrist will:

1. Deny the Deity of Jesus.
2. Deny that Jesus Christ is the Son of God.
3. Deny the relationship between the Father and the Son.

Believe it or not, hear it or not, but *"All that live Godly in Christ Jesus shall suffer persecution"* (2 Timothy 3:12), especially during the Tribulation Period. Even now, we hear of mass shootings and bombings in houses of worship of all denominations all around the world. Christians and Jews are the most hated ones, and we are the ones that Satan will attack the most. You can say one thing about Satan, he doesn't discriminate, he hates all of God's people!

From Revelation 13:1-18, we read where John saw the revision of the Holy Roman Empire in the Rise of the Antichrist. As you read the prophecy, please keep in mind that the "beast" or "creatures" represents a world power, he could be a person or an empire.

The Mark of the Beast:

John, the Revelator says that the Beast of the earth will force everyone to be marked, *"in their right hand or on their forehead"* [with a tattoo or the number 666], during the Tribulation Period (Rev. 13:15-17). Why the number 666? Because it is the number of man (Rev. 13:18). Man was created on the sixth day, God gave mankind [human government] a six thousand years of rule upon the earth and the Antichrist will be revealed at the sounding of the sixth trumpet (Rev. 9:14). I personally believe that the number 666 will be applied to everyone's social security number, and if that person doesn't have the number attached to it, then they will not be able to *"buy or sell."*

Furthermore, if the number isn't applied to the person's credit or debit cards then they wouldn't be able to spend any money, (i, e. 'buy or sale') they will be excluded from the economy. Jesus will return at the seventh [last trumpet] to "Rapture" His Saints, the church out of the world (1 Corinthians 15:51,52; Rev.11:15). Unfortunately, this will occur, *"Immediately after the Great Tribulation"* (Matt. 24:29-31), therefore, again, the church must go through the whole seven (7) years of the Tribulation Period.

Six comes before seven! Therefore, the Antichrist will come on the scene first, which will usher in the Tribulation Period, [The 1,260 days or 42 months or 3 ½ years all refers to the last half of the tribulation]. And Jesus is returning at the sounding of the seventh (last) trumpet on the 1,290[th] day to: Rapture His Saints out of the world where we will stand before Him at His Judgment Seat whereas, we will get our rewards for our work here on earth. Jesus will return to earth on the 1,335th day to set up His one thousand years Millennium Reign, which will have no end. The number eight in Scriptures represents, "new beginning."

After Jesus overthrows man's government, destroys the Antichrist with His Second Coming; He's going to set up His Eternal Kingdom (on the 8th day). John foresaw the *new beginning.* He said, *" I saw a new heaven and a new earth; for the first heaven and the first earth were passed away; and there were no more sea. And I John saw the holy city, the new Jerusalem, coming down from God out of heaven, prepared as a bride adorned for her husband. And I heard a great voice of heaven saying, "Behold the tabernacle* [dwelling place] *of God is with men, and He will dwell with them, and they shall be his people, and God himself shall be with them, and be their God, And God shall wipe away all tears from their eyes; and there shall be no more death, neither sorrow, nor crying, neither shall be any more pain: for the former things are passed away"* (Rev. 21;1-4).

A Cashless Society:

A cashless society will be implemented during the reign of the Antichrist. In the world of digital technology, it will be easy for Satan to push his agenda on people. The Bible says, he will "cause" people to accept his "Mark" because if they don't, then, they will not be able to buy or sell, not only that but many will be killed for their faith and opposition to the government of the Antichrist! (Rev. 13:15-18). Personally, I believe this will be a microchip placed in the recipient's hand or in the body. This technology is already in our credit and debit cards and in all cellular phones. But one can lose or deliberately leave those 'tracking devices' at home preventing their actual whereabouts to be known; but if a "chip" is placed in the person's body, then, their whereabouts will always be known. Hollywood and science fiction movies are portraying Satan's plan and agender. I saw a movie played by actor Will Smith; he had tracking devices in every item of clothing that he had on and in everything in his possession, and his every movement and whereabouts was known. But when he discarded everything, he was no longer able to be tracked. Again, Hollywood movies shows us things to come, it's not just entertainment, it gives us an insight into what is coming, not only in America but the whole world.

Like it or not but Satan has already planned your future, whether you're a Saint or a sinner, he has a trap set for you; and if you don't follow the instructions and warnings from the Bible, which is the Word of God, then you will not survive the coming crisis. Bankers, merchants, and credit card companies wants you to take advantage of "easy shopping and banking." You no longer will have to write a check, mail it, or go to the bank to make a deposit or wait seven to ten business days for your transactions to process, it can be done within seconds!

While consumers are being lured in by the cashless convenience and retailers are discovering the cost effectiveness of the debit and credit card system. Banks are continuing to increase their profits and while society is finding reasons to embrace this "convenient and modern" way of doing business; most people will be eager to accept it.

Many people used to write a check knowing that the funds weren't in their account, but it would be deposited before the check clears the bank. Not anymore, those days are in the past. With the new technology one can write a check for a purchase, it will be inserted through the merchant's cash register and within seconds, the cashier will hand you your check back as a receipt!

This technology is a boom for banks, they don't have to worry about the expenses of returning checks marked, "insufficient funds" and you doesn't have to pay "overdraft fees" anymore. The technology was developed because financiers have something to gain from it. First, they can cut down on labor, payroll taxes and the cost of insurance and benefits that they would otherwise have to pay for their employees.

Because of the high cost of insurance that employers must pay for their employees, many have gladly advanced this technology because it also reduces the threat of physical violence to employees which could result in high medical costs. Yes, the future of banking is here. One can make "Electronic" funds transfers or pay bills from their bank accounts while sitting and waiting in their car at a traffic light. Electronic banking is much cheaper for the banks because it cuts down on labor cost of all the reasons stated above. Furthermore, you can do your grocery shopping and have the funds transferred directly from your checking account to the store's bank account.

Therefore, the use of debit and credit cards are a big advantage to the retailer. The consumer's card is scanned by the store clerk; within seconds, the money is transferred directly from the consumer's account to the store's account on the spot. No waiting, no paperwork, no risk of checks being returned due to NSF (non-sufficient funds).

Another reason that retailers are advancing a cashless society is because it reduces the chances of employee theft. Because there will be no cash to steal, and with bar codes on every item sold; one cannot switch pricing on products and the retailers doesn't have to worry about armed robberies and check fraud. Furthermore, retailers knows that a person will spend more with a debit or a credit card because they won't have to worry about carrying a lump sum of cash to make a purchase.

Colleges and universities welcome credit and debit cards because they lessen the chances of their students to purchase alcoholic beverages, cigarettes, drug dealing and drug activities while on campus. Most students have a debit card that stores monetary value on it, where it is convenient in purchases at vending machines, dining programs, copiers, laundries, and the school's library.

Universities also welcome it because the debit cards eliminate the use of coins which is a magnet for vandalism of their vending machines. An All-card system whether it's for pre-paid, stored value or a "smart card" is most convenient for merchants, every kind of purchases including bus fares. A person won't have to carry around a pocket full of coins, they can download an app on their phones and their bus fare will be paid.

Parents love it because they don't have to worry about their child carrying cash on campus. I'm sure that most parents would rather put money into their child's account rather than having them walking around campus and throughout neighborhoods with a pocket full of cash which induces the chances of armed and strong- arm robberies against their children!

Police departments will gladly embrace a cashless society because it will reduce crime, especially in low-income neighborhoods. Because cash will not be in circulation, therefore their persuasive argument will be that in a cashless society drug dealing, prostitution and armed robberies will cease to exist.

I have a neighbor who is in law enforcement, he claims that "drug trafficking can be eliminated in a cashless society because, drug dealers carry out their business with a large amount of cash in suitcases and duffle bags, and if cash is eliminated the exchange for drug dealing will be a thing of the past." He said, "large scale transactions cannot be done through electronic banking because it will attract the attention of bank officials and, in turn, they must report all transactions over ten thousand dollars to the federal government." He also believes that black market activities "extortion, blackmail, kidnapping and prostitution" will be curtailed in a cashless society if there's no cash in circulation. Man has the technology to implant computer chips as small as a grain of rice in the body. I wouldn't mind if my pit bulldog Rover, has a chip implanted in him in case he gets lost, but I will never take one in my body. I think doctors and medical professionals are slipping chips into people's body through the flu shots vaccinations.

And now, because of the COVID-19 crisis the government has mandated that everyone to receive a COVID vaccination. What a clever way to "cause" people to receive the Mark of the Beast! I was once denied a life insurance policy by a major insurance company because I refused to be vaccinated for a flu shot. I told the agent that, "I know what their agenda is, and for my soul's sake, that I was not going to take their shot." I didn't know her religious beliefs, if any, and I didn't ask; but I quoted Revelation 13: 15-18 to her and she told me that, "I wouldn't be issued their insurance policy", in anger she tore up my application and left my house!

Several years ago, I also refused a shot at the hospital when I went to get my yearly physical. The nurse said that she needed to, "draw blood" in order to check my vital signs. I told her, "No" and I ask her to give me a knife, that I will cut myself and she can get a sample and test my blood."

People in the room laughed at me, I heard someone say that "I was insane", but one lady, a health care worker, whom I perceived to be a Christian, silently confirmed my suspicions regarding the technology. I didn't have my physical checkup and I haven't had one since.

If this was done during the Tribulation Period, then I would have to submit to the rule of the Antichrist to get health services, even if it went to the extent of "denying" Jesus! Jesus warned us of this persecution in the last days (Matt. 19:16-23). He said, *"Whosoever shall deny Him,* [in order to buy or sell or to get health or government services] during the Tribulation Period that *He will deny them before the Father and the angels* (Matt. 10:32,33; Mark 8:38). Jesus is addressing the church; many of the world has already rejected Him. Therefore, He is not warning the world, but He's warning His Bride, His Ambassadors, His Body of Baptized Believers, His "Elect" of things to come.

God knows the end from the beginning. He warned ancient Israel not to "paint", [tattoo] any markings on their bodies (Leviticus 19:28). Most people that I see today have tattoos on their body. I believe the devil is going to use his "Mark" [tattoo] to identify his subjects in the last days. Therefore, the church will not be caught up, i.e., "Raptured" until after the Mark of the Beast is forced upon mankind!

It would be wise to heed to the instructions left to us in the Holy Bible. It is the Word from our God and Creator. Everyone should read, learn, and obey the warning that God has set forth for us.

Your eternal soul is at stake, you and only you can determine your eternal future. *"God is not willing that any should perish"* therefore, He gave us His laws, ordinances, and instructions, He even went to the extent of sacrificing His Only Begotten Son that we might have eternal life and that more abundantly.

Our God is eternal, meaning He has no beginning, and He has no ending, God has always existed, and He will forever exist! He is above all course of time. Psalm 90:1,2, is a prayer of Moses, where he said," *LORD, thou hast been our dwelling place* (refuge) *in all generations...Before the mountains were brought forth, or ever thou hadst formed the earth and the world,* (gave birth to) *even from everlasting to everlasting, thou art God."*

The Bible declares that we too are eternal beings, where we spend eternity is totally up to us, God will not enforce His Love, Goodness and Mercy upon us. He created us to be free mortal agents. He gave us the power to choose or reject Him. He said, *"Death and life are in the power of the tongue"* (Proverbs 18:21). In all of God's creation, only man can have fellowship with God. We do that by living a righteous, holy life.

We are made in the image of God, we are a trinity-body, soul, and spirit. In 1 Thess. 5:23 Paul told the church, *"And the very God of peace sanctify you wholly; and I pray God your whole spirit and soul and body be preserved blameless unto the coming of our Lord Jesus Christ."*

Many are going to be left out of the promises of God because they will allow Satan to deceive them, having them to believe in the lie of a Pre -Tribulation Rapture of the church. If this is your belief, then you need to hear the Word of the Lord Jesus Christ, Again, He said, *"Immediately after the tribulation of those days shall the sun be darkened, and the moon shall not give her light, and the stars shall fall from heaven, and the powers of the heavens shall be shaken..."* (Matt. 24:29-31).

Many have rejected the Words and instructions of our Heavenly Father. People don't like to be told what to do, some are so hardhearted and rebellious that they don't believe in nor obey the wisdom of the Bible. Many have suppressed the Bible and they will condemn you because you are a believer and you're trying to live by the Words of our Holy God.

The Apostle Paul said, *"For the wrath of God is revealed from heaven against all ungodliness and unrighteousness of men, who hold* (suppress) *the truth in unrighteousness; Because that which may be known of God is manifest* (evident) *in them; for God has shown it to them. For the invisible things of him from the creation of the world are clearly seen, being understood by the things that are made, even his eternal power and Godhead; so that they are without excuse. Because that, when they knew God, they glorified him not as God, neither were thankful; but became vain in their imaginations, and their foolish heart was darkened...*

Professing themselves to be wise, they became fools (Romans 1: 18-22). Some have argued that God doesn't exist, but on judgment day they will find out that God does exist! He sits on His throne judging the affairs, hearts, and minds of men. They knew right from wrong but because of the hardness of their hearts, and their stubborn and rebellious attitude towards God, their unrighteousness will be exposed, and their eternal punishment will be in the lake of fire. They will be without excuse.

Paul goes on the tell us their problem, he said in Romans 8: 7, *"Because the carnal mind is enmity against God: for it is not subject to the law of God, neither indeed can be. So then they that are in the flesh cannot please God."* Those that rejects the True teaching of Christ regarding the timing of the rapture will find out that they were deceived by Satan and his agents; (false teachers in the church). This will not excuse them because Jesus told them, *"Take my yoke upon you, and learn of* [from] *me"* (Matt.11:29).

Jesus was giving us the great invitation of our salvation, but many will turn a deaf ear to it and perish in the lake of fire! Christ appeared once-He will appear again. Hebrews 9:26b declares, "... *but now once in the end of the world* (ages) *hath he appeared to put away sin by the sacrifice of himself.*"

Jesus appeared as a babe in a manger, "...*because there was no room for them in the inn*"(Luke 2:7). He *"grew, and waxed strong in spirit, filled with wisdom: and the grace of God was upon Him"* (Luke 2:40). He *"increased in wisdom and stature, and in favor with God and man"* (Luke 2:52).

When the time came for Jesus to enter His public ministry He appeared where John the Baptist was baptizing in Jordan, and God then and there placed His seal of approval upon His Son and upon His Son's ministry: *"And Jesus, when He was baptized, went up straightway out of the water: and lo, the heavens were opened unto Him, and he* (John) *saw the Spirit of God descending like a dove, and lighting upon Him:* (Christ) *and lo a voice from heaven, saying, This is my beloved Son, in whom I am well pleased"* (Matt. 3:16,17).

From that day forward, Jesus walked with His eye singled on Calvary. He knew why He came into the world, and He was determined to march on to that moment when His work should be accomplished, and He could give His cry of victory: *"It is finished!"* (John 19:30).

Jesus is going to appear again at the end of the ages, not as a babe, but as Judge of the universe. He appeared and offered one sacrifice for sins, the sacrifice that satisfied God completely; and that sacrifice will never be offered again, nor will any other. Just as surely as He appeared the first time to put away sin, so will *He "appear the second time without sin unto salvation"* (Hebrews 9:28).

We are redeemed through His precious blood; we are saved through His life. *"For if, when we were enemies, we were reconciled to God by the death of His Son, much more, being reconciled, we shall be saved by his life"* (Romans 5:10).

Rise of the Antichrist: (part 2)

The First Beast:

Revelation Chapter 13:

Vs.1 *"And I stood upon the sand of the sea, and saw a beast rise up out of the sea,* [the sea represents people, Gentile nations that will accept the Antichrist as their king] *having seven heads and ten horns, and upon his head ten crowns,* [the revision of the Holy Roman Empire] (ref. Daniel 7:8, 20-25) *and upon his heads the name of blasphemy* [a blasphemous name].

Vs. 2 *"And the beast which I saw was like unto a leopard* [representing the nation of Germany]. *and his feet were as feet of a bear,* [the bear represents Russia] *and in his mouth as the mouth of a lion,* [the lion represents Babylon] *and the dragon* [Satan] gave him [the Antichrist] *his power, and his seat,* [throne] *and great power."*

Special Note: This is a two-fold prophecy, Great Britten also uses the symbol of a Lion [strength] of which the United States came out of in 1776. Our nation's symbol is an eagle, [swiftness] *eagles' wings were plucked off of the lion and was lifted up from the earth, and was made to stand upon the feet* [two feet] *as a man, and a man's heart was given unto it.* [our government was formed i.e., "Uncle Sam"].

Vs. 3 *"And I saw one of the heads as it were wounded to death;* [the Antichrist will be opposed, wounded and left for dead but he will be revived by Satan, imitating the Resurrected Christ] *and his deadly wound was healed: and the world wondered after the beast* [people will marvel at the revived one].

Vs. 4 *"And they worshiped the dragon* [Satan] *which gave power* [authority] *to the beast: and they worshiped the beast, saying, Who is like unto the beast? who is able to make war with him?*

Vs. 5 *"And there was given unto him a mouth speaking great things and blasphemies; and power was given unto him to continue forty and two months* [3 ½ years of the Great Tribulation].

Vs. 6 *"And he opened his mouth in blasphemy against God, to blaspheme His name, and His tabernacle,* [the church Colossians 2:8-10] *and them that dwell in heaven."*

Vs. 7 *"And it was given unto him to make war with the saints,* [persecute the church] *and to overcome them: and power* [authority] *was given him over all kindreds, and tongues, and nations* [the whole world].

Vs. 8 *"And all that dwell upon the earth shall worship him, whose names are not written in the book of life of the Lamb slain from the foundation of the world."*

Vs. 9 *"If any man have a ear, let him hear."*

Vs. 10 *"He that leadeth into captivity shall go into captivity: he that killeth with the sword must be killed with the sword* [Matthew 16;25;26:52]. *Here is the patience and the faith of the saints."*

These passages of Scriptures are further proof that: There is no "Pre" Tribulation Rapture of the Church!

The Second Beast:

Vs. 11 *"And I beheld another beast* [the false prophet, (16:13; 19:20; 20:10) whose role is to bring people to worship the first beast [he is a deceiver vs. 14] *coming up out of the earth; and he had two horns like a lamb,* [presenting himself as gentle and harmless Matt. 7:15} *and he spake as a dragon."* [His dragon speech depicts his empowerment by Satan, he is given full exercise of the power of the first beast, who is the political ruler. His priestly role identifies him as a religious power or leader. He promotes global worship of the Antichrist].

Vs. 12 *"And he excerciseth all the power* [authority] *of the first beast before him* [in his presence] *and causeth the earth and them which dwell therein to worship the first beast, whose deadly wound was healed."*

Vs. 13 *"And he doeth great wonders,* [signs and miracles] *so that he maketh fire come down from heaven on the earth in the sight of men.*

Vs. 14 *"And deceiveth them that dwell on the earth by the means of those miracles which he had power* [was granted] *to do in the sight of the beast; saying to them that dwell on the earth, that they should make an image to the beast, which had the wound by as word, and live."*

Vs. 15 *"And he had power to give life* [breath] *unto the image of the beast, that the image of the beast should both speak, and cause that as many as would not worship the image of the beast should be killed* [ref. Daniel 3:6; Rev.16:2].

Vs. 16 *"And he causeth all, both small and great, rich or poor, free or bound* [imprisoned] *to receive a mark* [tattoo or a computer chip] *in their right hand, or on their forehead* [*tattoo* - Lev. 19:28].

Vs. 17 *"And that no man might buy and sell, save* [except] *he that hath the mark, or the name of the beast or the number of his name* [ref. Rev. 14:9-11].

Vs. 18 *"Here is wisdom. Let him that hath understanding count the number of the beast: for it is the number of a man; and his number is six hundred threescore and six* [666].

Note Again: Man was created on the 6th day, God has given mankind a 6,000-year rule on earth and the Antichrist in coming at the sounding of the 6th trumpet, (Rev. 6: 12-14) thus #666. Furthermore, as I've already explained during the Tribulation Period when the Antichrist will arise, rule, and reign the number 666 will be attached to everyone's social security number, their debit, credit, and store cards. Without it no one will be able to get or hold a job, open a bank account, fly on a commercial airplane or go into a federal building. No one will be allowed to obtain a passport in order to leave the country. If a person doesn't have it, they will not be allowed to buy or sell!

Matters not how much money that one may have in their bank account, if they don't have the number 666 attached to their account number, they won't be able to make any withdrawals. Cash will be done away with and become worthless and obsolete because by this time we would have become a total "cashless society." This is another way that the Antichrist, will *"cause"* people to receive his mark and number (vs. 16). *"Here is the patience and the faith of the saints"* (vs.10 b). Question again for you "Pre-Tribulation Rapture" believers: If the Rapture of the Church have already occurred, why then would the 'Saints' need "patience and faith" during the Tribulation Period?

I want to say again, who are you going to believe, man in his finite wisdom or the Wisdom of our Eternal God? Are you believing your false teachers or the architect of the universe? There will be no finger pointing when you stand before God at His Great White Stone Judgement Seat! You can't blame your false teachers and claim that you were deceived in believing the lie (of the pre-tribulation rapture) when our Eternal God gave you the truth in the volume of His Book, the Holy Bible.

But if you turn a deft ear to the eternal Word of God, then you are doomed for all eternity! There is no repentance from the grave, there are no second chances. If the rich man could have been saved after his physical death, then he would have a place in the eternal kingdom of God. But his fame and his fortune couldn't redeem him from hell's fire, neither could he buy a ticket into the kingdom of God!

God cannot be bought nor bribed. Salvation is a free- gift through our Lord and Savior, Jesus Christ (Ephesians 2:8). It calls for us to sacrifice the things of the world for our eternal blessings, but Satan has blinded the hearts and minds of many with the luxuries and pleasures of this life. That's why Jesus warned, *"For what is a man profited, if he shall gain the whole world, and lose his own soul? Or what shall a man give in exchange for his soul?"* (Matt. 16:26).

The Time of the End: (Matthew 24; Mark 13; Luke 21 and Daniel 12).

Matthew 24:1-31

In the Olivet discourse the disciples asked Jesus, *"Tell us, when shall these things be?" and what shall be the sign of thy coming,* (Greek -Parousia, His coming, appearing] *and the end of the world?* [human history] (Matt. 24:3). They were asking for clarification of the end of the church age and man's six thousand years of rule of the earth. Jesus answered their questions by warning them of things yet to happen before the end of the church age, and the Rapture of the church.

He warned them:

Vs. 4, 5 That religious deception and many false prophets would arise.

Vs. 6 Of wars and rumors of wars.

Vs. 7 Of nations fighting one another, famines, pandemics, and earthquakes.

Vs. 8, The beginning of sorrows.

Vs. 9, The Tribulation Period [first 3 ½ years].

Vs. 10, (a) Many saints will be offended at Him, they were expecting a "Pre-Tribulation Rapture (2 Peter 3:4), instead of persecution (ref. Rev. 2:10,11).

Vs. 10, (b)- 12. Denominational difference and false prophets will arise causing Saints to hate one another.

Note: This is another misunderstood passage of Scripture that many Saints uses to teach the Pre-Tribulation Rapture of the church. The first ones to be *taken* will be taken by the Antichrist (vs. 40, 41; Luke 17:34).

Vs. 13, True believers, *"he that endures until the end,* [of the Great Tribulation] *shall be saved"*

Vs. 14, Worldwide evangelism will occur before the Rapture of the Church.

Vs. 15, The temple in Jerusalem will be rebuilt and the Antichrist will set himself up in it pretending to be God (ref. 2 Thess. 2:1-4).

Vs. 16-20, Jesus warns the residence of Jerusalem to, *"flee into the mountains"* to escape the Great Tribulation.

Vs. 21, Great Tribulation begins [last 3 ½ years].

Vs. 22, Great Tribulation Period shorten for the *elect's* [churches sake].

Vs. 23-26, Religious deception will continue at an enormous rate.

Vs. 27, The Lord's Coming will be as sudden as a flash of lighting [after these events come to pass, at the last [7th trumpet] (1 Cor. 15:51, 52).

Note: World War III and two hundred million demons will be released from the Abyss to wage war against mankind where 1/3 of the earth's population will perish (ref. Rev. 9:1-16).

Vs. 28, Jesus said, "Eagles" [vultures] will eat the flesh of the slain dead (ref. Ezekiel 39:17-20; Rev. 19:17,18).

Vs. 29-31, The Rapture of the Church will be, *"Immediately after the* [Great] *Tribulation."*

Vs. 32-35, Jesus compared the end times signs with the parable of the fig tree. He said we will know the time of the end after the occurrence of these events.

Vs. 36, *No one knows the day* [of the week] *nor the hour* [of the day] that the Rapture will occur, *no one knows but the Father.*

Vs. 37, Jesus compared End Time events to the days of Noah, where everyone ignored the warnings and was going about their daily lives and routines and not concerned about their eternal future, and when the flood finally came, they were caught unprepared!

Timeline of the Rapture of the Church:

We just learned from Matthew 24:1-31 that the Rapture occurs at the end of man's six thousand years of rule on the earth. According to God's timetable, the Antichrist is going to rule from the, [yet to be rebuilt] temple in Jerusalem for "forty- two" months or a time, times and the dividing of time, or 1,260 days", i.e. 3 ½ years. The Rapture of the Church will be thirty (30) days later after the Great Tribulation is over at the 1,290[th] day. During these 30 days period, *"the sun will not shine and the moon will not give its light"* (vs. 29-31).

At this time, we will go to the Marriage Supper of the Lamb, (Rev.19:6-9) and the Judgment Seat of Christ to get our rewards.

Jesus' Second Coming will be forty (45) five days afterwards on the 1,335th day; "the time of the end" (Daniel 12:9-13). Thirty (30) plus forty -five (45) = seventy (75) five. Therefore, according to Scripture, the "time of the end" (Matt. 24:3) will be seventy- five days after the Great Tribulation is over.

Special Note: Remember the Bible was written to the church (Rev. Chapters 2-3), from Matt. 24:29-31 these three verses of Scripture tell us:

1. The [Great] Tribulation Period would be over when the Lord returns (vs. 29).
2. Jesus will appear from heaven with power and great glory (vs. 30).
3. Jesus will send His angels to gather [Rapture] His 'elect' [the church] from the four corners of the earth (vs. 31).

"A great sound of a trumpet" is the last (7th) trumpet that will sound to signal the Lord's return (1 Cor. 15:52; 1 Thess. 4:16; Rev. 8:2). I want to reiterate that we can know from prophecy that the Rapture will occur on the 1,290th day.

The 1,260th day [3 ½ years or 42 months] marks the end of the Great Tribulation Period; the Rapture will occur thirty- days later on the 1,290th day, and the Lord's Second Coming (Parousia) to usher in His one-thousand-years Millennium Reign will be forty-five days after the Rapture on the 1,335th day.

We will be "kings and priests" in His kingdom (Rev. 1:6). The Judgment Seat of Christ will determine our position of authority in the Millennium Kingdom, that's why Jesus gave us the parable of the talents (Matt. 25:14-34).

A Perfect Example of the Rapture of the Church and the Second Coming of Christ:

We elect our president in November of an election year, but he doesn't take office until January of the following year, exactly seventy (75) five days after the election. What happens in the meantime? The president-elect is getting his ruling cabinet together, everyone on his team will know their jobs and duties when their leader takes office. So will it be with the Second Coming of Christ. He will send His angels to gather [Rapture] the church (Matt. 24:29-31) on the 1,290th day; we will go to before the Judgment Seat of Christ (Rom. 2:16; 14:10) to get our rewards: this event is also described in Scripture as "The Marriage Supper of the Lamb" (Rev.19:6-9).

When the Lord returns to earth to rule in His 1,000 years Millennium Reign, (7th) day (Rev. 19:11-16 we will know our authority and our positions in His kingdom. James and John wanted a high position in the Lord's kingdom, one wanted to sit on His right hand and the other one on His left (Mark 10:35-37). Their mother also asked this of Jesus. We will help Him judge the world and the angels that sinned (1 Cor. 6: 2-3; Jude 6, 14-16). In the flesh, although we are saved, sanctified, by the Blood of the Lamb and filled with the precious gift of the Holy Ghost, and have been justified in God through Christ, yet we aren't perfect in ourselves, therefore, *we are not to judge nothing before the time, until the Lord come"* (1 Cor.4: 4, 5).

We know that the Book of Revelation is not written in chronological order, therefore, I believe that the *"silence in heaven for about the space of half an hour"* (Rev. 8:1) is when we will get our assignments and appointments in Christ's Kingdom rule. I mainly believe this because as I've stated many times, that the number seven (7) in Scripture represents completeness, this will occur at the opening of the 7th seal and at the sounding of the 7th trumpet (Rev. 10: ref. 1 Cor. 15: 51, 52; 1 Thess. 4:16).

I'm not judging those who teach the Pre-Tribulation Rapture Doctrine, the Word of God has already done that. I didn't write the message, [the Bible] I'm just merely the messenger. My King James Version of the Bible was translated into English in 1611, I wasn't born until 1952, therefore, I couldn't have written it. I tell people if they have an issue with God or His Word then they can present their case in His court at the Great White Stone of His judgement.

The books will be open, and they will be judged by the things that they have said and done in their lifetime (Rev. 20:11-15). Throughout this book I am delivering the written message to all that, *"Has an ear to hear what the Spirit saith unto the churches"* warning them that their doctrine of the Rapture doesn't agree with the author of the Bible- God, the Holy Scriptures are the Words of God. Again, I am *"crying aloud"*, I am *"sparing not"*, I am *'lifting up' my voice as a trumpet and* trying to *"show God's people their transgression"* (Isaiah 58:1).

The Time of the End (Mark 13)

Mark 13:1-37

This is called the Olivet Discourse, having been delivered by Jesus on the Mount of Olives where He had private time with His disciples.

Vs. 1. When Jesus left the temple one of His disciples referred to the huge stones of the temple built by Herod the Great, which begun in 20 B.C. and completed eighty-four years later.

Vs. 2. Jesus prophesied that the temple would be destroyed. (It was leveled by the Romans in A.D. 70).

Vs. 3, 4. Four of Jesus' disciples asked Him privately, "When was this to happen and what sign would be fulfilled?

Vs. 5-8. Jesus answered them with a warning of religion deception, wars, rumors of wars, earthquakes, and troubles [before the Rapture i.e. the church age and human history, man's six thousand years of man's rule on the earth]. He told them, *"These are the beginning of sorrows."*

Vs. 9-13. Jesus warned them of the coming seven years of tribulation upon the earth and the church. The first 3 ½ years of that *"time of trouble"* Jesus described it as *"Tribulation"*, the last 3 ½ years He described as *"Great Tribulation"* Compared to Matt. 24:9-12 and vs. 21, 22). Jesus plainly told His disciples, (The church) would experience Tribulation and Great Tribulation, whereas brethren, [saints of different denominations] will rise and hate one another; even betraying them to death.

Vs. 14-19. Jesus warned them of the Great Tribulation, [the last 3 ½ years] He told them to, *"pray that they wouldn't have to flee in the winter,* [because bad weather would hinder their travels] *nor on the Sabbath Day."* [Because many Orthodox Jews will be restricted by the Sabbath's travel law.

Vs. 20. Jesus promised that the Great Tribulation period will be shorten, *"for the elect's* [churches] *sake."*

Vs. 21-23. Jesus warned them of false Christs and false prophets who will arise with great signs and wonders, [performing miracles deceiving the unlearned].

He said, *"if it was possible, even the elect* [chosen ones, true believers in the churches] *would be deceived."* I again question, how would this passage of Scripture be fulfilled if the church has already been taken out of the world in a Pre- Tribulation Rapture?

Vs. 24-25. Jesus said, *"After the tribulation period is over the sun and the moon will not shine, and the stars of heaven shall fall."* (ref. Isiah 13:10; 34:4).

Vs. 26. Jesus will come with great power and glory.

Vs. 27. Jesus will send His angels, and they *"shall gather together* [Rapture] His elect, [the church] *from the four winds* [north, south, east, and west] *from the uttermost part of the earth to the uttermost part of heaven."*

Note: Jesus will not *come down* and "Rapture" His saints, He won't set foot on the earth until He returns to set up His Millennium Reign. Instead, He will send His angels down to do it. Afterwards, *"we will meet the Lord in the clouds"* [the air] after the gathering [Rapture] (1 Thess. 4:16,17).

Vs. 28-33. Jesus gave us the parable of the fig tree, where He explained that we will know the closeness of His coming when we see these things come to pass; but like the fig, no one knows the *day* [of the week] nor the *hour* [of the day] that the fruit will fall to the ground, only the Father knows.

Vs. 34-37. Jesus wants His church: the Saints, the body of Baptized Believers, the Elect, the Ecclesia, to watch [be on guard] that He doesn't find us sleeping [unaware] of the signs of the time on His (Parousia) -return (ref. Rev. 22:11- 16).

The Time of the End: (Luke 21)

The Gospel of Luke [a Gentile] was written primarily to Gentile believers. Luke was *"the beloved physician"* mention in Colossians 4:14, he also penned the Book of Acts, and he was a onetime travel companion to the Apostle Paul (2 Timothy 4:11).

Because of the racial divide of the day, [ethnical and religious] many Jewish believers was offended that the Gentiles had received the Gospel of Our Lord and Savior Jesus Christ. So much so that they rosed up an opposition against the apostles, [Paul and Barnabas] for preaching to the Gentiles (Acts 13:44-52). *"God is not willing that any should perish"* therefore, He chose Luke to appeal to Gentile believers [in every generation] who have accepted Christ as their Lord and Personal Savior.

Luke gives us, *"Signs of the end"* [of the church age and man's six -thousand years of human history, rule upon the earth] in the 21st chapter of his Gospel.

Vs. 5-7. Jesus answered His disciples' question about the end of the church age and His Second Coming to set up His Millennium kingdom.

Vs. 8-11. Jesus warned them of religious deception, wars, earthquakes, famines, pestilences [diseases, pandemics] and signs from heaven before His return.

Note: During the writing of this book the world is in the pandemic time of COVID-19. Many of your "false teachers" would have you to believe that the church would be Raptured before we experience these troublesome times! *News Flash- THE CHURCH IS STILL HERE AND THEY ALL HAD TO BE CLOSED!* I wouldn't be surprised if many small and "store front" ones operating on shoe-string budgets will not reopen!

Vs.12. Jesus warns us of the Tribulation period where His Saint's fate would be put on trial. He said, *"But before all these, they shall lay their hands on you, [arrest you] and persecute you, delivering you up to the synagogue, and into prisons, being brought before kings and rulers for my name's sake."*

Vs. 13-15. Saint's faith will be put on trial [tested] we're not to premeditate what we will answer, instead, we must allow the Lord to speak through us. Anyone who doesn't allow the Holy Spirit to speak through them during the Tribulation Period would be guilty of committing the *"unpardonable sin"*, they would have denied the Only One qualified to save them which the Bible declares as *"Blasphemy against the Holy Ghost"* (Matt.10:32, 33; Matt. 12:31,32).

Laws will be passed during the Tribulation Period where people will be arrested, even put to death because of their faith in Christ. Family members, friends and loved ones will turn against true Christians just to save their own skin.

Vs. 16-17 Jesus said, *"And ye shall be betrayed by both parents, and brethren* [Saints of different denominations] *and kinsfolk, and friends; and some of you shall they cause to be put to death...And ye shall be hated of all men for my name's sake."*

Vs. 18 Jesus promised protection to His faithful followers, not only for the Jews but also for all believers, [the universal church]. We will be sealed with the seal of God (Rev. 7:3-9; 9:1-4).

This passage of Scripture is further proof that, there is no truth to the "Pre-Tribulation Rapture Doctrine." Question: Why would the Saints be sealed here on earth [for protection during the tribulation period] if the church is already gone up in the Rapture?

Vs. 19 Jesus warns us that "faith" in Him and our "patience" during the tribulation period will be a soul saving issue. As I've previously said, many will 'Deny' our Lord and Savior because of the laws that will be passed by the government of the Antichrist.

They will not be able to "buy or sell" unless they receive the Mark of the Beast or the number of his name (Rev. 13:15-18).

Vs. 20-24 Jesus warns of the future fall of Jerusalem, those living in the city are warned to, *"flee into the mountains"* to escape the destruction when the Antichrist sets up his rule in the future temple.

The end times destruction of the temple will be far worse than its previous destruction by Titus, the Roman general in A.D. 70. *"Until the times of the Gentiles be fulfilled"* marks the end of human government, man's six thousand years of rule on the earth and the end of the church age.

Vs. 25-28 The coming of the Son of man: *"And there shall be signs in the sun, and in the moon, and in the stars; and upon the earth distress of nations, with perplexity; and the sea and the waves roaring; "Men's heart failing them for* [from] *fear and for looking after* [expectation of] *those things which are coming on the earth: for the powers of heaven shall be shaken, "And then shall they see the Son of man coming in a cloud with power and great glory. "And when these things began to come to pass, then look up, and lift up your heads; for your redemption draweth nigh."*

This passage of Scripture is self-explanatory. There will be signs of Christ's return and the Rapture of the Church! His "coming without warnings" is a false doctrine which I believe is one of those, "old wives fables" that the Apostle Paul warned the church to be aware of (1Timothy 4:7). Paul said, "refuse" [reject] them, therefore, I reject the Pre-Tribulation Rapture doctrine because it does not line up with the Holy Scriptures!

Vs. 29-33 The parable of the fig tree:
Jesus often spoke and taught in parables, He used the fig tree as an explanation of the Rapture and His Second Coming.

He said: *"Behold the fig tree, and all the trees; When they now shoot forth, ye see and know of your own selves that summer is now nigh* [near] *at hand. So likewise ye, when you see these things come to pass, know ye that the kingdom of God is nigh at hand. Verily I say unto you, This generation [those that are still alive at that time] shall not pass away, till all be fulfilled. Heaven and earth shall pass away; but my words shall not pass away."*

Vs. 34-36 We are warned to Watch and Pray: *"And take heed to yourselves, lest at any time your hearts be overcharged [weighed down] with surfeiting [carousing] and drunkenness, and the cares of this life, and so that day come upon you unawares. For as a snare shall it come on all them that dwell on the face of the whole earth. Watch ye therefore, and pray always, that ye may be accounted worthy to escape all these things that shall come to pass, and to stand before the Son of man."*

Note: This is another passage of Scripture that people falsely take out of context to teach the "Pre-Trib" doctrine. The "escape" is not in a Rapture, but rather in our sealing for protection (Rev. 7: 1-17).

Rise of the Antichrist:

The Time of the End: (Daniel 12)

For thousands of years people have been fascinated with predictions of the end of the world. There have been date setters in every generation, each one has failed, and this false teaching has brought profound disappointment to many well-meaning and sincere individuals. Despite centuries of disappointments, they haven't put an end to attempts to associate world events and conditions with Biblical prophecies concerning the end times.

We hear almost daily in the news and social media of mass shooting, wars and rumors of wars. Many will say, "The Bible says, the love of many will wax cold, Jesus could come and Rapture the church any time now." But as Jesus prophesied, *"These are the beginning of sorrows."* Therefore, anyone who is expecting the Rapture to occur before the Tribulation Period is either deceived or they don't know the Scriptures. From the 12th Chapter of Daniel, you will learn that the *"Time of the End"* refers to the end of man's six thousand years of rule of the earth and the end of the church age, the Rise and Fall of the Antichrist, the Rapture of the Church, and Christ's Second Coming.

Here is wisdom from the 12th Chapter of Daniel.

- The Rapture of the Church will be at the end of the Great Tribulation Period.
- 1,260 days equals 3 ½ years of the Great Tribulation (vs.7).
- 1,290th day will be the Rapture of the Church.
- 1,335th day (vs. 12) marks the day of Christ's Second Coming (Parousia) to establish the 1,000 years of His Millennium Reign on earth.

Word of caution: Don't get these passages of Scriptures confused with what Jesus taught in Matthew 24:36 Jesus was teaching that no one knows the day *of the week* nor *the* hour *of the day* of His return. Therefore, if someone tell you that Jesus will come on a certain day and at a certain time of the day, then rest assured that he or she is a false teacher! But since, *"knowledge shall be increased"* and the *signs* of Christ's returned will be seen (Matt. 24: 29-31) we can know that the time by counting the days of prophesied events.

Vs. 1 *"And at that time* [after God delivers Israel from enemy armies and the destruction of the Antichrist] *shall Michael stand up, the great prince which standeth* [stands watch over] *for the children of thy people: and there shall be a time of trouble,* [tribulation] *such as never was since there was a nation even to that same time: and at that time thy people shall be delivered, every one that shall be found written the book"* [the Book of Life].

Vs. 2 *"And many of them that sleep in the dust of the earth shall awake, some to everlasting life, and some to shame and everlasting contempt* [abhorrence- damnation].

After the Great Tribulation there will be two resurrections, one for the righteous which died trusting in Jesus Christ, our Lord and Savior and another one for the unrighteous that died unsaved, without confessing a hope in Christ. They will also awake, but to everlasting damnation, separated from God and His Great Mercy forever; they will be cast into the lake of fire (Rev. 20:11-15). These two resurrections are one-thousand years apart (Rev. 20:4).

Vs. 3 *"And they that be wise shall shine as the brightness of the firmament; and they that turn many to righteousness as the stars for ever and ever."*

Regardless of the social movements, the bickering of our political leaders, and the religious deception of this world, we have a great job to complete. If the world is going to be evangelized, it must come from the church. It is our commission and responsibility to be clear, honest, and polite in our efforts to win lost souls to Christ. Remember what Jesus said in Matthew 24:14? How can the *"Gospel of the kingdom"* be preached to the whole world if the church is 'caught up' in a Pre-Tribulation Rapture? We will be rewarded in our efforts to win the lost at the Judgment Seat of Christ.

We are not called to judge the sinner, but rather, we are to approach them in a loving and humbling manner and to explain the purpose and the hope of the coming Kingdom of God as Jesus did. He set the example for us, therefore, as soul winners for Christ, we must remain faithful to Him and complete our earthly mission: if we do so, we, like Daniel will inherit eternal rewards for our works for Him.

Vs. 4 *"But thou, O Daniel, shut up the words, and seal the book, even to the time of the end: many shall run to and fro, and knowledge shall be increased."*

It was impossible to understand the significance of these things in Daniel's lifetime, but God promised that at the Time of the End many will be able to understand them.

Vs. 5-6 Daniel saw three men, [angels] Michael (vs. 1); and two others, two of them was standing on each side of the river [Heddekel i.e. Tigris Dan. 10:4]. And one [Michael, *clothed in linen*] was standing over the river. One of them asked the one standing over the river, [Michael] *"How long shall it be to the end of these wonders?*

Vs. 7 The man [Michael] answered him that it will occur at the end of the Great Tribulation Period, *"after the power of the holy people are scattered"*; *time* (1 year), *times* (2 years.) *and a half* (6 months) i.e., 3 ½ years. Again, this period of time is also revealed as: 42 months (Rev.11:2) and 1,290 days (vs. 11).

Vs. 8-9 Daniel did not understand the things revealed to him, he asked, *"O my Lord, what shall be the end of things?* He was told, *"Go thy way Daniel,"* [go on about your life]: *for the words are closed and sealed until the time of the end."*

Jesus is the only One qualified to break the seals and read the book (Rev. 5).

Vs. 10 Daniel was assured that, *"Many shall be purified, and made white,* [righteous, through Our Lord and Savior Jesus Christ] *and tried;* [refined, endured through the Tribulation Period] *but the wicked shall do wickedly: and none of the wicked shall understand; but the wise shall understand."*

Note: During the rise of the Antichrist, he will set himself up in the (yet to be rebuilt) Temple in Jerusalem and resume the daily sacrifices once held by the children of Israel (Matthew 24:15).

Vs. 11-13 *"And from the time that the daily sacrifices shall be taken away, and the abomination that maketh desolate set up, there shall be a thousand two hundred and ninety days. Blessed is he that waiteth, and cometh to the thousand three hundred and five and thirty days. But go thy way till the end be: for thou shall rest, and stand in thy lot at the end of the days."*

Understanding Daniel's Prophecy:

From verse 7 we learn that the Great Tribulation will last for 3 ½ years [1,260 days], the Rapture of the Church will be 30 days later, on the 1,290th day, where we [Saints] will be caught up [Raptured] to go before the Judgment Seat of Christ to get our rewards (2 Cor. 5:10; Rev. 19:6-10). The Lord's Second Coming will be 45 afterwards on the 1,335th day, where we will come back with Christ to rule and reign with Him in His Millennium Kingdom (Rev. 19:11-21). We, and every believer in Christ and those that died looking for the promise alone with Daniel will, *"stand in our lot"* [arise to our inheritance] in Christ's Eternal Kingdom.

Note: The number eight (8) in Scripture represents a new beginning. John was shown what will happen on earth after man's time and rule of the earth is completed, the destruction of the Antichrist and all of God's enemies are thrown into the lake of fire.

John said, *"And I saw a new heaven and a new earth: for the first heaven and the first earth were passed away, and there was no more sea. And I John saw the holy city, new Jerusalem, coming down from God out of heaven, prepared as a bride adorned for her husband. And I heard a great voice out of heaven saying, Behold, the tabernacle [dwelling place] of God is with men, and he will dwell with them, and they shall be his people and God himself shall be with them, and be their God. And God shall wipe away all tears from their eyes, and there shall be no more death, neither sorrow, nor crying, neither shall there be any more pain, for the former things are passed away. And he that sat upon the throne said, Behold, I make all things new. And he said unto me, Write: for these words are true and faithful"* (Rev. 21:1-5).

Three Traditional Views of the Rapture of the Church:

There are three traditional views of the Rapture of the Church, which one did Jesus teach? Bible scholars, theologians and Christian believers teach that there "will be" a Rapture of the Church; however, they can't conclude when it will occur.

The Three Traditional Views of the Rapture are:

- The Pre- Tribulation view which teaches the Rapture will occur before the Tribulation Period.
- The Mid- Tribulation view which teaches the Rapture will occur in the middle of the Tribulation Period.
- The Post Tribulation view which believes that the Rapture will occur after the Tribulation Period is over.

Your "Pre- Trib" teachers and many illiterates in Scriptures and uninformed Bible scholars will have you to believe that the Rapture can occur at any given moment, even before you finish reading this book! The "Mid" Tribulation teachers will tell you that the church will go through the first half of the Tribulation Period and that Jesus will send His angels to rescue [Rapture] His Saints after 3½ years of trouble and persecution. The "Post" Tribulation believers [of which I am one of them] believes the church will be Raptured after the Great Tribulation is over.

There will be a Rapture of the Church, however, all of these cannot be right, therefore, somebody is wrong! I consult the Holy Scriptures and I follow Jesus' teachings to get the truth. By doing so,

He said, *"And Ye shall know the truth, and the truth shall make you free"* [from false teaching and religious deception, emphasis mine].

It is written; *"All Scripture is given by inspiration of God, and is profitable for doctrine, for reproof, for correction, for instruction in righteousness: that the man of God may be perfect, thoroughly furnished unto all good works"* (2 Timothy 3:16,17). So then, with that said, which view did Jesus teach? Apparently, Jesus was a Post Tribulationists. He said, *"Immediately after the tribulation of those days* [the Great Tribulation] *that He will send His angels to gather* [Rapture] His elect [the church] (Matt. 24:29-31).

I've sided with Jesus, the Son of God. He was *"God in the flesh"*, He came down from heaven to be a propitiation for our sins (1 John 2:2). Therefore, I'm trusting in *Him* for my eternal salvation, I accept, believe, and I follow *His* teachings. That is why I don't put anything nor anyone's teachings above the teachings of our Lord and Savior Jesus Christ. It's also the reason that I've question many popular and well-known pastors, teachers, believers and so called, "Bible scholars" regarding their false view and teachings of the Rapture of the Church!

Jesus plainly said, *"And this gospel of the kingdom shall be preached in all the world for a witness unto all nations; and then shall the end come"* (Matt. 24: 14). Question: How will this portion of the Holy Scriptures be fulfilled if the church is suddenly caught up (Raptured) in a "Pre" or "Mid" Tribulation? I'll give you the same words that Our Lord and Savior Jesus Christ said in Matt. 24: 4, *"Take heed that no man deceive you."*

11

CHAPTER

Revelation Chapter 14

Armageddon and Judgment Day:

Here is a quick overview of God's Judgment of the nations, however, you should read Revelation Chapters 14 thru 20 to get a full understanding of what is to come. Armageddon is a Greek pronunciation of the Hebrew words 'har Megiddo', or 'mountain of Megiddo', a location in the Jezreel Valley north of Israel. In ancient times, all roads connecting Africa with Asia and Europe passed near Megiddo, and its strategic position ensured that many important battles would be fought here, including the 'final battle' between good and evil (Rev. 16).

I've already explained the meaning of the Day of the Lord in chapter four of this book, that it is not the Rapture of the Church nor Christ's Second Coming, but rather it is Judgment Day, when God's wrath will be unleashed upon mankind for our wickedness and disregards of His Holy ways. To get a full understanding of Judgment Day you should re-read Revelation Chapter 6 at the opening of the 6th seal.

Remember that *"Judgment is going to begin at the House of God"* (1Peter 4:17, 18). Question: With your false teaching and beliefs where will you fit in? Will the Lord say to you, *"Come ye blessed of My Father, inherit the kingdom prepared for you from the foundation of the world"* (Matt.25:34) or will He say, *"Depart from me ye workers of iniquity"* (Matt.7: 23).

Understand the 14th Chapter of Revelation:

Vs.1-5. John said, *"And I looked, and, lo, a Lamb* [Christ] *stood on the mount Zion,* [in Jerusalem] *and with him a hundred forty and four thousand,* [from Ch. 7] *having his Father's name written in their foreheads...And I heard a voice from heaven, as the voice of many waters, and as the voice of a great thunder; and I heard the voice of harpers harping with their harps: And they sung as it were a new song before the throne, and before the four beast,* [living creatures] *and the elders: and no man could learn that song but the hundred and forty and four thousand, which were redeemed from the earth. These are they which were not defiled with women; for they are virgins. These are they which follow the Lamb whithersoever he goeth. These were redeemed from among men, being the first fruits from God and to the Lamb. And in their mouth was found no guile:* [deceit] *for they are without fault before the throne of God."*

The Everlasting Gospel Preached to Mankind:

The message of the angels:

Vs. 6-8. *"And I saw another angel fly in the midst of heaven, having the everlasting gospel preached unto them that dwell on the earth, and to every nation, and kindred,* [tribe] *and tongue and people,* [ref. Matt. 24:14] *Saying, with a loud voice, Fear God, and give glory to him; for the hour* [time] *of his judgment is come: and worship him that made heaven, and the earth, and the sea, and the fountains of waters. And there followed another angel, saying, Babylon* [USA- see Ch 17, 18] *is fallen, is fallen, that great city, because she made all nations drink of the wine of the wrath of her fornication."*

The everlasting gospel is the "Good News" that Christ will win, and the Beast will be judged. There will be two avenues to this Good News: (1). Positively- it focuses on redemption through Christ and the coming of His kingdom. (2). Negatively- it has three parts: (1) the hour of judgment is come (v. 7); (2) Babylon [USA] is fallen (v. 8); (3) those who "worship the beast" will be punished "forever" (vs. 9-11). The whole world is commanded to Fear [reverence] God and to give glory to Him.

Vs. 9-11. *And the third angel followed them, saying with a loud voice, If any man worship the beast and his image, and receive his mark in his forehead, or in his hand, The same shall drink of the wine of the wrath of God, which is poured out without mixture into the cup of his indignation; and he shall be tormented with fire and brimstone in the presence of the holy angels, and in the presence of the Lamb.*

All who receives the mark of the beast, the number of his name or worship him will receive God's eternal punishment in the lake of fire (ref. Rev. 13: 16-18; Matt. 25:41; Rev. 20:15). This includes unbelievers and unfaithful Christians who "denies" the Lord Jesus during the Tribulation period.

True believers must have *"patience"* to *"endure unto the end"* of the Great Tribulation (Matt. 24: 13; Luke 21:19; Rev. 2:10, 11). The *wine of the wrath of God* is God's righteous anger (cf. Job 21:20; Ps 75:8; Isaiah 51:17; Jeremiah 25: 15- 38).

Vs. 12-13. *"Here is the patience of the saints: here are they that keep the commandments of God, and the faith of Jesus. And I heard a voice from heaven saying unto me, Write, Blessed are the dead which die in the Lord from henceforth: Yea, saith the Spirit, that they may rest from their labors; and their works do follow them."*

Is further proof that the church is still on earth during the Tribulation period. *Patience* here is perseverance or endurance. The assurance of the judgment of God's enemies is a basis for the perseverance of the Tribulation believers to continue following Christ. Remember, true believers will be sealed with the seal of God for protection during this time (Rev. 7: 1-17).

The Harvest of the Earth, (Rapture of the Church) and the judgments that follows.

Vs.14-16. *"And I looked, and behold a white cloud, and upon the cloud one sat like unto the Son of man, having on his head a golden crown, and in his hand a sharp sickle. And another angel came out of the temple, crying with a loud voice to him that sat on the cloud, Thrust in thy sickle, and reap: for the time is come for thee to reap; for the harvest of the earth is ripe. And he that sat on the cloud thrust in his sickle on the earth; and the earth was reaped.*

The *Son of man* is Jesus Christ, the Messiah (cf. Rev. 1:13; Dan. 7:13; Matt. 26: 53,64). The *cloud* relates to Christ's second coming (cf. Dan. 7:13; Matt. 24:30; Acts 1:9-11). The *crown* pictures Him as the ruler of the earth, and the *sickle* symbolizes judgment as an instrument of the harvest (cf. John 5:27). *The time is come* to finish the judgment of the earth. The second coming of Christ includes more judgment. To *reap* and harvest *the earth* is to judge and punish its people (cf. Jerimiah 51:33; Hosea 6:11; Matt. 13:30, 40-42).

Vs. 17-20. Whereas verses 14-16 picture Christ's judgment as a grain harvest, verses 17-20 symbolize the wrath of God as a grape harvest with the treading of the grape *clusters* as an immense *winepress.* Again, the sickle depicts judgment. *The clusters of the vine of the earth* represents unbelievers of the earth, and those who have followed and worshiped the Beast (vs. 8-11). *Her grapes are fully ripe* (at the prime) in that the time for God's judgment of the earth is now! The *great winepress of the wrath of God* pictures the violence and intensity of God's coming judgment on the earth (cf. 19:15; Isaiah 63: 2-6; Lam. 1:15; Joel 3: 12-14). The *city* is Jerusalem, God's future headquarters (Joel 3:12-14; Zech. 14:1-4; John 19:20; Heb. 13:12).

In reference to the coming Battle of Armageddon (16:14-16) that will be fought in Palestine the *blood* is the human blood that will be spilled in the final battle, it will stretch *a thousand and six hundred furlongs* [184 miles] which is the full length of Palestine. The blood will be the height of a horses' bridles [about four feet] this can be characterized as "a river of blood" (emphasis mine). The winepress is an anticipation of the vial or bowl of God's judgments of Chapter 16.

Preparations for the Seven Vials
[Bowls of God's Wrath]

Revelation 15:1-8

This passage of Scripture gives us the scenario for the preparation of the seven bowls of God's wrath which is to be poured out on the earth before the Rapture of the Church. Since the fall of man in the Garden, God has shown His Great Love, Goodness, Mercy and Patience towards mankind throughout every generation, however, because of the rebellion of His creative beings, He must also pour out His Wrath upon all who opposes Him and refuse to accept and live by His laws, statues and ordinances.

GOD IS LOVE, love is the very essence of God's nature: He does not simply "love" He IS Love. He is the source of all love, and if we cannot come into the right relationship with God, we cannot know perfect love. It is through our Lord and Savior, Jesus Christ that makes it possible that we can love God and show love for each other.

GOD IS HOLY, the essential nature of God is holiness. He is pure, free from all defilement. He cannot be tempted with evil (James 1:13). King David declared that God is Holy; in Psalm 99:5, 9, he said, *"Exalt ye the Lord our God, and worship at his footstool; for he is holy. Exalt the Lord our God, and worship at his holy hill; for the Lord our God is holy."*

Therefore, being His offspring, [in the flesh, "He became flesh and dwelt among us" John 1 :14]. He expects His children to be holy as well. 1 Peter 1:14-16 tells us, *"As obedient children, not fashioning* [conforming] *yourselves according to the former lusts in your ignorance. But as he which hath called you is holy, so be ye holy in all manner of conversation;* [conduct] *Because it is written, Be Ye HOLY; FOR I AM HOLY."*

GOD IS MERCIFUL-Throughout the whole Bible we read of God's Great Mercy. *"Many sorrows be to the wicked: but he that trusted in the Lord, mercy shall compass him about"* (Psalm 32:10). Since God is not willing that any should perish, he renews and extends His Mercy toward us daily. His mercy is manifested toward all who love Him. His mercy is extended on all who serve Him and walk in His paths of righteousness. God knows the end from the beginning; He knows the transgressors that will eventfully come to Him in faith and be saved from His judgment and wrath which is to come upon this sinful world. In King Solomon's prayer of the dedication of the temple built [financed] by David, his father, he (Solomon) built a bronze platform before the whole congregation so that everyone could see him.

The platform was five cubits long, five cubits broad and three cubits high, [eight square feet by five feet high] King Solomon kneeled before the whole congregation and prayed: *"O Lord God of Israel, there is no God like thee in heaven, nor in the earth, which keepest covenant, and showest mercy unto thy servants, that walk before thee with all their hearts: Thou which hast kept with thy servant David my father that which thou hast promised him, and spakest with thy mouth, and hast fulfilled it with thine hand, as it is this day"* (2 Chronicles 6:12-15).

King David was a man after God's own heart, who recognized God's goodness, grace, and mercy, he said, *"The Lord is merciful and gracious, slow to anger and plenteous in mercy, He will not always chide:* [rebuke for past sins] *neither will he keep his anger forever. He hath not dealt with us according to our iniquities.* [sins and short comings] *For as the heaven is high above the earth so great is his mercy toward them that fear* [reverence] *him. As far is the east is from the west, so far has he removed our transgressions from us. Like a father pitieth his children, so the Lord pitieth them that fear him. For he knoweth our frame; he remembereth that we are dust. As for man, his days are as grass: as a flower of the field, so he flourisheth. For the wind passeth over it, and it is gone; and the place thereof shall know it no more. But the mercy of the Lord is from everlasting to everlasting upon them that fear him, and his righteousness unto children's children; To such as keep his covenant, and those that remember his commandments to do them"* (Psalm 103:8-18 KJV).

A Personal Testimony: From my own experience, I now know that God knew that I would stray away from my upbringing; but in His own time, that I would accept my calling and get back on His path of righteousness. Therefore, He didn't allow me to die in my sins, but rather, He kept me by His Grace and Mercy. I've learned not to 'write people off' because of their seemly; lack of the knowledge and acceptance of God. He's still showing His Great Mercy to the sinner just as He showed His Great Mercy towards me during my young, reckless, and wayward lifestyle.

GOD IS ALSO PATIENT, but there will come a time when the patience of God will run out, and then He must and will punish His enemies with eternal damnation in the Lake of Fire. The Devil, his demons and all mankind from every generation who rebelled against the Almighty will have their day in God's court at the Great White Throne Judgment Seat (Rev. 20:1-15).

Revelation Chapter 15

The Seven Seals

Vs. 1 The wrath of God begins with the opening of the seven seals (Ch. 6) and will be finished with the Seven last plagues, which are seven vials (Rev. 15:7).

Vs. 2-4 The sea of glass was before God's Throne in Rev.4:6. The victory over the beast is won through our faith in Christ, we will have the victory over the evil one by our refusal to submit to the rule of the Antichrist (Rev. 2:7,11,17, 26; 1 John 4:1-6).

The song of Moses refers to the praise of Israel after God's triumphal deliverance from Egypt and the overthrow of Pharaoh's army, (Exodus 15; Deuteronomy 32) which prefigured the deliverance of the Tribulation Saints from the Antichrist. They praise and worship God for His power and His righteousness where all nations will come and worship God, through Christ in the Millennial Kingdom.

Vs. 5-8. The seven angels prepare to administer the seven last tribulation judgments of Christ, which concludes with the seven vials (Ref. 16:1-7; 17:1; 21:9). God has a right to judge because He is the Eternal One, the Almighty. Again, His judgment is going to begin in the House of God, [the church] therefore, the church must still be on earth when this occurs.

The Temple represents the presence of God Himself. The smoke is like the incense that filled the Holy of Holies in the Tabernacle. The Tabernacle [God's dwelling place] was a temporary structure, it was moved each day as the children of Israel journeyed in the wilderness. It contained the Ark of the Testimony and the Mercy Seat. No one, Saint nor sinner will be allowed to enter the Temple when God is present (vs. 8).

Note: A future Temple will be rebuilt and destroyed again when the Antichrist will set himself up in it claiming to be God (ref. Matt. 24:1-2, 15; 2 Thessalonians 2:1- 8).

From Exodus 25: We learn that the Israelites were to bring an offering unto God (vs. 1-7) where God communicated to the children of Israel in the Tabernacle from the Holy of Holies. Vs. 8-22 states, *"And let them make me a sanctuary;* [a sacred place] *that*

I may dwell among them. According to all that I show thee, after the pattern of the tabernacle, and the pattern of all the instruments thereof, even so shall ye make it."

The Ark of the Testimony and the Mercy Seat was to be placed in the Tabernacle as well.

Vs. 10 *"And they shall make an ark* [a chest] *of shitten* [acacia] *wood: two cubits and a half shall be the length thereof, and a cubit and a half shall be the breadth thereof, and a cubit and a half the height thereof* (about 3 ¾ ft long x 2 ½ ft wide x 2 ¼ ft high)."

Vs. 11 *"And thou shall overlay it with pure gold, within and without* [inside and out] *shall thou overlay it, and shall make upon it a crown of gold round about."*

Vs. 12 *"And thou shalt cast four rings of gold for it, and put them in the four corners thereof; and two rings shall be in the one side of it, and two rings in the other side of it."*

Vs. 13 *"And thou shall make staves* [poles] *of shittim wood, and overlay them with gold."*

Vs. 14 *"And thou shalt put the staves into the rings by the side of the ark, that the ark may be borne with them."*

Vs. 15 *"The staves shall be in the rings of the ark: they shall not be taken* [removed] *from it".*

Vs. 16 *"And thou shalt put into the ark the testimony* [tablets of the law] *which I shall give thee."*

Vs. 17 *"And thou shalt make a mercy seat* [atonement cover] *of pure gold: two cubits and a half shall be the length thereof and a cubit and a half shall be the breath thereof."*

Vs. 18 *"And thou shalt make two cherubim of gold, of beaten work* [hammered gold] *shall thou make them, in the two ends of the mercy seat".*

Vs. 19 *"And make one cherub on the one end, and the other cherub on the other end: even of the mercy seat shall ye make the cherubim on the two ends thereof."*

Vs. 20 *"And the cherubim shall stretch forth their wings on high, covering the mercy seat with their wings and their faces shall look one to another; toward the mercy seat shall the faces of the cherubim be."*

Vs. 21 *"And thou shalt put the mercy seat above upon the ark; and in the ark thou shalt Put the testimony* [law] *that I shall give thee."*

Vs. 22 *"And there I will meet with thee, and I will commune* [speak] *with thee from above the mercy seat, from between the two cherubim which are upon the ark of the testimony, of all the things which I will give thee in commandment unto the children of Israel."*

Revelation Chapter 16

The Seven Vails [Bowls] of God's wrath poured out:

In this chapter of God's Word, we read of the seven plague- wielding angels who pours out their bowls upon the earth. By reading Chapter 16 in its entirety, we will learn what the Bible says about the severity of God's wrath. *"The Lord is merciful and gracious, slow to anger, and plenteous in mercy"* (Psalm 103:8). However, during the Tribulation period, after God has given mankind space to repent and, *"turn from their evil ways"*; most living during that time will not repent of their evil and outright rebellion against God. Being the Righteous Judge that He is, He must punish mankind for their rejection and rebellion of Him. In this chapter of God's Word, no repentance is invited nor shown.

Regarding this period, Jesus said, *"He that is unjust, let him be unjust still: and he which is filthy, let him be filthy still: and he that is righteous, let him be righteous still: and he that is holy, let him be holy still"* (Rev. 22:11). Just as one cannot repent from the grave (Luke 16: 19-31), likewise, it will be too late to make a last-minute confession and be saved; [like the thief on the cross] that door of opportunity will be closed as described in the parable of the ten virgins (Matt.25:1-13).

The Emptying of the Bowls:

The vails [bowls] of the wrath of God represents the climax of God's punishment of sinners during the Tribulation period. From Revelation Chapter 16, we learn that God is going to unleash His wrath upon mankind in the form of plagues upon the earth.

Vs. 1 John heard the voice of God from the temple instructing the seven angels to: *"Go your ways, and pour out the vials of the wrath of God upon the earth."*

Vs. 2 The first bowl of God's wrath inflicts sores upon those who bares the Mark of the Beast and worships his image.

Vs. 3 The second angel poured out his bowl upon the sea, turning it to blood as a contaminated dead person and killing all sea creatures.

Vs. 4 The third angel poured out his bowl upon the rivers and springs of water turning them into blood.

Vs. 5 The angel that poured out his bowl upon the waters praised God saying, *"Thou art righteous, O Lord, which art and wast, and shalt be because thou hast judged thus...*

Vs. 6 *"For they have shed the blood of saints and prophets, and thou hast given them blood to drink; for they are worthy."*

Vs. 7 John hears another angel praising God saying, *"Even so, Lord God Almighty, true and righteous are thy judgments."*

Vs. 8 The fourth angel's bowl of God's wrath was [will be] poured out on the sun creating intense heat that scorched people with fire.

Vs. 9 Those affected by the heat blasphemed the name of God and they did not repent nor give Him the glory.

Vs. 10 The fifth angel poured out his bowl of God's wrath upon the seat [throne] of the beast [Antichrist] and his kingdom became dark and people gnawed their tongues in pain.

Vs. 11 Those affected by the plagues of God's wrath blasphemed God's name, and they did not repent of their sins.

Vs. 12 The sixth angel poured out his bowl upon the Euphrates River drying it up, so that enemy armies could cross over it, preparing for the battle of Armageddon.

This allows kings from the east and their armies to cross this great natural barrier to fulfill the prophecies of Zachariah 14:1-4 that, *"All nations will come against Jerusalem to battle."* (ref. Matt.24; Mark 13; Luke 21).

Vs. 13 John saw three unclean spirits of demons that supports the activities of Satan, the beast and the false prophet which represents an evil trinity, counterfeiting the True and Righteous Trinity of the Father, the Son and the Holy Spirit.

Vs. 14 Their mission was to go out into all the world performing miracles before kings and nations deceiving them and gathering them into the battle of Armageddon.

Vs. 15 Is an exhortation from Christ to the surviving believers to be watchful and alert during this time of intense crises and persecution, that their righteous garments [spiritual preparedness] don't be transformed to nakedness and shame (ref. Matt.24:32-25:13).

Vs. 16 *"And he* [Christ] *gathered them* [the enemy armies] *together to Armageddon"* [for the final battle against good and evil].

Vs. 17 The seventh bowl was poured out in the air and John heard a voice from the temple in heaven saying, *"It is done."* Vs. 18-21 Is the climax of it all, the greatest earthquake ever witnessed by mankind occurs. If these things happen in our lifetime and if we want to escape the calamities which are to come upon this sinful world then, we need to seek God for life, protection, and salvation.

If we, as a Christian nation; [at least it started out that way by our founding fathers], with our anti-God ways of living don't repent and, *"turn from our evil ways"* God will surely punish us in a great tribulation. Jesus said, *"It will be more tolerable for the land of Sodom and Gomorrah in the day of judgment than for those whose God's judgment will fall upon"* (Matt. 10:15).

You may be thinking, "Why would it be more tolerable for the sinful cities of Sodom and Gomorrah than for this present generation? Those cities were totally destroyed by God." It will be so because Jesus said that it would. That was Old Testament, and people were under the law, we're living under a New Covenant- GRACE (God's Riches At Christ's Expense).

Jesus had not come in the flesh to shed His precious soul saving Blood for that generation. His Sacred Blood was shed for New Testament believers. All that did not die in faith, looking for the promised Savior will have their part in the Lake of Fire on Judgment Day! The same God who destroyed the wicked world in Noah's day and sent fiery brimstone upon Sodom and Gomorrah, also sent His Only Begotten Son to die on the Cross for our sins (John 3:16,17).

Therefore, the reason for more severe judgment is because Jesus Christ, the Savior of humanity, the Lamb of God, whom God the Father had proposed to be the Savior of the world had not shed His precious Blood for that generation. Now that Jesus has paid the price for our sins; He suffered and died for our salvation. But mankind has given God a, "one finger salute" to His laws and ordinances and adopted their own way of life and lifestyle, therefore, God's wrath will be more severe on this generation than for those that lived during those, Old Testament times.

God reveals His love for humanity in a well-documented balance between justice and mercy. Bible history proves that God is longsuffering (2 Peter 3:9). He extends His mercy to sinners and His disobedient children (Saints) day after day, year after year. God's patience with defiance and rebellion is limited, therefore, He justifiably responds in His wrath to deal with defiant and rebellion; both inside the household of faith as well as those on the outside.

It is written, *"For the time is come that judgment must begin at the house of God: and if it first begin at us, what shall the end be of them that obey not the gospel of God? AND IF THE RIGHTEOUS SCARCELY BE SAVED, WHERE SHALL THE UNGODLY AND THE SINNER APPEAR?"* (1 Peter 4:17,18). Romans 6:23 declares, *"The wages of sin is death; but the gift of God is eternal life through Jesus Christ our Lord."*

GOD IS RIGHTEOUS AND JUST. There are two judgments of God, every person will receive justice at the hand of God Almighty. Everyone who ever lived will be dealt with justly and righteously. Whether you're a Saint or a sinner, you will stand before God and you will receive exactly what is just and right. We must stand before God and give account for everything that we said or did in our lifetime (Matt. 12: 36, 37).

In man's corrupt justice system, people have been wrongly accused, convicted; and spent many years in incarceration, and some have been put to death for crimes they didn't commit. And on the other hand, some have committed heinous crimes, and because of their fame, and financial status they have escaped man's justice system.

But the judgment of God will be exactly right. God is no respecter of persons, He cannot be bribed or bought; all will be dealt with justly and righteously. God's character declares it; He cannot judge wrongly. *"Everyone will be judge out of those things which were written in the books, according to their works"* (Rev. 20: 12).

The Saints of God will go before the Judgment Seat of Christ where we will get our rewards from our works here on earth (1 Cor. 3:11-15; 2 Cor. 5:10; Rev. 19:6-9). Our judgment will be of stewardship rather than salvation. We are saved because of our faith and confession in Christ. Once we become Christians, we are obligated and commissioned to do good works unto the Lord, for His kingdom and for His Glory.

Romans 14:11,12 declares, *"For it is written, AS I LIVE SAITH THE LORD, EVERY KNEE SHALL BOW TO ME, AND EVERY TONGUE SHALL CONFESS TO GOD, So then every one of us shall give an account of himself unto God."*

Psalm 96 Is a call for Converted and Saved Saints to Praise God:

"Oh SING unto the Lord a new song: sing unto the Lord, all the earth. Sing unto the Lord, bless his name; show forth his salvation day by day. Declare his glory among the heathen, his wonders among all people. For the Lord is great, and greatly to be praised: he is to be feared above all gods. For all the gods of the nations are idols; but the Lord made the heavens. Honor and majesty are before him: strength and beauty are in his sanctuary. Give unto the Lord, O ye kindreds of the people, give unto the Lord glory and strenght. Give unto the Lord the glory due unto his name, bring an offering, and come into his courts. O worship the Lord in the beauty of holiness: fear before him, all the earth. Say among the heathen that the Lord reigneth: the world also shall be established that it

shall not be moved: he shall judge the people righteously. Let the heavens rejoice and the earth be glad; let the sea roar, and the fullness thereof.

Let the field be joyful, and all that is therein: then shall all the trees of the wood rejoice before the Lord: for he cometh, for he cometh to judge the earth: he shall judge the world with righteousness, and the people with his truth."

And the sinners (unsaved souls who rejected and neglected the Gift of God, (Jesus Christ) will be judged at the Great White Throne Judgment Seat of God. They, the devil, and all his demons will be sentenced and condemned into eternal damnation in the Lake of Fire (Rev. 20:11-15).

God sent His Son into the world to save sinners. The apostle Paul declared, "Christ died for our sins according to the Scriptures" (1 Cor. 15:3). The death of Jesus Christ our Savior is mentioned approximately two hundred times in the New Testament, and the Old Testament Scriptures contain many prophetic and typical references to His death. Christ's death on the cross was not an incident in His life; but rather, it was God's supreme purpose that was planned before the foundation of the world!

God knew from the beginning that mankind was going to fall, therefore, He provided a way for His prized creation to be redeemed. Jesus was 'lifted up' on the cross that we might sit with Him in heavenly places (ref John 3:14,15).

12

The United States of America
A Nation Gone Astray:

The United States of America today is not the 'Christian Nation' [in character] as established by our founding fathers who acknowledged God in every aspect of their lives. And they encouraged the citizenry to do likewise; but this nation has spiraled down morally from its conception. We're more divided than ever, yet we call ourselves, "One Nation Under God" but our character isn't in the words that we proclaim. It is reported that in the beginning of World War II that President Theodore Roosevelt prayed for the nation right before allied forces invaded Normandy, France on D-Day June 6, 1944, in his prayer he prayed-

"My fellow Americans: In this poignant hour, I ask you to join me in prayer: "Almighty God, our sons, pride of our nation, this day have set upon a mighty endeavor, a struggle and our civilization, and to set free a suffering humanity. Lead them straight and true, give them strength to their arms, stoutness to their heart, steadfastness to their faith. They will need thy blessings. Their road will be long and hard. The enemy is strong. He may hurl back our forces. Success may not come with rushing speed, but we shall return again and again; and we know that by Thy Grace, and by the righteousness of our cause, our sons will triumph. They will be sore tired, by night and by day, without rest-till the victory is won. The darkness will be rent by noise and flame. Men's souls will be shaken with the violence of war. These are men lately drawn from the waves of peace. They fight not for lust of conquest. They fight to end conquest. They fight to liberate. They fight to let justice arise, and tolerance and good will among all Thy people. They yearn but for the end of battle, for their return to the haven of home. Some will never return. Embrace these, Father and receive them, Thy heroic servants, into Thy kingdom... And for us at home- fathers, mothers, children, wives, sisters, and brothers of brave men overseas, whose thoughts and prayers are ever with them-help us, Almighty God, to rededicate ourselves in renewal faith in Thee in this hour of great sacrifice. Many people have urged that I call the nation into a single day of special prayer. But because the road is long and the desire is great, I ask that our people devote themselves in continuance prayer. As we rise each new day, and again when each day is spent, let words of prayer be on our lips, invoking Thy help to our efforts. Give us strength, too-trough in our daily task, to redouble the contributions we make in the physical and material support of our armed forces. And let our hearts be stout, to wait out the long travail, to bear sorrows that may come, to impart our courage unto our sons wherever they may be... And, O Lord, give us faith. Give us faith in Thee; faith in our sons; faith in each other; faith in our united crusade. Let not the keenness of our spirit ever be dulled. Let not the impacts of temporary events, of temporal matters of but fleeting moment-let not these deter us in our unconquerable purpose. With Thy blessing, we shall prevail over the unholy forces of our enemy. Help us to conquer the apostles of greed and radical arrogances. Lead us to the saving of our country, and with our sister nations into a world unity that will spell a sure peace-a peace invulnerable to the scheming of unworthy men. A peace that will let all men live in freedom, reaping the just rewards of their honest tool.

Thy will be done Almighty God, Amen."

We had godly and righteous leaders in those days who wasn't 'politically correct' but acknowledged God in everything. My prayer today is: Almighty God, make this nation "Great Again", and give us godly leaders who will stand before You and that they, In all of their ways will acknowledge You, and to encourage the citizens of this nation to repent of their sins and follow Your Laws, Statutes and Ordinances, in that this nation might prosper; and with Your blessings, we will live in freedom, peace and harmony. Help us O Lord God, to seek Your leadership as our forefathers did? You have promised us, in all our ways, if we would acknowledge You, that You will direct our paths.

The Word of God declares, *"Blessed is the nation whose God is the Lord; and the people whom he hath chosen for his own inheritance"* (Psalm 33:12). With all the racial prejudice, economic and social divisions and hostility among the people that's going on in America today, it seems somewhat hypocritical for us to claim that we are, "One Nation Under God" while there is so much hatred and division among us. We have not followed the precepts of our founding fathers. They drafted in our Constitution that, "All men are created equal" yet many have violated it with their hatred of people of certain races, creeds, and color. Not only is this hatred shown among the people, but most of it comes from our top elected officials who should be examples for others to follow. The Bible declares, *" A house or a kingdom divided against itself cannot stand"* (Mark 3:24, 25).

We have not followed the precepts of our founding fathers, here is some more examples that they and others political leaders set for us.

PRESIDENTS:

It is reported that our first president George Washington said, "IT IS THE DUTY OF ALL NATIONS TO ACKNOWLEDGE THE PROVIDENCE OF ALMIGHTY GOD, TO OBEY HIS WILL, TO BE GRATEFUL FOR HIS BENEFITS, AND HUMBLY, TO IMPLORE HIS PROTECTION AND FAVOR."

John Adams was quoted saying, "WE HAVE NO GOVERNMENT ARMED WITH POWER CAPABLE OF CONTENDING WITH HUMAN PASSIONS UNBRIDGED BY MORALITY AND RELIGION, OUR CONSTITUTION WAS MADE ONLY FOR A MORAL AND RELIGIOUS PEOPLE. IT WAS WHOLLY INADEQUATE TO THE GOVERNMENT OF ANY OTHER."

James Madison was quoted saying, "BEFORE ANY MAN CAN BE CONSIDERED AS A MEMBER OF CIVIL SOCIETY, HE MUST BE CONSIDERED A SUBJECT OF THE GOVERNOR OF THE UNIVERSE."

Thomas Jefferson was quoted as saying,"...AND CAN THE LIBERTIES OF A NATION BE THOUGHT SECURE WHEN WE HAVE REMOVED THEIR ONLY FIRM BASIS. A CONVICTION IN THE MINDS OF THE PEOPLE THAT THESE LIBERTIES ARE OF THE GIFT OF GOD? THAT THEY ARE NOT TO BE VIOLATED BUT WITH HIS WRATH? INDEED, I TREMBLE FOR MY COUNTRY WHEN I REFLECT THAT GOD IS JUST: THAT HIS JUSTICE CANNOT SLEEP FOREVER."

John Quincy Adams-Referring to the birth of the nation on July 4, 1776, was quoted as saying: "IT IS NOT THAT THE CHAIN OF HUMAN EVENTS, THE BIRTHDAY OF THE NATION IS INDISSOLUBLY LINKED WITH THE BIRTHDAY OF THE SAVIOR? THAT IT FORMS A LEADING EVENT IN THE PROGRESS OF THE GOSPEL DISPENSATION? IT IS NOT THAT THE DECLARATION OF INDEPENDENCE FIRST ORGANIZED THE SOCIAL COMPACT ON THE FOUNDATION OF THE REDEMMER'S MISSION UPON EARTH? THAT IT VALID THE CORNERSTONE OF HUMAN GOVERNMENT UPON THE FIRST PRECEPTS OF CHRISTIANITY?

FOUNDING FATHERS:

"TO THE KINDLY INFLUNCE OF CHRISTIANITY WE OWE THAT DECREE OF CIVIL FREEDOM, AND POLITICIAL AND SOCIAL HAPPENESS, WHICH MANKIND NOW ENJOYS...WHENEVER THE PILLARS OF CHRISTIANITY SHALL BE OVERTHROWN, OUR PRESENT REPUBLICAN FORMS OF GOVERNMENT-AND ALL BLESSINGS WHICH FLOW FROM THEM- MUST FALL WITH THEM." Jedidiah Morse

Patrick Henry was quoted saying, "AN APPEAL TO ARMS AND TO THE GOD OF HOSTS IS ALL THAT IS LEFT US!...SIR, WE ARE NOT WEAK IF WE MAKE A PROPER USE OF THOSE MEANS WHICH THE GOD OF NATURE HAD PLACED IN OUR POWER...BESIDES SIR, WE SHALL NOT FIGHT OUR BATTLES ALONE, THERE IS A JUST GOD WHO PRESIDES OVER THE DISTINIES OF NATIONS, AND WHO WILL RAISE UP FRIENDS TO FIGHT OUR BATTLES FOR US,...IS LIFE SO DEAR, OR PEACE SO SWEET, AS TO BE PURCHASED AT THE PRICE OF CHAINS AND SLAVERY? FORBID IT, ALMIGHTY GOD! I KNOW NOT WHAT COURSE OTHERS MAY TAKE BUT AS FOR ME, GIVE ME LIBERTY OR GIVE ME DEATH!"

Benjamin Franklin, "I HAVE LIVED, SIR, A LONG TIME, AND THE LONGER I LIVE, THE MORE CONVINCING PROOFS I SEE OF THIS TRUTH; THAT GOD GOVERNS THE AFFAIRS OF MEN. AND IF A SPARROW CANNOT FALL TO THE GROUND WITH HIS KNOWLEDGE, IS IT PROBABLE THAT AN EMPIRE CAN RISE WITHOUT HIS AID? WE HAVE BEEN ASSURED, SIR, IN THE SACRED WRITTINGS THAT EXCEPT THE LORD BUILDS THE HOUSE, THEY LABOR IN VAIN THAT BUILD IT. I FIRMLY

BELIEVE THIS; AND I ALSO BELIEVE THAT WITHOUT HIS CONCURRING AID WE SHALL SUCCEED IN THIS POLICITIAL BUILDING NO BETTER THAN THE BUILDERS OF BABEL."

SUPREME COURT JUSTICES:

John Jay: First Chief Justice- "THE BIBLE IS THE BEST OF ALL BOOKS, FOR IT IS THE WORD OF GOD AND TEACHES US THE WAY TO BE HAPPY IN THIS WORLD AND IN THE NEXT. CONTINUE THEREFORE TO READ IT AND TO RELATE YOUR LIFE TO IT'S PRECEPTS." He was also quoted as saying, "PROVIDENCE HAS GIVEN TO OUR PEOPLE THE CHOICE OF THEIR RULERS, AND IT IS THE DUTY, AS WELL AS THE PRIVILEGE AND INTEREST OF OUR CHRISTIAN NATION, TO SELECT AND PREFER CHRISTIANS FOR THEIR RULERS."

James Wilson: Original Justice on the U. S. Supreme Court was quoted as saying, "HUMAN LAW MUST REST ITS AUTHORITY ULTIMATELY UPON THE AUTHORITY OF THE LAW WHICH IS DIVINE...FAR FROM BEING RIVALS OR ENEMIES, RELIGION AND LAW ARE TWIN SISTERS, FRIENDS, AND MUTUAL ASSISTANTS, INDEED THESE TWO SCIENCES RUN INTO EACH OTHER."

Joseph Story, U. S. Supreme Court Justice said, "ONE OF THE BEAUTIFUL BOASTS OF OUR MUNICIPAL JURISPRUDENCE IS THAT CHRISTIANITY IS A PART OF THE COMMON LAW...THERE NEVER HAS BEEN A PERIOD IN WHICH THE COMMON LAW DID NOT RECOGNIZE CHRISTIANITY AS LYING AT ITS FOUNDATION,..I VERILY BELIEVE CHRISTIANITY IS NECESSARY TO THE SUPPORT OF CIVIL SOCIETY."

CONGRESS:

"WE ARE A CHRISTIAN PEOPLE NOT BECAUSE THE LAW DEMANDS IT, NOT TO GAIN EXCLUSIVE BENEFITS OR TO AVOID LEGAL DISABILITIES, BUT FROM CHOICE AND EDUCATION; AND IN A LAND THUS UNIVERSALLY CHRISTIAN, WHAT IS TO BE EXPECTED, WHAT DESIRED, BUT THAT WE SHALL PAY DUE REGARD TO CHRISTIANITY?" Senate Judiciary Committee Report, January 19, 1853

House Judiciary Committee Report, March 27, 1854.

"AT THE TIME OF THE ADOPTION OF THE CONSTITUTION AND THE AMENDMENTS THE UNIVERSAL SENTIMENT WAS THAT CHRISTIANITY SHOULD BE ENCOURAGED, IN THIS AGE THERE CAN BE NO SUBSTITUTE FOR CHRISTIANITY, THAT WAS THE RELIGION OF THE FOUNDERS OF THE REPUBLIC AND THEY EXPECTED IT TO REMAIN THE RELIGION OF THEIR DESENDANTS."

EDUCATION:

"LET EVERY STUDENT BE PLAINLY INSTRUCTED AND EARNESTLY TO CONSIDER WELL THE MAIN END OF HIS LIFE AND STUDIES IS TO KNOW GOD AND JESUS CHRIST IN WHICH IS ETERNAL LIFE (John:3) AND THEREFORE TO LAY CHRIST IN THE BOTTOM AS THE ONLY FOUDATION OF ALL SOUND KNOWLEDGE AND LEARNING AND SEEING THE LORD ONLY GIVEN WISDOM, LET EVERYONE SERIOUSLY SET HIMSELF BY PRAYER IN SECRET TO SEEK IT OF HIM (Proverbs 2:3). EVERYONE SHALL SO EXERCISE HIMSELF IN

READING THE SCRIPTURES TWICE A DAY THAT HE SHALL BE READY TO GIVE SUCH AN ACCOUNT OF HIS PROFICIENCY THEREIN." Harvard 1636 Student Guidelines

Yale Student Guidelines 1787:

"ALL THE SCHOLARS ARE REQUIRED TO LIVE A RELIGIOUS AND BLAMELESS LIFE ACCORDING TO THE RULES OF GOD'S WORD, DILIGENTLY READING THE HOLY SCRIPTURES, THAT FOUNDATION OF DIVINE LIGHT AND TRUTH, AND CONSTANTLY ATTENDING ALL THE DUTIES OF RELIGION."

SUPREME COURT RULING:

"THERE IS NO DISSONANCE IN THESE [legal] DELCLARATIONS, ...THESE ARE NOT INDIVIDUAL SAYINGS, DECLARATIONS OF PRIVATE PERSONS: THEY ARE ORGANIC [legal governmental] UTTERANCES..."

In today's society- we, the United States of America is leading the whole world in rebellion against God. We have removed prayer from our public schools, removed most Scriptures and references of God from many public places and buildings.

We have sanction laws that allows women and teenage girls to legally kill their unborn babies. Because of this, millions of our children have been brutally killed in our abortion mills called, 'planned parenthood.' Rest assured, God is going to hold those 'murders' accountable on Judgment Day, when He said, *"Thou shalt not kill"*, He also had innocent unborn babies in mind; their blood is, *"crying out to God from the ground"* (Genesis 4:10).

It's ironic to me that our so called "justice system", will charge women and girls with murder for killing a baby after its born but that same person can legally kill the child any time she wishes after its conception! To this I say, "Hypocritical America" murder is murder in the eyes of God, matters not whether the child is killed before or after its birth!

God loves the unborn children, they are part of His creation, the women and girls who have murdered their unborn babies and the doctors who performed those procedures are going to answer to God on Judgment Day! (Revelation 20:1-15).

Jesus warned, *"Whosoever shall offend* [cause to sin or murder] *one of these little ones which believe in Me, it were better for him that a millstone were hanged about his neck, and that he were drowned in the dept of the sea"* (Matthew 18:6). God's eternal judgment will be worse; they will be cast into the lake of fire- FOREVER! (Rev. 21:8). This nation has become so prideful and arrogant that it has forgotten the very God that established it. The Bible declares, *"Pride goeth before destruction and a haughty spirit before a fall"* (Proverbs 16:18).

In our ignorance and arrogance, we have called "good evil and evil good." There was a group that I read about several years ago that was trying to have IN GOD WE TRUST taken off our currency. Also, there was a young Christian lady who was chosen Valedictorian at her graduation, everyone knew her and her Christian beliefs and character, therefore, she was warned not to mention God or Jesus Christ in her presentation; she rightly and justifiably refused to participate.

Also, I read in the newspaper several years ago that a Military Chaplin who was conducting a memorial service for the fallen, he was told, "not to pray in the Name of Jesus!" Our constitution guarantees us 'freedom of religion', but we have a group of *God haters* who has established a cult that calls for "freedom from religion." And many in this [once] Christian nation, which was given to us by God and that our forefathers dedicated on the citizenry to live by godly principles and belief in God; seems to have adopted that same view!

Again, how hypocritical we are as a nation. Furthermore, many employers don't allow their employees to share their Christian faith and beliefs with fellow co-workers. But as soon as there's a mass shooting or some other crisis in the workplace, what do they do? They call in pastors and Christian counselors to comfort, console and encourage the survivors; Oh, how hypocritical we have become!

By the same token, they have taken prayer out of our public schools, but when there's a mass shooting in schools, they call in pastors and Christian counselors to console the kids. Again, Hypocritical America! God is going to destroy those that don't allow Him to rule and reign supreme in their lives. We were created free mortal agents, God wants us to love, honor and obey Him but He's not going to force Himself on us. He wants us to love, honor and reverence Him freely; to do it willingly and lovingly so that He can get the Glory out of our lives. After all, we were created in His image and likeness but many, even some which call themselves Christians have adopted the way of Cain, they have gone their own ways rather than the ways of our Holy God.

The Apostle Paul warned those who have turned a deft ear to God's laws, statues and ordinances and have adopted their own way. Paul said, *"For the wrath of God is revealed from heaven against all ungodliness and unrighteousness of men, who hold the truth in unrighteousness; Because that which may be known of God is manifest in them; for God had shown it unto them. For the invisible things of him from creation of the world are clearly seen, being understood by the things that are made, even his eternal power and Godhead; so that they are without excuse; Because that, when they knew God, they glorified him not as God, neither were thankful; but became vain in their imaginations, and their foolish heart was darkened. Professing themselves to be wise, they became fools, And changed the glory of the incorruptible God into an image made like to corruptible man, and to birds, and four-footed beast, and creeping things. Wherefore God also gave them up to uncleanness through the lust of their own hearts, to dishonor their own bodies between themselves: Who changed the truth of God into a lie, and worshiped and served the creature more than the Creator, who is blessed for ever. Amen. For this cause God gave them up unto vile affections: for even their women did change* [exchanged] *the natural use into that which is against nature: And likewise also the men leaving the natural use of the woman, burned in their lust one towards another; men with men working that which is unseemly,* [shameful] *and receiving in themselves that recompense* [penalty, HIV-AIDS] *of their error which was meet* [due]. *And even as they did not like to retain God in their knowledge, God gave them over to a reprobate* [debased] *mind, to do those things which were not convenient;* [fitting] *Being filled with all unrighteousness, fornication, wickedness, covetousness, maliciousness; full of envy, murder, debate, deceit, malignity, whispers, backbiters, haters of God, despiteful, proud, boasters, inventers of evil things, disobedient to parents, Without understanding, covernantbreakers, implacable,* [unforgiving] *unmerciful: Who knowing the judgment of God, that they which commit such things are worthy of death, not only do they the same, but have pleasure* [approve of] *in them that do them"* (Romans 1:18-32).

The passage of the Holy Scriptures that you just read didn't come from me but from my heavenly Father. He inspired men to pin His Word that it may be preserved and available to every generation until the return of Our Lord and Savior, Jesus Christ (2 Timothy 3:16, 17). 2 Peter 1:20-21 tells us, *"Knowing this first, that no prophecy of the scripture is of any private interpretation....*

...For the prophecy came not in old time by the will of man: but holy men of God spake as they were moved by the Holy Ghost." In other words, the Bible is God breathe, directly from the mouth of God rather than by a group of men who got together and decided to write the Bible. Man printed it because of the invention of the modern printing press, but the Old Testament writers wrote by hand, they were inspired by God what to write what He dictated to them, and because they were "holy men" they didn't add their own words to it (Rev. 22:18,19).

Again, our Supreme Court have passed laws legalizing the murder of unborn children through abortions, which God has declared to be "murder". Our politicians have sanctioned "Gay Pride" through parades and festivals. And we, as a nation are dumb enough to wonder why this nation is suffering morally from immorality! I can plainly see why Jesus Christ, Our Lord and Savior said, *"I say unto you,* [U.S.A.] *That it shall be more tolerable for the land of Sodom in the day of judgment, than for thee"* (Matthew 11:24) [emphases mine]. Many citizens in this country have called for, "separation of church and state", that isn't based on what you have just read from our founding fathers nor earlier politicians, but from ignorant men and women who wants their own way by ignoring the Words of our Creator. I say unto all that don't want to live up to God's standards that He will allow you to, "do your own thing" but in the end, it will cost you your eternal soul in the lake of fire!

If anyone would study their Bible, they will learn that God always sent His prophets [the church] to warn the king [the state] of their wrongdoings. God sent His prophet Samuel, to warn King Saul. He sent Nathan, to rebuke King David. He sent Jonah, to warn the City of Nineveh to repent or perish. He sent Daniel to interpret the dream of King Nebuchadnezzar and to warn him that his kingdom was going to fall. Daniel was also sent to interpret the handwriting on the wall of King Belshazzar, grandson and successor to King Nebuchadnezzar who held a great banquet and desecrated the holy vessels that were taken from the temple in Jerusalem. Daniel warned the king that his kingdom would fall that very night. And it did just as the prophet of God said that it would! (Dan. Ch 5).

And in the New Testament when the early church was born, God converted Saul of Tarsus, whom the Lord renamed Paul. God spared Paul's life on many occasions so that he would appear before the ruling authorities to deliver God's message. Paul was sent to Felix, the governor [Roman procurator serving in Judea], and Festus who was governor in Samaria, Paul was also sent by God to Augustus and King Agrippa. *"There is nothing new under the sun", God, is the same yesterday, today and forever, He changes not."* Therefore, His prophets [the church] are still to warn [the state] and it's citizenry to, *"turn from their wicked ways and live"* (Ezekiel 33:1-6).

I'm reminded in the story that Jesus told of the dialogue between Abraham and the rich man. Lazarus, a poor beggar full of sores showed up at the rich man's gate daily begging for the crumbs that fell from the rich man's table. Lazarus didn't ask to be invited in, he just desired the leftovers, the food that the rich man most likely was going to throw out. But the rich man had no compassion for him. It seems that the dogs cared more for him than the rich man, they came and licked his sores. Lazarus eventually died *saved,* and he was carried into paradise by the angels. The rich man also died but he died *unsaved,* was buried and he went straight to hell and found himself in the torments of hell's fire! He asked Abraham to send Lazarus, whom he had neglected daily to, *"dip the tip of his finger in water to cool his tongue."* All he was asking for was one drop of water. If a snowball can't stand a chance in hell, how much would one think that a single drop of water could do?

The rich man sault salvation and comfort after his death but it was too late! His next request was to send Lazarus to his father's house to warn his five *unsaved* brothers that there is life after death and if they didn't repent and be saved before their death that they would end up in hell as well. But Abraham told him, *"they have Moses and the prophets* [church folks] *preaching and teaching God's Word; let them hear them"* (Luke 16:19-31).

The message of salvation and the deliverance of God Word should come from His church, yet we have "nay Sayers" and "God haters" who have call for "separation of church and state." They have turned a deft ear to God and His Word. Why is that? It's because, *"man loved* [loves] *darkness rather than light, because their deeds were* [are] *evil."* Some might say, "keep your religion in your church" but as soon as there is a crisis they reach out to the churches for comfort and support! How hypocritical those *God haters* are! I can truly understand why Jesus said, *"Let the dead bury their dead"* (Luke 9:60). They will regret their defiance of God on Judgment Day!

Again, I say we, as Believers in Christ, will be judged; our judgment won't be to determine whether we're saved or lost, but rather, it will be for our stewardship (as rulers and our positions) in Christ's Millennium Kingdom and for all eternity here on earth. All too many Christians fail to understand that they must give an account for their stewardship. Many of today's pastors and teachers fail to convey the message to their congregation. Jesus taught in many parables explaining the Kingdom of God and our stewardship and rewards. For those who fail to *"search the Scriptures"* and relying on their "blind and deceived" pastors and teachers will be disappointed when they stand before Christ in judgment.

Therefore, Jesus said, *"Not every one that saith unto me, Lord, Lord, shall enter into the kingdom of heaven; but he that doeth the will of my Father which is in heaven…Many will say to me, in that day,* (at the judgment seat of Christ) *Lord, Lord, have we not prophesied in thy name? and in thy name have cast out devils? and in thy name done many wonderful works?…And then will I profess unto them, I never knew you: depart from me, ye that work iniquity"* (Matt. 7:21-23).

These are "church folks" who did great works in the Lord's name, but they were never saved. Therefore, they will be rejected and cast out! God accepted their works because, *"He is not willing that any should perish."* Had they been saved and fell short, they would have been called, *"the least in the kingdom of heaven"* (Matt. 5:19). The apostle Paul became all things to all men, he related to all on their level. He said, *"For though I be free from all men, yet have I made myself servant unto all, that I might gain the more. And unto the Jews I became as a Jew, that I might gain* (win) *the Jews:…To them that are without the law* (Gentiles) *that I might gain them…To the weak because I as weak, that I might gain the weak: I am made all things to all men, that I might by all means save some…But I keep under my body, and bring it into subjection: lest that by any means, when I have preached to others, I myself should be a castaway."* (1 Corinthians 9:19-27).

13

Revelation Chapter 17

UNITED STATES OF AMERICA: *"MYSTERY BABYLON THE GREAT, THE MOTHER OF HARLOTS AND ABOMINATION OF THE EARTH"*

As I've stated before, the United States of America is leading the world into sin. Everyone wants to pattern themselves after us. We have freedoms and constitutional rights that was written into our constitution and bill of rights that the citizens of most other nations of the world wants to enjoy, we have freedoms that they only dream of. Our land is blessed beyond measure with rich land that produces an abundance of foods, land rich with raw materials for our resources. Along with our God given freedom and rights, should also come responsibility. Responsibility to God our Creator, God sanctioned this nation [as with the Nation of Israel] to be a God-fearing nation and set a godly standard for others to follow. God allowed this nation to be established to fulfill His promised to Abraham, that through him, *"All nations would be blessed."* Therefore, we have immigrants from every nation around the globe who have come to this nation to enjoy religious and economic freedoms that others only dream of.

I strongly believe that the United States of America is the "MYSTERY BABYLON THE GREAT, THE MOTHER OF HARLOTS AND ABOMINATIONS OF THE EARTH" as prophesied in [read] Revelation 17:5. Most Pre-Tribulation Rapture believers think the old city and nation of Babylon will be revised and once again restored to its former glory and prominence. They are half right, Babylon will be revised and restored at the revising of the Holy Roman Empire but not to its former glory because it will be under the leadership of the Antichrist and his "little" kingdom will only last for seven years.

We learn from the Bible, which is the Word of God that the Persians [modern day Iran] conquered Babylon in 539 B.C. on the night that Belshazzar held an idolatrous feast with his entire noble invited guest, they drank wine from the Holy vessels that was looted from the temple in Jerusalem. In their partying they broke the first four commandments. As they partied and defiled the Holy vessels of God, they praised the gods of gold, silver, brass [bronze] iron, wood and stone (Daniel 5:1-5).

The king saw fingers of a man's handwriting on the wall which terrified him, he sought an interpretation from his astrologers, prophets, and wise men of his kingdom but no one in his kingdom could interpret the writings. Daniel was eventually called in at the request of the queen who remembered his encounter with king Nebuchadnezzar (Belshazzar's grandfather) to interpret the writings. Daniel warned the king that his kingdom would fall that very night and will be divided and be given to the Medes and the Persians (vs. 13-31).

The old city of Babylon was never restored to its former glory as prophesied by Isaiah (13:19-20). Isaiah saw the immediate destruction in 539 B.C. as well as its future destruction as recorded in Rev. 14:18. The nation flourished during the reign of Darius the Median and Cyrus the Persian who signed a decree which allowed the Jews to return to their homeland and to rebuild their wall, temple and city. There were other rulers who ruled and reigned in Babylon, but not to the prestigious point as with its former glory. The most prominent conqueror and ruler was a Greek named Alexander the Great, of whom it is said, "that by the age of thirty-three he had conquered all the known world and cried because there was no more land to conquer."

"The nations that forgets God is doomed for failure" (ref. Job 8:13, 14; Psalm 9;17). The free nations of the world want to pattern

their lives and lifestyle after us. More nations today have embraced the homosexual lifestyle that Hollywood propagates through their television shows and TV advertisements. Many TV shows and commercials portrays or sell products that are geared to the homosexual lifestyle. They even show same sex couples engaging in scenes meant for a male and a female. What do you see when you turn on the TV set? You see men kissing men, and women kissing women. I even witnessed a TV show that had two men having anal sex.

What an abomination to God! And mankind, especially citizens of this nation are dumb enough to think that God doesn't exist, they think there is no God that rules and reigns over the whole universe. God declares, *"The fool hath said in his heart, There is no God. They are corrupt, they have done abominable works, there are none that doeth good"* (Psalm 14:1). But one day, those "fools" are going to realize that there IS a HOLY GOD, and His judgment is going to fall upon them! (Rev. 6:9-17).

In Revelation Chapter 17, John describes for us the rising and falling of great empires, from the Middle Ages up to now our time.

I believe this is a twofold prophecy, it not only depicts the revising of the Holy Roman Empire, but it also predicts the doom and destruction of *"MYSTERY BABYLON THE GREAT, MOTHER OF HARLOTS AND ABOMINATIONS OF THE EARTH"* i.e. The United States of America. Again, our history books prove that the Word of God is true as supported by the Holy Scriptures. In the revising of the Holy Roman Empire, I believe Germany, with its power and prestige seems to be growing worldwide and it is becoming a central figure in Europe and that nation will have a prominent role in this End Time Bible *Prophecy*. Come walk with me through the 17th Chapter of Revelation and I will show you how this prophecy relates to the United States of America.

Note: Because of *"political correctness"*, I'm not allowed to quote verbatim this passage of the Holy Scriptures, therefore, (read it) and I will explain its meaning.

Vs. 1- The United States of America is the only nation on the globe that, *"sits upon many waters."* We have five Great Lakes, the Atlantic and Pacific Ocean, the Gulf of Mexico, and the Mississippi River which is 2,348 miles long and runs from Lake Itasca, Minnesota to the Gulf of Mexico just to name a few large bodies of 'waters' [lakes] within our country. Not only that but the State of Minnesota is known as, "the land of ten thousand lakes." In my state, the state of Wisconsin, we probably have as many lakes and rivers as Minnesota does. I'm sure that whatever city and state that you live in there are lakes, rivers, streams, parks with fishing ponds and lagoons in them, i.e. *"Many Waters."*

Vs. 2 *"With whom the kings of the earth have committed fornication, and the inhabitants of the earth have been made drunk with the wine of her fornication."*

The "waters" also represents people, the immigrants of various people of nations that have made the United States of America their home. "She sitteth upon them" represents worldwide influence. Her harlotry and fornication refer to the moral decline of the nation in physical immorality and spiritual adultery-apostasy. The following Scriptures are prophecies against the Nation of Israel, but they also apply to the United States because like Israel, we have, "gone the way of Cain" and have forgotten the Lord that established us as a nation (cf. Isaiah 1:21; 23:16; 17; Jer. 2: 20-37; 13:27; Ezekiel 16: 15-43; Nahum 3:4-6).

Vs. 3 *"So he carried me away in the spirit into the wilderness: and I saw a woman sit upon a scarlet colored beast, full of names of blasphemy, having seven heads and ten horns.*

Vs. 4 *"And the woman was arrayed in purple and scarlet color, and decked with gold and precious stones and pearls,* [wealth and attractiveness] *having a golden cup in her hand full of abominations and filthiness of her fornication:* [passing laws allowing abortions and sanctions of same sex marriages, etc.] which are abominations to God.

Vs. 5 *"And upon her forehead was a name written,* MYSTERY BABYLON THE GREAT, THE MOTHER OF HARLOTS AND ABOMINATIONS OF THE EARTH."

Vs.6 *"And I saw the woman drunken with the blood of the saints, and with the blood of the martyrs of Jesus: and when I saw her, I wondered* [marveled] *with great admiration"* [amazement].

Vs. 7 *"And the angel said unto me, Wherefore didst thou marvel? I will tell thee the mystery of the woman, and of the beast that carried her, which hath seven heads and ten horns."*

Note: John was shown the revising of the Holy Roman Empire headed by the Antichrist.

Vs. 8 *"The beast that thou sawest was,* [existed in the form of the ancient Roman Empire] *and is not;* [will not rule again until the Antichrist comes to power and gains worldwide authority] *and shall ascend out of the bottomless pit* [Satan will raise up the Antichrist as his false messiah and give him worldwide rule (Rev. 11:7;13:3,4) *and go into prediction:* [Antichrist and the false prophet along with Satan will be cast into the lake of fire Rev. 19:20] *and they that dwell on the earth shall wonder whose names are not written in the book of life from the foundation of the world, when they behold the beast that was, and is not and yet is"* [Unbelievers will wonder in amazement" at this revival of the power and glory of the Revised Holy Roman Empire].

Vs. 9 *"And here is the mind which hath wisdom. The seven heads are seven mountains, on which the woman sitteth."* The seven heads of the beast are depicted as mountains, [nations] the woman represents seven idolatrous, anti-God civilizations, and will be centered at Rome and it will have worldwide influence vs. 15.

Vs. 10 *"And there are seven kings: five are fallen, and one is, and the other is not yet come; and when he cometh, he must continue a short space."*

Note: Seven kingdoms or empires throughout history has ruled over Israel and much of the known world. The five fallen ones were: Egypt, Assyria, Babylon, Medo-Persia, Greece *"and one is"* Rome, which was in power when John was given this vision, *"and the other is not yet come"*, [the Revised Holy Roman Empire which will be ruled by the Antichrist] ...*"he must continue a short space"* [the rule of the Antichrist will last seven years divided into two periods of time, 3 ½ years of the Tribulation Period and 3 ½ years the Great Tribulation Period].

Vs. 11 *"And the beast that was, and is not, even he is the eighth, and is of the seven, and goeth into perdition."*

The beast, the final world kingdom ruled by the Antichrist, is the eighth king or kingdom. He is of the seven in that he is the culmination of all the previous, pagan, idolatrous empires. But he will go into perdition, in the lake of fire (vs. 8; 19:20).

Vs. 12 *"And the ten horns which thou sawest are ten kings, which have received no kingdom as yet; but receive power as kings one hour with the beast."*

The ten horns on the Beast represent ten kings of the future revived Roman Empire (Daniel 2:41-44; 7:24). Their worldwide power will come in the association with the beast. *"One hour"* *indicates* a relatively short time (18:10; 17,19).

Vs. 13 *"These have one mind, and shall give their power and strength* [authority] *unto the beast."*

Vs. 14 *"These shall make war with the Lamb, and the Lamb shall overcome them: for he is Lord of lords, and King of kings: and they that are with him are called chosen and faithful."*

These rulers of a ten-nation federation will unitedly give their political authority and military power to the beast to conquer the earth and make war against Christ (16:14; 19:19). The purpose of Satan through the beast and fellow kings is to establish an invincible kingdom that Christ cannot overcome when He returns. But Christ is the *"King of kings"* and will be victorious over the beast and his kingdom (19:11-21). Those who follow Christ are called faithful and chosen by Him (19:7,8,14). (Read) Vss.15 & 16 *"The waters that thou sawest, where the* [expletive] *sitteth, are peoples, and multitudes, and nations and tongues." "And the ten horns which thou sawest upon the beast, these shall hate the* [expletive] U.S.A. *and shall make her desolate and naked, and shall eat her flesh, and burn her with fire"* [nuclear weapons].

Vs. 17 *"For God hath put it in their hearts to fulfill his will, and to agree,* [be of one mind, One World Government or New World Order] *and give their kingdom unto the beast, until the words of God shall be fulfilled."*

Vs.18 *"And the woman which thou sawest is that great city,* [New York City- financial capital of the U.S.A.] *which reigneth over the kings of the earth."*

Verses 15-18 Is a two-fold prophecy describing the Revised Holy Roman Empire and the empire of the idolatrous United States of America. The U.S.A. has been described as sitting upon many waters (v.1), on the beast (v.2), and on seven mountains (v.9). Here the waters are again identified as, peoples, and multitudes, and nations and tongues, indicating the worldwide influence and authority of the [expletive]. In vs. 18 she is identified as that great city, which reigneth over the kings of the earth [worldwide idolatrous, pagan system influenced by the Antichrist and centered at Rome].

Near the end of the Tribulation period, the ten kings (vs. 12) will destroy the [expletive] system (18:6-24). They will do this as

God's will and will turn their total devotion and worship to the beast (13:12; 17:13; Dan. 11:36-39). The ten kings will be God's instrument to destroy the [expletive], [Babylonian system, which includes the U.S.A. and the Revised Holy Roman Empire].

Note: Many Bible prophecy teachers have ascribed the *"City with sits on seven hills"* as Rome. But this prophecy is against the United States! New York, City is our financial center of the nation which have seven boroughs, (*cities*) they are:

1. Manhattan- North,
2. Manhattan- South,
3. Brooklyn-North,
4. Brooklyn- South,
5. The Bronx,
6. Queens,
7. Staten Island.

Revelation Chapter 18

The Fall of Babylon [United States of America] Predicted:

Again, as a nation, God is fed up with our sins, pride and arrogance. He is going to allow our enemies to conquer and devour us just as He did with the Nation of Israel after their journey into the promise land. God warned them that they should be the, a "Holy Nation" that He established to proclaim His love, goodness, and mercy throughout the whole world. By the same principle, God allowed this nation to be established to fulfill the promise that He had made through Abraham, that, *"through him all nations would be blessed."*

God allowed the Europeans and the early settlers to take over this land from the Native Americans [who was worshipping idols] that they should establish a "Christian Nation" where all people, regardless of their ethnicity, people from all nations to freely come here to worship and honor Him. God preserved this nation for His purpose as a paradigm of heaven, so that, *"His will be done on earth as it is in heaven."*

As I stated earlier, Ancient Babylon will never be restored to its greatness and glory, not even during the yet to be Revised Holy Roman Empire. Therefore, this prophecy is against the United States of America; again, God calls us, "MYSTERY BABYLON, THE GREAT, THE MOTHER OF HARLOTS AND ABOMINATIONS OF THE EARTH."

Vs. 1 *"And after these things I saw another angel come down from heaven, having great power;* [authority] *and the earth was lightened* [illuminated] *with his glory."*

Vs. 2 *"And he cried mightily with a strong* [loud] *voice, saying, Babylon the great is fallen, is fallen, and is become the habitation of devils,* [demons] *and the hold of* [a prison for] *every foul spirit, and a cage to every unclean and hateful* [hated] *bird."*

Vs. 3 *"For all nations have drunk of the wrath of the wine of her fornication, and the kings of the earth have committed fornication with her, and the merchants of the earth are waxed* [have become] *rich through the abundance of her delicacies* [luxury]."*

Verses 1-3- That city [nation] Babylon [USA] in Chapter 18 is the same [expletive] in Chapter 17. It is shown by; (1) The parallels between the two (ref. 17:1-6; 15-18; with 18: 2, 3; 6- 8, 12, 18-24).

(2) The identification of the [expletive] as the "great city" in 17;18; (3) The summary of Babylon's judgment in 19:2, 3; (4) The fact that the imagery in both chapters comes from the Old Testament references to Tyre, Nineveh, and Babylon (ref. Isaiah 13,14,23; Ezekiel 26-28; Jeremiah 50, 51).

The language of chapter 18 is highly figurative and is a twofold prophecy. The phrase *"after these things"* shows that chapter 18 is a further revelation concerning "Mystery Babylon" [United States of America] and the results of her destruction.

In verse 2 her doom is announced: *"Babylon the great is fallen"* (Cf. Isaiah 21:9).

The reference to devils (demons) and every foul spirit shows the total and utterly destruction of the [expletive] system. "All nations"- the system had worldwide influence and control. *"For the wine of her fornication"* [partakers of her idolatrous system] (ref 17:2). "Rich"- the merchants of the earth have become wealthy through the apostate, idolatrous system that will be centered at Rome but heavily influenced by the United States of America!

Vs. 4 *"And I heard another voice from heaven, saying, come out of her, my people, that ye be not partakers of her sins, and that ye receive not of her plagues."*

This Is a call for Believers to separate themselves from the [expletive] system otherwise, they will be found to share in her sins (ref. Ephesians 5:1-7).

Vs. 5 *"For her sins have reached unto heaven, and God hath remembered her iniquities.*

At this time, judgment day has arrived, and God is going to send down His wrath on the sinful world destroying His enemies, i.e., Satan, the Antichrist and the false prophet, and overthrowing man's religious and political systems to usher in Christ's Kingdom which will have no end.

Vs. 6 *"Reward her even as she rewarded you, and double* [repay] *unto her double according to her works: in the cup which she hath filled fill to her double."*

The double judgment emphasizes full punishment for her [U.S. A.'s] sins.

Vs. 7 *"How much she hath glorified herself, and lived deliciously,* [luxuriously] *so much torment and sorrow give her: for she hath saith in her heart, I set as a queen, and am no widow, and shall see no sorrow."*

In our arrogance, self-confidence and pride, [of our military might] as a nation, we think that we are above any possibility of self-sorrow. We have relied heavily on our strong, armed forces rather than our God who allowed this nation to exist.

But our military might couldn't prevent the attacks in New York City, our financial capital on Sept. 11, 2001! It is written, *"pride goeth before destruction and a haughty spirt before a fall."* (Proverbs 16:18).

Vs. 8 *"Therefore shall her plagues come in one day, death, and mourning, and famine; and she shall be utterly burned with fire: for strong is the Lord who judges her."*

Again, because of our pride and arrogance, God is going to bring His judgment upon this nation by allowing our enemies to attack and overcome us; to show us that He is in full control! He did the same of the Nation of Israel for their arrogance, pride, haughtiness, and disobedience. God is still, *"The same yesterday, today and forever."*

Vs. 9 *"And the kings of the earth, who have committed fornication and lived deliciously* [luxuriously] *with her, shall bewail* [weep for] *her, and lament for her, when they shall see the smoke of her burning,*

Vs. 10 *"Standing afar off for the fear of her torment, saying, Alas, alas, that great city Babylon,* [U.S.A.] *that mighty city!* [New York] *for in one hour is thy judgment come."*

Vs. 11 *"And the merchants of the earth shall weep and morn over her; for no man buyeth their merchandise anymore:"*

Vs. 12 *"The merchandise of gold, and silver, and precious stones, and of pearls, and fine linen, and purple, and silk, and scarlet and all thyine* [citron- costly] *wood and all manner of vessels of ivory, and all manner vessels of most precious wood, and of brass, and iron and marble,"*

Vs. 13 *"And cinnamon, and odors,* [incense] *and ointments,* [fragrant oil] *and frankincense, and wine, and oil, and fine flour, and wheat, and beast,* [cattle] *and sheep, and horses,* [machinery] *and chariots,* [automobiles] *and *slaves, and souls of men."*

Vs. 14 *"And the fruits that thy souls lusted after* [longed for] *are departed from thee, and all things which were dainty* [riches] *and goodly* [splendid] *are departed from thee, and thou shall find them no more at all."*

Vs. 15 *"The merchants of these things, which were made rich by her, shall stand afar off for the fear of her torment, weeping and wailing,"*

Vs. 16 *"And saying, Alas, alas, that great city,* [nation] *that was clothed in fine linen, and purple, and scarlet, and decked* [adorned] *with gold, and precious stones, and pearls!*

Vs. 17 *"For in one hour so great riches are come to nought* [nothing]. *And every shipmaster, and all the company of ships, and sailors, and as many as trade by sea, stood afar off,"*

Vs. 18 *" And cried when they saw the smoke of her burning, saying, What city* [nation] *is like unto this great city!* [nation].

Vs. 19 *"And they cast dust on their heads, and cried, weeping and wailing, saying, Alas, alas that great city,* [nation] *wherein were made rich all that had ships in the sea by reasons of her coastlines!* [wealth] *for in one hour she is made desolate"* [a wasteland].

Vs. 20 *"Rejoice over her, thou heaven, and ye holy apostles and prophets; for God hath avenged you on her."*

Vs. 9-20. God, our Righteous judge is going to judge this nation for our sins and disobedience to His laws, statues and ordinances. These verses consist of three laments over the fallen city of Babylon, [Babylonian system, United States of America] from the perspective of kings [presidents and rulers of allied nations], (vs. 9, 10), merchants (11-16), and seamen (17-19).

The laments picture the results of God's judgment, it will be shown on world news. Our allies and merchants *"standing afar off"* watching this nation's demise from the attacks of nuclear weapons from our enemies, [possibly Russia, North Korea, China, Iran, and Muslim nations that has labored us, "the great Satan."

Note: *During the Tribulation period people will be put in debtor's prison for personal debts that they cannot pay, (vs. 13) they will become 'slaves' to foreign nations (Cf. Matt. 5:25-26; 18: 25-30). There are nuclear suicide bombers already planted in the United States waiting for orders to strike. In one hour, this nation will be destroyed by nukes from our enemies; it will be viewed on world news outlets and the rest of the world will witness the demise of, "MYSTERY BABYLON THE GREAT, THE MOTHER OF HARLOTS AND ABOMINATIONS OF THE EARTH." i.e. The United States of America!

Vs. 21 *"And a mighty angel took up a stone like a great millstone,* (asteroid) *and cast it into the sea, saying, Thus with violence shall that great city Babylon* [USA] *be thrown down, and shall be found no more at all."*

Vs. 22-24 *"And the voice* [sound] *of the harpers, and musicians, and the pipers* [flutists] *and trumpters, shall be heard no more at all in thee; and no craftsman, of whatsoever craft he be, shall be found any more in thee; and the sound of the millstone shall be heard no more at all in thee; And the light of a candle...* [lamp-our electrical grid]*...shall shine no more at all in thee; and the voice of the bridegroom and of the bride shall be heard no more at all in thee: for thy merchants were the great men of the earth; for* *by thy sorceries* [power and influences] *were all nations deceived. And in her were found the blood of the prophets, and of saints, and of all that were slain upon the earth"* (ref Matt. 24:7-12; Luke 21:16-19; Rev. 6:9-11).

Note: Russia, "the king of the north" (*Rosh*, of the land of Gog and Magog, Ezekiel 38 & 39). Is north of the United States, the Russian tyrant has threatened to use nuclear weapons if the west [USA] and its allies intervenes in his quest to conquer and annex the Sovereign nation of Ukraine.

If an EMP [electromagnetic pulse] is released over the United States, it will knock out our power grid, which will spiro us back into the dark ages. Jobs will have to close because nothing electrical will work anymore, automobiles, electric lights, computers, cash registers etc. will cease to function. This will cause confusion, panic, and a rise in crime. Worst of all, we won't be able to lunch a counterattack because our military relies heavily on computers.

These verses of Scripture pictures the results of the collapse of the Babylonian system [USA]. The finality of its destruction is shown by the sixfold repetition of the phrase, *"no more at all."* The stone [asteroid] cast into the sea depicts the violence and permanence of the destruction. These passages of Scriptures give us three reasons why God is going to allow our enemies to destroy this nation to fulfill His judgment. They are (1) our arrogance, (2) deceptions of nations, (3) and persecution and martyrdom of His people.

Revelation Chapter 19

Those in Heaven praise God:

Vs. 1 *"And after these things I heard a great voice of much people* [a great multitude] *in heaven, saying, Alleluia; salvation, and glory, and honor, and power, unto the Lord our God:*

Vs. 2 *"For true and righteous are his judgments: for he hath judged the great* [expletive], [USA] *which did corrupt the earth with her fornications, and hath avenged the blood of his servants at her hand* [shed by her].

Vs. 3 *"And again they said, Alleluia. And her smoke rosed up for ever and ever."*

Vs. 4 *"And the four and twenty elders and the four beast* [living creatures] *fell down and worship God that sat on the throne, saying, Amen; Alleluia.*

Vs. 5 *"And a voice came out of the throne, saying, Praise our God, all ye his servants, and ye that fear* [reverence] *him, both small and great."*

The Marriage Supper of the Lamb:

Vs. 6-7 *"And I heard as it were the voice of a great multitude, and as the voice of many waters, and as the voice of many thundering, saying, Alleluia: for the Lord God omnipotent reigneth...Let us be glad and rejoice, and give honor to him: for the marriage of the Lamb is come, and his wife* [the church] *hath made herself ready."*

Vs. 8 *"And to her was granted that she should be arrayed in fine linen, clean and white:* [bright] *for the fine linen is the righteousness* [righteous acts] *of saints."*

Vs. 9 *"And he saith unto me, Write, Blessed are they which are called unto the marriage supper of the Lamb. And he saith unto me, These are the true saying of God.*

Vs. 10 John prostrated himself to worship the angel but he wasn't allowed to. He was told, *"See thou do it not: I am thy fellow servant, and of thy brethren that have the testimony of Jesus: worship God: for the testimony of Jesus is the spirit of prophecy."*

The Rider on the White Horse (Jesus Christ):

Vs. 11-13 This rider on the white horse is not the same as the one described in Rev. 6:2. The rider of Rev. 6:2 is the Antichrist; he's coming first to deceive the nations. Jesus is the *True Messiah*; He returns victoriously to overthrow the government of the false one.

Jesus is *Faithful* to His Word and promises. He will fulfill the twofold role of judge and warrior. His judgment of the earth will be totally righteous (cf. 16:5-7; 19:2; Ps. 96:13). *"His eyes were as a flame of fire."* The *fire* depicts His glory and judgment. The *crowns* indicate total sovereignty and authority (contrast 12:3; 13:1). The secret *name* expresses the mystery and greatness of the person of Christ (cf. 2:7; 3:12; 19:13,16; Phil. 2:9-11).

The *blood* represents the judgment of Christ's enemies (cf. 14:14-20; Isaiah 61:1-6). The name *Word of God* presents Christ as the revelation of God Himself (cf. John 1:1, 14; 1 John 1:1). In His first advent, Jesus revealed the love and grace of God (cf. John 1:17; Romans 5:8). But in His second advent, He will reveal the holiness, justice, and judgment of Almighty God (cf. Hebrews 4:12).

Vs. 14-16. The *armies which were* in heaven that follows Him are believers in every generation that died in faith, they include the angels mention in Zech. 14:5; Matt. 26:53; Hebrews 12:22-24; and the Raptured church, including those that overcame the Great Tribulation period.

Vs. 17-18. *The supper of the great God* is different from the marriage supper of the Lamb (vs. 9). Here, God calls the fowls or birds of the sky to gather to eat the flesh of those who have died in the Battle of Armageddon (cf. 16:14, 16; 19:21; Ezekiel 39:17-20). *All men* indicate "all kind of men", not only those that died in the Battle of Armageddon but also those in the church that didn't live up to their calling (cf. Matthew 25: 31-46). In this passage of Scripture, Jesus was addressing 'church folks' who had done mighty works in His name (ref. Matt. 7: 21-23). The Lord will accept the souls of those won by false ministers, but He reject those works that were not done in faith (cf. Jeremiah 6:30; 7: 29, 30; 1 Cor, 9:27).

Vs. 19-21. The armies of the beast and of the kings of the east [and of all the earth] will gather in Palestine at Armageddon (cf. 16:12-16) to attempt to prevent the return and kingdom of Christ. Christ will immediately defeat and capture the beast and the false prophet (Cf. Ch. 13). These will become the first inhabitants of the lake of fire (cf. 20:10). The rest of the kings and armies will be killed by the Word of Christ, and their flesh will be eaten by birds (vs. 17,18). The unbelieving survivors of the Tribulation period will be judged by Christ and sentenced to everlasting fire (Matt. 25:41, 46).

This is a judgment of separation: sheep on His right...goats on His left. At this judgment all nations (all Gentiles and unfaithful confessed Christians) stand before Christ who then separates the sheep (saved) from the goats (lost) in a manner reminiscent of the wheat and tares parable (Matt. 13: 24-30).

Revelation Chapter 20

Satan bound for a thousand years:

Satan will be bound in the bottomless pit during the time of Christ's Millennium Reign on earth.

Vs. 1- 3 The bottomless pit, [the abyss] is the abode of evil spirits (cf. 9:1-11; Luke 8:31). The *key* shows authority, and the *chain depicts* imprisonment and binding. Before the Millennium Kingdom begins, Satan (cf. 12:9) is bound in the abyss. The *seal* indicates God's authority and guarantee that Satan will not be released until the thousand years have passed.

During the Millennium Reign of Christ, Satan will not be able to tempt or deceive the nations. His fallen comrades [demons] will also be imprisoned (ref. Isaiah 24: 21-23). Any temptation to sin during the Millennium must come from within those people who are born after the kingdom begins. If a person lives to be a hundred years old, he / she will be considered a child (compare Isaiah 65:20). Jesus Christ will reign on earth without opposition, and His kingdom will be characterized by righteousness, peace and love (cf. Isaiah 2:3,4; 11:3-5; 35:1,2; Dan. 7:14; Zech. 14:9). After the thousand years are over Satan will be released for a short while (vs. 7-9).

Vs. 4 The *thrones* represent the administration of the messianic kingdom. Those whom John sees comes to life after the Tribulation martyrs, who refuse to worship the beast (Rev. 13:15). They will rule the earth with Christ for a thousand years. Christ will rule through three classes of kingdom administrators: (1) Old Testament Saints (cf. Isaiah 26:19; Dan. 12:2), who will be resurrected at this time; (2) The apostles and the church (cf. Matt. 19:28, 29; and (3) The Tribulation Saints (cf. Luke 19:12-27). Only believers will enter the Millennium at its beginning, (cf. John 3:3, 5). God promises to Abraham (Gen. 12: 2, 3) and David (2 Samuel 7:16) will be fulfilled (cf. Luke 1: 31-33; Romans 11:15, 29). After the Millennium, Christ will deliver the kingdom to God the Father and will then be appointed Ruler forever (cf. 1 Cor. 15: 24-28).

The Two Resurrections:

Vs. 5-6 There will be two resurrections, one for the Saints and one for sinners. The first part of verse 5 is a parenthesis and comes chronologically after verse 11. The *first resurrection* is the resurrection included in verse 4, it has three principal phases; (1) The resurrection of Christ (the first fruits- 1 Cor. 15:23 cf. Rev.1:5) (2) The resurrection of the church (the dead in Christ 1 Cor. 15:23;

1 Thess. 4:16); and (3) The resurrection of Old Testament and Tribulation Saints (v. 4; Isaiah 26:19; Dan. 12:2). The *rest of the dead* (unbelievers) will be raised in the second resurrection, described in verses 12 and 13.

The first resurrection is a resurrection of life (cf. John 5: 28, 29), whereas the second resurrection is a resurrection to death. The *second death* is eternal punishment in the lake of fire (verse 14).

Vs. 7-10 At the end of the Millennium Satan and his demons will be released from their imprisonment and they will make another attempt to defeat Christ. Satan will once again deceive the nations into rebellion against God. The reference to Gog and Magog [modern day Russia and Germany] will be heavily influenced by Satan to join the battle against Christianity.

From Ezekiel chapters 38 and 39 we learn that Gog, was the prince of *Rosh*, (Russia) he and his allies the Assyrians, Scythians, Meshech and Tubal were enemies to ancient Israel. Magog, with his allies; Persia, [modern day Iran] Ethiopia, Libya, Gomer, were all defeated by God in a battle. God once again will defeat the enemies of His Chosen People, the nation of Israel once again in the final battle.

The *beloved city* is the earthly Jerusalem, headquarters of Christ's Millennium kingdom (cf. Isaiah 60:1-22; Zachariah 14:1-20). The rebels will be quickly destroyed by fire from God. Satan and his army of demons, the false prophet and the Antichrist will all be cast into the lake of fire where they will be tormented forever.

The Judgment Seat of God:

Vs. 11"*And I saw a great white throne, and him that sat on it, from whose face the heaven and the earth fled away; and there was found no place for them.* "The *throne* depicts divine government and judgment (cf. Dan. 7: 9,10, 26, 27). The *white* or shining in appearance (signifying glory, purity and holiness). The judge is God, who will judge the world in righteousness, He will have the final judgment. Christ will judge His people (the church) at the "Judgment Seat of Christ" (Romans 14:10; 2 Corinthians 5:10).

Vs. 12 *"And I saw the dead, small and great, stand before God; and the books were opened: and another book was opened, which is the book of life: and the dead were judged out of those things which were written in the books, according to their works."*

Vs. 13 *"And the sea gave up the dead which was in it; and death and hell* [hades, the abode of the unsaved dead- Luke 16:19-31] *delivered up the dead which were in them: and they were judged every man according to their works."*

The *dead* are the unsaved dead of all ages, which includes the "rest of the dead" mentioned in verse 5. They were [will be] judged from two sets of books. The *books* contain the record of every person's life.

Each unsaved person is judged in accordance with his / her *works* (cf. Romans 2:6, 16), which will clearly show that each one is a guilty sinner (cf. Romans 3:9-19) deserving of eternal death (cf. Romans 3:23; 6:23).

The *book of life* contains the name of every person who has received eternal life through faith in Christ alone (cf. John 20:31; 1 John 5:11-13). These unsaved people are shown that they did not take advantage of salvation offered to them by God through the sacrifice of His Only Begotten Son (John 3:16,17; Romans 9:32;10:3).

Vs. 14, 15 *Death and hell* [the resurrected body and the unsaved soul] will experience the *second death* which is eternal punishment in the lake of fire. Once the final judgment is passed there will be no further need for neither death nor hell [hades] (cf. Rev. 1:18; 6:8; Is. 25:8; 1 Cor. 15: 26, 55). An eternal separation is now made between those who have *life* and those who have "death" (cf. Daniel 12:2; John 5:29).

Revelation Chapter 21

John is shown the new beginning (eight-day creation). This is the eternal state of the earth following the Millennium Reign of Christ and the final judgment centering in the New Jerusalem as the eternal habitation of the saved (cf. Heb. 11:10; 12:22-24). The first heaven and the first earth will be replaced by a new heaven and a new earth as predicted by Isaiah (cf. Isaiah 65:17; 66:22). The present universe will be cleansed from all the effects of sin (cf. 2 Peter 3:7, 10-13).

The present world consists of about three quarters of water, but since there will be no more sea, the increased land space will be fully capable of handling a vast number of redeemed people from all ages (from Adam and Eve to the last person born into this present world). Even hell itself will be enlarged (Isiah 5:14) to accommodate the multitudes that neglected the message and gift of salvation.

The New Jerusalem is fully described in 21:10-22:5. It is (will be) a holy city, totally separated from sin (cf. vs. 8, 27; 22:15. It is being prepared (cf. John 14:3) as the habitation of the bride of Christ (v. 9).

Let's do a walkthrough of the vision as God showed it to His prophet John?

The New heaven and the New Earth:

Vs. 1 *"And I saw a new heaven and a new earth: for the first heaven and the first earth was passed away; and there was no more sea."*

Vs. 2 *"And I John saw the holy city, new Jerusalem, coming down from God out of heaven, prepared as a bride adorned for her husband."*

Remember, the church is depicted as the *"bride of Christ."* He is the *"bridegroom."*

Vs. 3 *"And I heard a great voice out of heaven saying, Behold, the tabernacle* [dwelling place] *of God is with men, and he will dwell with them, and they shall be his people, and God himself shall be with them, and be their God."*

Vs. 4 *"And God shall wipe away all tears from their eyes; and there shall be no more death, neither sorrow, nor crying, neither shall there be any more pain: for the former things are passed away."*

We will be "Born Again" in our glorified bodies in our eternal state and in our eternal home. The presence of God will be with His people, and He will forever dwell with them. God's purpose of redemption through Christ will be accomplished. We will be able to see the Shekinah Glory of God, His very essence. Sin prevented us from seeing Him in His Glory, therefore, Christ became the *"image of the invisible God"* that through Him, we will be reconciled to God the Father and able to reside in our eternal home in the New Jerusalem (cf. Col. 1:15-22).

Vs. 5 *"And he that sat upon the throne said, Behold, I make all things new. And he said unto me, Write: for these words are true and faithful."*

Vs. 6 *"And he said unto me, It is done. I am Alpha and Omega, the beginning and the end. I will give unto him that is athirst of the fountain of the water of life freely."*

Vs. 7 *"He that overcometh* [those redeemed from the earth and those that bore faith and patience during the Tribulation period] *shall inherit all things; I will be his God, and he shall be my son."*

Vs. 8 *"But the fearful,* [cowardly] *and unbelieving, and the abominable and murderers, and whoremongers,* [sexually immoral] *and sorcerers,* [witchcraft] *and idolaters,* [worshippers of idols instead of God] *and all liars, shall have their part in the lake which burneth with fire and brimstone, which is the second death."* This is the death of the soul, externally separated from God and His Mercy!

The New Jerusalem:

Our eternal home inhabited by believers from all generations including the New Testament church, [the bride of Christ] those redeemed from the earth and overcomers of the Tribulation period. Verses 9-21 John describes the beauty of the city. The wall shows its security and protection. Its gates show accessibility, saved Israel is also present. The city will be a square cube twelve thousand furlongs (1,500 miles in each direction with a wall of 1,500 miles high. The walls of the city will be a hundred and forty-four cubits (about 200 ft thick).

Vs. 9 *"And there came unto me one of the seven angels which had the seven vials* [bowls of God's wrath] *full of the seven last plagues, and talked with me, saying, Come hither, I will show the bride, the Lamb's wife."*

Vs. 10 *"And he carried me away in the spirit* [Holy Spirit] *to a great and high mountain, and showed me that great city, the holy Jerusalem, descending out of heaven from God."*

Vs. 11 *"Having the glory of God: and her light was like unto a stone most precious, even like a jasper stone, clear as crystal.*

Vs. 12 *"And had a wall great and high, and had twelve gates, and at the gates twelve angels, and names written thereon, which are the names of the twelve tribes of the children of Israel:*

Vs. 13 *"On the east three gates, on the north three gates; on the south three gates."*

Vs. 14 *"And the wall of the city had twelve foundations, and in them the names of the twelve apostles of the Lamb."*

Vs. 15 *"And he that talked with me had a golden reed to measure the city, and the gates thereof and the walls thereof."*

Vs. 16 *"And the city lieth four square, and the length is as large as the breadth: and he measured the city with the reed, twelve thousand furlongs. The length and the breadth and the height of it are equal."*

Vs. 17 *"And he measured the wall thereof, a hundred and forty and four cubits, according to the measure of a man, that is of the angel."*

Vs. 18 *"And the building of the wall of it was of jasper: and the city was pure gold, like unto clear glass."*

Vss. 19, 20 *"And the foundations of the wall of the city were garnished with all manner of precious stones. The first foundation was jasper; the second, sapphire; the third, a chalcedony; the fourth, an emerald."*

Vs. 21 *"And the twelve gates were twelve pearls; every several* [individual] *gate was of one pearl: and the street of the city was pure gold, as it were transparent glass."*

Vs. 22 *"And I saw no temple therein: for the Lord God Almighty and the Lamb are the temple of it."*

Vs. 23 *"And the city had no need of the sun, neither of the moon, to shine in it: for the glory of God did lighten it, and the Lamb is the light thereof."*

Note vss. 22, 23: There will be no temple in the New Jerusalem, since both the Father and the Son will be present in their fullest manifestation. Its light will be provided by the Shekinah glory of God and of Christ.

Vs. 24 *"And the nations of them which are saved shall walk in the light of it: and the kings of the earth do bring their glory and honor into it."*

Vs. 25, 26 *"And the gates of it shall not be shut at all by day: for there shall be no night there. And they shall bring the glory and honor of the nations into it."*

Vs. 27 *"And there shall in no wise enter into it any thing that defileth, neither whatsoever worketh* (causes an) *abomination, or maketh a lie: but they which are written in the Lamb's book of life."*

The glory of God in the New Jerusalem (in eternity) will light the whole earth just as it will be during Christ's Millennium Reign (cf. Isiah 60). The nations ruled by virous kings and levels of earthly authorities, will honor the heavenly city as the dwelling place of God.

The open gates show that security measures will no longer be necessary (cf. Isiah 60:11). Day is continuous since darkness never comes. Only redeemed and glorified people will have access to or dwell in the New Jerusalem (cf. v. 8; 22:15; Isiah 52:1; Ezekiel 44:9; 1 Corinthians 6:9,10; 2 Peter 3:13). No sinful thing that" defileth" will enter God's presence.

Revelation Chapter 22

Vs. 1 *"And he showed me a pure river of water of life, clear as crystal, proceeding out of the throne of God and of the Lamb."*

Vs. 2 *"In the midst of the street of it, and on either side of the river, was there the tree of life, which bare twelve manner of fruits, and yielded her fruit every month: and the leaves of the tree were for the healing of the nations.*

These verses depict the abundant life and continuous blessing of the New Jerusalem: one river, containing water of life (cf. 7:17; 21; 22:17), comes from God's throne and waters the entire city (cf. similar millennial blessings in Ezekiel 47:1-12; Joel 3:18; Zech.14:8). The tree of life pictures eternal sustenance and immortality (cf. v. 14; Gen. 2:9; 3:22). Both the variety and abundance of fruit are emphasized. The healing of the nation's indicates physical healing by God in the eternal state.

Vs. 3-5 *"And there shall be no more curse; but the throne of God and the Lamb shall be in it; and his servants shall serve him: And they shall see his face; and his name shall be in* (on) *their foreheads. And there shall be no light there; and they need no candle* (lamp, i.e., no electricity), *neither light of the sun; for the Lord God giveth them light: and they shall reign for ever and ever."*

The effects of the post-Edenic curse (cf. Gen. 3:14-19) will be totally gone forever. God's saints will serve Him (cf. 7:15) and reign with Him forever (Daniel 7:18-27). The greatest blessing of eternity is that we will see His face (cf. Matt.5:8; Heb. 12:14). This is impossible for an unglorified human being (cf. Exodus 33:20), it will occur in the eternal state. The name of God in their foreheads shows ownership and consecration (cf. 3:12; 13:16; Ex. 28:36-38). In the New Jerusalem God is always present. His glory makes all other sources of light unnecessary (cf. 21;23; Is. 60: 19, 20; Zech. 14:7).

Vs. 6, 7 *"And he said unto me, Theses sayings are faithful and true: and the Lord God of the holy prophets sent his angel to show unto his servants the things which must shortly be done." Behold, I come quickly: blessed is he that keepth the sayings of the prophecy of this book."*

Verses 8-11. John certifies that he has actually seen and heard everything that he has written in the book. He again makes the mistake of worshipping the messenger (angel) of God rather than

God Himself (cf. 19:10). Angels are simply fellow servants of God (cf. Ps. 103:20; Dan. 7:10; Heb. 1:14). We are forbidden to worship them (Zeph. 1:5; Deut. 5: 7, 8).

In contrast with Daniel, who was told to "seal" up his book of prophecy (since the time of the end is still in the distant future-cf. Dan. 12:4,9, 13), John is told to leave his book open (Seal not). The Messiah has come, Jesus' Second Advent will bring judgment upon all that will not adhere to the Words (prophecy) of his book.

Verse 11 is a warning to those who turns a deft ear to the prophecy of Jesus Christ. Unlike the thief on the cross, it will be too late to make a last-minute decision to follow or seek Christ. Character tends to become fixed and unchangeable, determined by a lifetime of habitual action. The arrival of the end will prevent any change of destiny.

When Christ returns, the deliberate choice of each person will have fixed his eternal fate! *"He that is unjust, let him be unjust still: and he which is filthy, let him be filthy still: and he that is righteous, let him be righteous still: and he that is holy, let him be holy still."*

Verses 12, 13 Again Christ encourages His followers to remain faithful and obedient to Him, that they may receive their rewards. Reward is always based on work (cf. Jer. 17:10; Rom. 2:6; 1 Peter 1:17). For believers, there is the Judgment Seat of Christ (2 Cor. 5:10; cf. Dan. 12:2 for Old Testament saints). For unbelievers there are various judgments, culminating in the Great White Throne judgment (20:11-15; Matt. 25:31-46).

Verses 14, 15 *"They that do his commandments"* are believers (cf. 12:17; 14:12; Matt. 7:13-21; 1 John 3:10). The *"tree of life"* indicates immortality and divine blessing (cf. 2:7; 22:2). To be able to *"enter in through the gates into the city"* is to have heavenly citizenship in the eternal dwelling place of God and redeemed mankind.

All unbelievers are *"without"* (outside the prominence of God) i.e., in the lake of fire-cf. v. 15; 21:8, 27. The *"dogs"* are impure and malicious people (cf. Deut. 23:17, 18; Phil.3:2). *"Sorcerers"* are those who practice witchcraft (Gr. *pharmakos*). *"Whoremongers"* are those who practices all kinds of sexual immorality (Gr. *pornos;* English, *pornography*).

Verse 16, 17 Jesus authenticates His angel through whom He has given this revelation to John (cf. 1:1). *"You"* is plural, indicates that the revelation is for all churches in every generation. As *"the root and the offspring of David"*, Jesus is the fulfillment of the messianic promise of Isaiah 11:1 (cf. 5:5; Rom. 1:3.)

As "the bright and morning star", Jesus will shortly bring in the new age: His messianic kingdom (cf. Num. 24:17; Rom 13:11, 12; 2 Peter 1:19). It will be accomplished after the overthrow of Satan's, New World Order and his "One World Government."

Verse 17 contains four invitations to the unsaved to come to Christ in faith for eternal life. The *"Spirit"* is the Holy Spirit, and the *"bride"* is the church (cf. 19:7-9). The Holy Spirit works through the church to evangelize the world. The *"water of life"* is eternal life, available *"freely"* by faith in Christ (cf. 7:17; 21:6; Isiah 55:1; John 4:14; 7:37).

Verses 18,19 Is a warning aimed against the willful distortion of the message of the book (cf. Deut. 4:2; 12:32; Prov. 30:6; Gal. 1:6,7). The speaker is Christ Himself (vs. 20). Jesus claims a canonicity for the book (and the entire New Testament) equal to that of the Old Testament. Anyone who willfully distorts the message of the Book of Revelation shows himself not to be a genuine believer and will not participate in eternal life or the blessings of the New Jerusalem.

Verses 20, 21. The final promise of Christ in the Bible is that His return is certain, *not imminent* as your false teachers will distort and have you to believe (vs. 7, 12). *"Amen"* means "truly" or "so be it." The believer's response is simply, "Come, Lord Jesus," which is equivalent of the Aramaic *Maranatha* (1 Cor. 16: 22).

Finally, Verses 6-21 form a conclusion or summary to the book of Revelation. They emphasize two themes: (1) the authenticity of the book as a revelation from God; and (2) the surety of the return of Christ. *These sayings* refer to the entire Book of Revelation.

They are authenticated as genuine by the angel whom God sent to give them through John and His servants, that is, the members of the churches (cf. 1:3, 11).

Quickly (Gr. *Tachu*) here vs. 12 (a) doesn't refer to the imminence of the Rapture of the Church, but rather, in God's own time: (1) after man's dominance of the earth, [his six thousand years of rule] (2) the rise and fall of the Antichrist, [overthrow of Satan and his One World Government i.e., the New World Order] (3) World War III [which will result in the annihilation of one-third of world's population] (4) the Day of the Lord, [Judgement Day]. All these events must take place before God Almighty ushers in Christ's Eternal Reign, which will have *"no end."*

In conclusion and based upon the evidence I've presented to you through the volume of the book, the Holy Bible; I say again to you false teachers, with this WARNING that, *THERE IS NO PRE-TRIBULATION RAPTURE OF THE CHURCH!*

Printed in the United States
by Baker & Taylor Publisher Services